Women Who Think Too Much

Women Who
Think Too Much

*How to Break Free
of Overthinking
and Reclaim Your Life*

Susan Nolen-Hoeksema, Ph.D.

HENRY HOLT AND COMPANY · NEW YORK

Case studies used in the book are either fictional,
or information about individuals has been changed
to protect their identity.

Henry Holt and Company, LLC
Publishers since 1866
115 West 18th Street
New York, New York 10011

Henry Holt® is a registered trademark of
Henry Holt and Company, LLC.

Copyright © 2003 by Susan Nolen-Hoeksema
All rights reserved.
Distributed in Canada by H. B. Fenn and Company Ltd.

Library of Congress Cataloging-in-Publication Data
Nolen-Hoeksema, Susan, date.
    Women who think too much : how to break free of overthinking
and reclaim your life / Susan Nolen-Hoeksema.
        p. cm.
    Includes index.
    ISBN 0-8050-7018-4
    1. Worry.   2. Negativism.   3. Peace of mind—Problems,
exercises, etc.   4. Women—Psychology.   I. Title.

BF575.W8 N65 2003
158'.082—dc21   2002027311

Henry Holt books are available for special promotions
and premiums. For details contact: Director, Special Markets.

First Edition 2003

Designed by Victoria Hartman

Printed in the United States of America
10   9   8   7   6   5   4

CONTENTS

Part I: An Epidemic of Overthinking

1. What's Wrong with Overthinking?   3
2. If It Hurts So Much, Why Do We Do It?   32
3. Women's Unique Vulnerabilities   48

Part II: Strategies for Overcoming Overthinking

4. Breaking Free   59
5. Moving to Higher Ground   80
6. Avoiding Future Traps   105

Part III: Triggers for Overthinking

7. Married to My Worries: Overthinking Intimate
   Relationships   133
8. Family Matters: Overthinking Our Parents and Siblings   152
9. The Parent Trap: Overthinking and Our Children   165

10. Always on the Job: Overthinking Work and Careers   184

11. Toxic Thoughts: Overthinking Health Problems   205

12. Can't Get Over It: Overthinking Loss and Trauma   221

13. Moving Our Society to Higher Ground   243

Notes   255

Resources   261

Acknowledgments   263

Index   265

Women Who Think Too Much

Part I

An Epidemic of Overthinking

What is overthinking and where does it come from? In Part I, I describe overthinking and our research on its negative consequences. I suggest several contributors to overthinking, particularly in women.

1

What's Wrong with Overthinking?

Over the last four decades, women have experienced unprecedented growth in independence and opportunities. We are freer to choose what kinds of relationships to have, whether and when to have children, what careers to pursue, and what lifestyles to lead—choices previous generations never dreamed possible. Advances in medical science have made us healthier than ever before and living longer. We have many reasons to be happy and confident.

Yet, when there is any pause in our daily activities, many of us are flooded with worries, thoughts, and emotions that swirl out of control, sucking our emotions and energy down, down, down. We are suffering from an epidemic of *overthinking*—getting caught in torrents of negative thoughts and emotions that overwhelm us and interfere with our functioning and well-being. Our concerns are about fundamental issues: Who am I? What am I doing with my life? What do others think of me? Why am I not happy and content? Answers do not come easily or quickly to such questions and so we search and ponder and worry even more. As our mood gets deeper and darker, we can identify still more concerns, big and small: Is my son taking drugs? Why am I still in the same dead-end job? How am I going to keep my spouse interested in me? Why can't I control my temper with my mother? These thoughts ebb and flow with our rapidly shifting moods, but we seldom reach any conclusions.

Even minor events can send us off on hours or days of overthinking and distress. Your boss makes a sarcastic remark to you and you spend days worrying about what he meant and about your feelings of guilt and shame. A friend makes a comment about your weight, and you get mired in thoughts about how you look and how insensitive the friend is. Your spouse is too tired to have sex one evening and you're up all night wondering what this means for your marriage.

This epidemic of morbid meditation is a disease that women suffer much more than men. My studies have found repeatedly that women are more likely than men to fall into overthinking and remain stuck there.[1] Take, for example, Veronica, a twenty-seven-year-old full-time mom with auburn hair and dancing brown eyes. Veronica adored caring for her toddler twins and being involved in community activities that she felt could benefit her twins and other children in her town. But when she wasn't teaching the twins how to swim, or at an organizational meeting for some fund-raiser for her community, or otherwise busy, Veronica would find herself slipping into the muck of negativity and concern we call overthinking:

> What's wrong with me that I never feel completely satisfied with what I'm doing? I just keep agreeing to more committees and arranging more activities for my kids. But nothing ever feels quite right. What's wrong with my life? Maybe it's something about my hormones. But it seems to last all month long. I don't know, maybe I've made the wrong choices in my life. I say I like being a stay-at-home mom, but do I really? Does Rick really appreciate what I do for our children?

As she continues to fret, Veronica's thoughts jump to her weight, then to her marriage, and then to her life before full-time motherhood:

> I'll never get rid of the pregnancy weight. I'm destined to be fifteen pounds too fat for the rest of my life, and it will only get worse with age. What if Rick meets some pretty young thing at work and gets sick of me? How would I ever manage alone with twins? And how would I ever get a good job again? It's not as though I had great job skills before I stopped working. I never liked that job and my boss never liked me.

Women can ruminate about anything and everything—our appearance, our families, our career, our health. We often feel that this is just part of being a woman—that it's a reflection of our caring, nurturing qualities. This may be partly true, but overthinking is also toxic for women. It interferes with our ability and motivation to solve our problems. It drives some friends and family members away. And it can wreck our emotional health. Women are twice as likely as men to become severely depressed or anxious, and our tendency to overthink appears to be one of the reasons why.

We do not have to be this way, however. We can rise above this epidemic of emotional oversensitivity and hypervolatility and learn to recognize and appropriately express the emotions we experience. We can keep these emotions under reasonable control, and deal effectively with the situations that upset us. We can maintain serenity and self-efficacy among conflict, confusion, tragedy, and chaos. We can stand strong and tall against the worst storms. We can be the directors of our own emotional lives.

Escape from Overthinking

Trying to overcome overthinking is like trying to escape from quicksand. The first step to freedom is to break the grip of your thoughts so that they don't continue to pull you down further, and eventually smother you. The second step is to climb up out of the muck onto higher ground where you can see things more clearly and make good choices about what directions you should go in in the future. The third step is to avoid falling into the trap of overthinking once again. At the core of *Women Who Think Too Much* is a set of practical strategies for accomplishing each of these steps—breaking the grip, moving to higher ground, and avoiding future traps.

Some people come by these strategies naturally. Take, for example, an incident in the life of Jenny, a thirty-two-year-old stockbroker who lives in New York. For the last year, Jenny has been dating Sean, a handsome botanist who works for the state environmental protection agency. Jenny and Sean have several mutual friends and enjoy cooking elaborate dinners for them, usually at Sean's small apartment on the outskirts of the city. On a Friday, Sean invited some of their friends to dinner at his apartment and asked Jenny if she would come a couple of hours early to help in the preparations. She happily agreed, but the afternoon of the dinner party she found herself far behind in preparing client invoices that had to go out by 6 P.M. At about 3 P.M., Jenny called to tell Sean she would be a bit late. She then got so frantic about finishing her invoices that she lost track of time, and looked up to see it was 5:45—only forty-five minutes before their guests were to arrive, and it was a half-hour drive to Sean's apartment. When Jenny ran breathlessly up the steps into Sean's apartment at 6:17, she immediately saw that his attitude toward her was cold as ice. When the guests left, he let her have it, saying she was obsessed with her career, self-centered, and uncaring. Jenny knew he would be mad at her for being late, but this was more grief than she expected. After Sean yelled at her for a half hour, she walked out, slamming the apartment door behind her.

All night, Jenny tossed and turned reliving her argument with Sean again and again. She couldn't believe the cruel things he'd said to her. She went over and over it, coming up with sarcastic retorts to his arguments, and examples of times Sean had disappointed her.

> He was completely out of line. Calling me a self-absorbed career-ist! I'm not self-absorbed at all. He has no idea how much work I have to do and he doesn't care. He's totally self-centered to invite people over when I'm so busy. All he thinks about is himself and having fun. I should have told him he was getting hysterical again. That would stop him in his tracks!

Jenny eventually fell asleep, but woke up in the morning with the same thoughts. As her body tensed, and her thoughts got wilder and wilder, she realized, "I'm doing it again. This is getting me nowhere. I've got to get a grip on this." She went for a jog along the river to clear her mind and lift her mood. After she returned home, she thought through the argument with Sean again. She could see ways in which he was right about her, but she could also see that he was exaggerating in the heat of the argument. Jenny realized that her relationship with Sean was very important to her and she didn't want this argument, or her response to it, to ruin the relationship. She thought of a couple of things she wanted to say to Sean—that she loves him, that she's sorry for what she's done to upset him, and that it upsets her when he yells accusations at her. She thought through what his reactions to each of these statements might be. After a while, she felt herself slipping back into angry thoughts about how nasty and unfair Sean could be when he got mad. Concerned that her thoughts and feelings were sinking deeper and deeper into dangerous territory, she decided to do something else for a while, something to get her mind off all this, and then go back to reconsider what she wanted to say to Sean. After calling a friend for some moral support, she looked back at the list and decided she was ready to call Sean. Her mood was good and her mind was clear. She was able to say what she wanted to Sean—including that she felt he had overreacted—but also to listen to him calmly. They patched things up over the phone and made a date to meet the next night.

Jenny's handling of this argument with Sean didn't start out well—she was only expanding her anger and distress with her thoughts about what he had said and what she should say back. If she had kept going down this road, she probably would have only gotten angrier and may have said things to Sean that did long-term damage to their relationship.

But Jenny was able to deal effectively with this conflict because she used a number of strategies to break the grip of her angry thoughts, to rise above them and develop an effective plan for overcoming her conflict with Sean and avoid slipping into ruminations once again. Specifically, Jenny broke free from her initial ramblings by giving them a rest. She used a healthy, active distraction—jogging—to release her mind from her negative thoughts. She moved to higher ground by raising her mind above the details of what he said and she said and focusing on her primary goal: maintaining her relationship with Sean, and considering some ways she could reestablish this relationship. She recognized when she was slipping into overthinking again and was proactive in stopping her descent by stepping away from her thoughts and getting active.

My research over the last twenty years has shown that a critical component of healthy living is not to allow our negative emotions rule our lives and undermine our efforts. Negative emotions exert powerful influences over our thoughts and behaviors. When you are sad, your brain has greater access to sad thoughts and memories, and you are more likely to interpret present circumstances in a sad way. Your actions are slowed down, your motivation is sapped. It is harder to concentrate, to make decisions, or to accomplish any task. In short, when sadness is amplified instead of managed, it can take you down paths to hopelessness, self-hate, and immobility.

Similarly, when you are anxious, you see threats very easily, including threats that may not actually exist, such as the threat that you have cancer, or the threat that your spouse will be unfaithful. Your mind flits from one thing to the next, and it's hard to focus long enough to evaluate what you should do. Your limbs feel jittery, your stomach churns, your heart races. You might act impulsively or not act at all, frozen in fear. When anxiety is amplified instead of managed, the results can be chronic arousal that wears down the body and makes you unable to deal with even mildly challenging situations.

When you overthink on top of sadness or anxiety or anger, you pay attention to the thoughts created by your mood, mulling them over, taking them very seriously, and letting them influence your decisions. The negative beliefs and bad decisions that result can ruin your life, impairing your mental well-being, your physical health, and your ability to function in the everyday world.

It is possible to pull out of snowballing thoughts and gain control over them, however, and in the second part of *Women Who Think Too Much* I describe specific strategies for doing just that. I've arranged these strategies into groups: initial strategies that help women pull out of overthinking; strategies that help women rise above these thoughts to think more clearly and make better choices for themselves; and strategies that help women avoid overthinking in the future.

Women overthink all sorts of situations, including loss and trauma, competition and success at work, the past, conflicts with others, and sexual and romantic satisfaction. In each of these situations, our thoughts can be compelling because they deal with concerns that are at the heart of our own self-concepts and the important relationships in our lives. It can be difficult to see how or why we should avoid these thoughts. But in each of these situations, overthinking can interfere with our ability to cope, damage our self-worth, and contribute to unwise decisions. The third part of *Women Who Think Too Much* focuses on these and other common overthinking situations or themes and strategies for breaking these thoughts and dealing more effectively with our concerns.

Exactly What Is Overthinking?

When you overthink, you go over and over your negative thoughts and feelings, examining them, questioning them, kneading them like dough. You may begin with thinking about a recent conflict with a friend: How could she have said that to me? you think. What does she really mean by that? How should I react? Sometimes we can answer these questions quickly—she was in a lousy mood, she's like that to everyone, I'm just going to blow it off, or I'm going to tell her how mad I am—and then move on.

But when we are caught in overthinking, these questions just lead to more questions—what I call the *yeast effect*: Is it okay for me to be mad? What if I can't confront her? What does she think of me? Just as yeasty bread dough will double in size after it's been kneaded, our negative thoughts expand, grow, and begin to take up all the space around them in our minds. At first the thoughts may be about a specific event, but then they spread to other events or situations in your life and to big questions you have about yourself. And they get more and more negative with time: If I can't handle conflicts like this, why do I think I could do well as a manager at my company? I let myself get walked on all the time. I'm sick of it, but I'm too weak to do anything about it. That one time I did blow my stack at work I made a fool of myself. My parents never taught me how to handle my anger. They couldn't handle their anger, either.

Franny, a darkly handsome, lanky fifty-five-year-old divorced woman, the daughter of Italian immigrants, succumbs often to the yeast effect. Franny's overthinking most often begins with thoughts about her work as a landscape designer. She has many wealthy and demanding clients and worries a great deal about whether they are going to be happy with her designs. In one particularly intense bout of overthinking, Franny began by thinking about recent interactions with a particular client:

> I wasn't persuasive enough in selling my ideas. I should have pressed harder. The objections he was raising were bull. I caved. He said maybe they were "salvageable." What did he mean? Why didn't I ask him what he meant? I can be such a wimp!

Then Franny moved to memories of past clients who have rejected her plans:

> It's just like that guy who called my plans "boring." What did he know? How could I have let him get away with that? He eventually accepted the plans. He was just flexing his muscles.

Many more clients have loved her plans, but Franny's mind always gravitates toward the bad memories, not the good ones. Unless her mental rampage is interrupted, Franny will eventually begin thinking about her relationship with her boyfriend Andrew, a handsome Armenian immigrant. Andrew is an extremely successful owner of a chain of high-class vegetarian restaurants, who always seems ready with a joke or a clever comment to amuse his patrons. Franny is absolutely smitten with Andrew, but wonders constantly what he really thinks of her:

> He could have any woman he wants—single or married— because he's handsome, wealthy, and totally captivating. I can't believe what I fool I made of myself with him last weekend. It was supposed to be a lovely day sailing off the coast. But I let myself get drunk and sunburned. I must have looked like an idiot wobbling around and slurring my words, embarrassing myself and him in front of his friends.

From her thoughts about Andrew, Franny will move on to thoughts about her sexual attractiveness, her health, and her twenty-year-old son. There are some positive things happening in these areas of her life—she had a clear health exam and a great dinner with her son last week. But most of Franny's thoughts will focus on unhappy thoughts—that her mother has leukemia, her inability to have an orgasm during a sexual encounter with Andrew a couple of days ago, and her worries about her son's drinking habits. Franny moves from one thought to another—they all seem connected somehow—and never really resolves much regarding any of these concerns. This yeasty overthinking causes Franny pain and creates paralysis in her life. If it continues, Franny runs the risk of destroying her relationship with Andrew and harming her career and health. But Franny could begin to climb out of this quagmire and improve the quality of her life by following some of the basic strategies that Jenny did.

Types of Overthinking

There are three primary types of overthinking. Some people specialize in one particular type; many of us occasionally engage in all three:

1. **Rant-and-rave overthinking** is the most familiar type and usually centers around some wrong we believe has been done to us. Rants and raves tend to take on an air of wounded self-righteousness and focus on designing a retribution that will severely sting our victimizers:

> They rejected my application to graduate school. I can't believe this. I'm more qualified than most people. I bet they let in the kids of their alumni even when their qualifications aren't as good as mine! I worked for this so long and hard, I deserve this. These people don't know what they're doing. Or else they are prejudiced. I'm going to sue those bastards!

We may be right and the people who have inflicted harm on us may be wrong. But rant-and-rave overthinking tends to paint others as terrible villains without considering the "other side of the story." It also can lead us to take impulsive actions in retribution against others that can backfire, such as filing an expensive and hopeless lawsuit or lashing out in physical violence.

2. **Life-of-their-own overthinking** begins innocently as we notice we're feeling upset or we ponder a recent event. Then we begin to entertain possible causes for our feelings:

> Maybe I'm depressed because I have no friends. Or maybe it's because I haven't lost any weight this month. Or maybe it's because of all those things that happened in my past. Maybe I'm angry because I keep getting walked on at work. Or maybe it's because my mother keeps making snide remarks to me. Or maybe it's because my life isn't turning out the way I want.

When we overthink, all these possibilities seem highly likely. We accept all the explanations we generate, especially the most dramatic ones, as equally plausible.

Unfortunately, overthinking can cause us to see problems that don't really exist, or at least aren't as big as our thoughts make them out to be—they take on a life of their own. They can also cause us to make bad decisions about these problems we feel we have. We confront others, we decide to quit our job or school, we cancel social outings, acting out of our bad moods and exaggerated concerns.

3. **Chaotic overthinking** occurs when we don't move in a straight line from one problem to another, but it is as if all kinds of concerns, many of them unrelated, flood our minds all at the same time:

> I can't cope with the pressure of my job. I'm totally overwhelmed. I'm doing a lousy job and I deserve to be fired. Joe has to go on another business trip next week. He's going on too many business trips, leaving me here with the kids alone. He cares more about his work than he does about his family. But I can't confront him because I can't face the possibility that he's gone all the time because he doesn't love me anymore. I'm a mess. I'm just a mess and I don't know what to do.

Chaotic overthinking can be especially immobilizing because we can't identify what we feel or think very clearly—we are just overwhelmed with feelings and thoughts that disorient us and often cause us to shut down or run away. People who drink alcohol or take drugs in response to overthinking may be trying to drown out jumbled-up thoughts because they can't zero in on any one thing to worry about or to do in the morass of their thoughts.

Test Your Overthinking Potential

In much of my research, I have used a short quiz to evaluate people's tendency to overthink and become stuck in repetitive negativity. You might want to try the quiz yourself to determine your overthinking potential.

✦ AM I AN OVERTHINKER? ✦

When you feel upset—sad, blue, nervous—how do you find yourself responding? For each possible response below, rate whether you generally engage in this response "never or almost never," "sometimes," "often," or "always or almost always" when you feel upset. Please rate what you generally do when you are upset, not what you think you should do.

1. I think about how alone I feel.
2. I think about my feelings of fatigue or achiness.
3. I think about how hard it is to concentrate.
4. I think about how passive and unmotivated I feel.
5. I think, "Why can't I get going?"
6. I go over and over a recent situation, wishing it had gone better.
7. I think about how sad or anxious I feel.
8. I think about all my shortcomings, failings, faults, and mistakes.
9. I think about how I don't feel up to doing anything.
10. I think "Why can't I handle things better?"

If you answered "never or almost never" to all of these, or "sometimes" to just a few, congratulations! You have developed excellent strategies of your own to combat overthinking. If you answer "often" or "always" to more than just a few of these questions, you may be prone to fretting about your feelings and your life instead of effectively managing your emotional life.

What Overthinking Is Not

People often confuse overthinking with simple worry. Worry involves the "what ifs" of life—anticipations of what might happen: What if I don't say the right thing? What if I can't make it through school? What if this date goes badly? Worriers spend tremendous energy anticipating everything that could possibly go wrong, thinking about what they should do, but worrying that they can't do what they should.

Overthinkers *are* terrific worriers, but they do much more than worry. Much of overthinking is focused not on things that might happen in the future but on things that have happened in the past—events that have happened, things you have done, situations you wish had gone differently. Worriers wonder if something bad is going to happen, but when you overthink, you become dead certain that something bad has already happened. After a while, you are absolutely confident that you are stuck in a mediocre job, that your marriage is failing, that your friends don't really like you, or that you are not the person you should be.

Overthinking is also not the same as obsessive-compulsive disorder (OCD). People with OCD have obsessional thoughts, but these thoughts tend to be focused on situations or events that are external to them, and they experience the thoughts as foreign and unwelcome, such as thoughts about germs. The person with OCD may believe that everything she touches is contaminated with germs or bacteria or dirt. She will then go to great lengths to avoid touching things with her bare hands. She may wash her hands a hundred times a day, but no amount of washing will quell the thought that her hands are dirty and contaminated. The doubts of people with OCD are about specific actions they did or did not take— Did I turn off the stove? Did I lock the window? Did I accidentally run over someone in my car without knowing it? These doubts often seem bizarre to people without OCD. Of course they didn't accidentally run over someone without knowing it. Yes, they did lock the window and, in fact, they have already checked that it is locked ten times. These are thoughts that people without OCD—including chronic overthinkers— can turn off easily. But people with OCD have a fundamental problem with turning off such doubts, and other obsessional thoughts that seem trivial to the rest of us.

Finally, overthinking is not the same as "deep thinking." When I talk to people about overthinking, they often say, "Isn't it good to be in touch with your emotions and to ponder the deep issues behind our emotions? Aren't nonoverthinkers just shallow people who never confront their problems and their past?"

Sometimes our negative emotions do provide clues about concerns that we are not facing. A considerable body of research over the years has shown that people who chronically block out negative feelings and thoughts—a process often called suppression—can suffer negative consequences, especially for their physical well-being. Chronic suppression has been linked to hypertension and cardiac diseases, and possibly to immune-system disorders. One antidote for suppression is to take our negative emotions seriously as possible signs of conflicts that we are not dealing with effectively. This kind of inner examination is healthy and can lead to a much happier life.

Negative emotions don't necessarily give us a direct line to our truest, deepest concerns, however. Instead of providing us with a clear window, negative emotions impose a lens that shows a distorted, narrow view of our world—what I've called the *distorted lens effect* of overthinking. We look through that lens, and instead of seeing the unvarnished reality of our past and our present, we see only what our negative mood wants us to see—the events in our past that are negative, the aspects of our present situation that are negative, the things that could go wrong in the future. "Look here at this bad event!" our negative mood says to our brain, "and here at this sad situation! But do *not* look there at the other, positive side of the situation!" As Sandy, a crusty fifty-year-old waitress from Brooklyn describes it:

> As soon as my mood gets dragged down a little bit, there's like three or four things I always feel—my brain goes right to them— and I think about how I want to have more friends, and I want a stronger support network. When I'm feeling good, I tend not to think about that stuff.

When you overthink you look through the distorted lens of your negative mood, then follow the brightly lit paths in your brain to the negative nodes. All these paths are connected by your negative mood, so as you leave one negative node, you immediately go down another brightly lit path to another negative node. You begin thinking about a fight with your son, which leads you to think about your short temper and your inability to control it. Then you think about your father's short temper and evaluate your childhood as unstable. You link that unstable childhood with your unstable career. As you think about your career, you name the string of incompetent bosses you've had. Pretty soon, you have accumulated a truckload of negative memories, thoughts, and expectations to ponder. You may also make some horrible decisions based on these negative thoughts.

So yes, chronic overthinkers do think about big issues—the meaning of their lives, their worth as individuals, the future of their relationships. But the quality of their thinking can be so colored by their negative mood that they gain a highly distorted view of these big issues.

By contrast, when we learn to recognize that we are overthinking, and develop strategies for overcoming that overthinking, our minds can be freed to ponder big issues in much more meaningful and effective ways.

Major League Effects

My conclusions about overthinking come from dozens of studies I've conducted over the last twenty years, with people from many walks of life. These studies have shown that overthinking

- makes life harder—the stresses we face seem bigger, we are less likely to find good solutions to our problems, and we are more likely to react to stresses in an intense and lasting way.
- hurts our relationships—others may become annoyed, even abandon us, and we have trouble understanding what we need to do to improve our relationships.
- may even contribute to serious mental disorders, including depression, severe anxiety, and alcohol abuse.

The powerful effects of overthinking on people's reactions to a traumatic event were evident in one of my early studies, conducted when I was a professor at Stanford University. You may remember the World Series Earthquake—the 7.1 quake that hit the San Francisco Bay Area in October 1989, right in the middle of a World Series game between the Oakland A's and the San Francisco Giants. This earthquake was the largest Northern California had experienced since the 1906 earthquake that leveled San Francisco. In the Bay Area, 62 people were killed, 3,757 were injured, and 12,000 were left homeless. More than 18,000 homes and 2,575 businesses were damaged. In the city of Oakland, the upper deck of a major highway collapsed onto the lower deck, crushing and killing people. A fire in the Marina District of San Francisco raged for hours. A section of the Bay Bridge, the major link between San Francisco and the East Bay, collapsed, rendering the bridge unusable.

This earthquake was high-grade fuel for rumination. The media was saturated for weeks with pictures of burning houses in the Marina District, injured people on the streets the night of the earthquake, cars that had nearly fallen into San Francisco Bay when the Bay Bridge fell, and stories of buildings that had unexpectedly collapsed on people days after the earthquake. Almost everyone had their own personal story of how the earthquake affected them—some were injured themselves or had their homes and property severely damaged, others had family members or friends who had suffered injuries or property damage.

By luck, I had given a version of my questionnaire on overthinking, and a questionnaire measuring depression and anxiety, to about 200 Stanford students several days before the earthquake. My former graduate student assistant, Jannay Morrow, and I soon realized we could go back to those students and see if their answers to our overthinking questionnaire predicted their emotional responses to the earthquake.

About ten days after the earthquake we were able to locate 137 of the students who had completed our pre-earthquake questionnaires and got them to fill out another depression questionnaire. We also asked them about their experiences of the earthquake: Did they experience any personal injury or loss of property? Did close family members or friends have injuries or property loss? We reasoned that those students who had more stress as a result of the earthquake would have more reason to be depressed, and so we should know about their stress. We then went back to these students again in December, seven weeks after the earthquake, to see if the overthinkers were still more depressed than the nonoverthinkers.

Chronic overthinking did indeed predict both short-term and long-term depressive reactions to the earthquake.[2] Those students who had a tendency to fall into overthinking before the earthquake were more likely to be depressed both ten days and seven weeks after the earthquake, regardless of how depressed they were before the quake or how much stress the quake had caused them. In addition, chronic overthinkers had more symptoms of post-traumatic stress disorder, such as anxiety, a feeling of numbness, and being watchful for danger.

Jill, a small, pencil-thin, Asian-American eighteen-year-old, was one student overthinker. The day of the earthquake, she was with her college roommate in their dorm room. The two young women were chatting animatedly about the upcoming midterm exams and their chemistry instructor, who had a reputation for "weeding out" students from his class with the first exam. Their dorm room was actually one of the safer places to be on campus, because the building had been fortified to withstand an 8.0 earthquake. Nonetheless, it rocked and rolled like everything else in the Bay Area the evening of the quake. Jill was a sophomore at Stanford, and had grown up in Los Angeles, so she was quite familiar with earthquakes. This only fed her post-earthquake ruminations, however:

> Why can't I get over this one? For heaven's sakes, it's not like I've never been in an earthquake! I can't get it out of my head, though. I keep playing back the moments when the earth was shaking. Our bookshelf nearly fell on my roommate and I just stood there screaming. She could have been killed and I did nothing. I should have known what to do. I should have made sure that bookcase was screwed to the wall in the first place—my parents have talked about earthquake safety all my life! What is wrong with me!

By contrast, Jill's roommate, Leila, was not an overthinker. Leila was from Colorado and had experienced only a couple of small earthquakes during the year or so she had been at Stanford. When this earthquake began, Leila's soft brown eyes grew as large as compact discs and she hurriedly hauled her slender 5' 2" frame over into a corner of the dorm room in an effort to be safe, milliseconds before the bookshelf fell on the bed on which she had been sitting. She was scared speechless just after the earthquake happened and then, like all the others in her dorm, chattered incessantly about it for the rest of the night and for the next few days. Within a week, however, Leila was sick of talking about the earthquake and just wanted life to get back to normal. Midterm exams had been delayed because of the earthquake and Leila was annoyed; she felt she had been prepared for her chemistry exam the day of the quake, and now had to get prepared again.

Mostly, however, Leila was tired of listening to Jill talk about the earthquake and her feelings about the trauma. Jill just couldn't seem to let it go. She kept berating herself for not securing the bookcase to the wall and apologizing to Leila for "nearly killing her." Leila assured Jill that she didn't hold her responsible for the bookcase, that she was fine, and that Jill would be fine, too. But Jill couldn't stop overthinking. After three weeks, Leila got so sick of Jill's effusions about the earthquake that she blew up at her and told her to grow up and get over it. This, of course, offended Jill deeply. She accused Leila of not caring about her or any of the people injured or made homeless by the earthquake, who were frequently in Jill's thoughts. After more harsh words, Leila stormed out of their room and didn't return that night. The two sophomores continued to live together for the rest of the semester but didn't speak to each other, and Jill moved to another room in January.

Jill's and Leila's experience illustrate both how differently over-thinkers and nonoverthinkers react to the same situation, and how difficult it can be for them to get along. Nonoverthinkers just can't understand why overthinkers don't "get over it," let go of their frets and fixations, and move on. Overthinkers can feel misunderstood by non-overthinkers, who seem unsympathetic, coldhearted, even superficial.

Overthinking and the Brokenhearted

When people lose a loved one to death, it's normal for them to experience grief-related depression. Severe depression that lingers for months and years after a loss can devastate an individual's life, however. My Bereavement Coping Project showed that chronic overthinkers are more likely to have long-lasting, severe depression following a loss. Their social relationships deteriorate more after a loss. And they have more trouble answering the profound questions that can arise after a loss, such as "Why did this have to happen to me?" I was joined in this project by Judith Larson, Ph.D., a therapist who specializes in bereavement counseling and education.[3]

Over a five-year period, Judi and I and our staff of interviewers talked with nearly five hundred people who had lost a loved one to a terminal illness, most often cancer, but also AIDS and advanced heart disease. The variety of experiences we heard about was staggering. We spoke with older women and men who lost their spouses to disease, who were trying to reconstruct a life without the person they had been with over the last fifty-some years. We also spoke with young people who lost their parents or siblings, and whose friends and coworkers didn't understand why they didn't "just get over" their loss within a couple of months. We spoke with people who had given up lucrative jobs to care for a dying friend in the last days of the friend's life. We heard heart-wrenching stories of mothers who had come from Iowa or New Jersey or South Carolina to care for their adult sons who were dying of AIDS.

We learned so much from these people. We learned that overthinking is especially toxic in the context of loss. People who were chronic overthinkers had more depressive symptoms while they were caring for their loved ones, shortly after the loss, and through the eighteen months we followed them after their loss. And these weren't just the pangs of grief that nearly all bereaved people feel. Almost 45 percent of the chronic overthinkers had severe enough symptoms of depression around the time of the loss that they could be diagnosed with a major depressive disorder, one of the most severe forms of depression. In contrast, people who weren't prone to chronic overthinking typically experienced some depression-like symptoms around the time of the loss and over the next year and a half. But for most, these symptoms were never overwhelming or long-lasting.

Overthinking nearly killed Karen, a forty-seven-year-old physical therapist whose sister, Amanda, had died of breast cancer during our study. You wouldn't know to look at them that Karen and Amanda were sisters—Karen was tall and blond and athletic, while Amanda was dark-haired, shorter, a bit overweight, and ten years older. But Karen and Amanda were devoted to each other. Amanda had taken a great deal of responsibility for Karen during their childhood, in large part because both of their parents drank heavily and neglected the girls in favor of alcohol several nights a week. As they became adults, the women leaned on each other for both practical and emotional support, and spent as much time together as their jobs and family obligations would allow.

When Amanda was diagnosed with breast cancer, the sisters vowed to remain optimistic and to fight it together. Whenever Karen was not with Amanda, however, she worried and ruminated, losing sleep, skipping meals, and getting increasingly depressed.

What am I going to do if Amanda dies? I can't live without her. Why couldn't it have been me who got cancer? Why is God doing this to us? We've suffered enough already. I can't stand this. I don't know if I can live without her.

Tragically, the best medicine on the West Coast couldn't save Amanda. Her cancer had spread too far before it was caught and continued to spread rapidly despite aggressive treatment. Within a year of her diagnosis, Amanda died.

Like many bereaved people, Karen was in a state of shock when Amanda actually passed away. She closeted herself in her house for days, eating almost nothing, barely responding to her husband when he tried to talk to her. As the shock slowly lifted, the pain of her loss grew more intense and Karen's overthinking became more virulent. She went over every conversation she had had with Amanda's doctors, replaying what they had said and what she had said, wondering if the doctors had done everything possible to save Amanda. Karen derided herself for not seeking out alternative treatments, such as experimental ones at the university, that could have helped Amanda. Surely there was something out there, some new medicine or surgical technique, that could have at least prolonged Amanda's life.

Karen's husband tried his best to be supportive of her. He listened for hours as she talked about Amanda and the wonderful times they had had together over the years. He gently responded to Karen's self-lashings as she went over everything she perceived she had done wrong in her relationship with Amanda, and tried to help Karen understand that she had done the best she could do and had been a very loving sister. He took over Karen's usual jobs around the house and with their children so she could have more time to herself, and for visiting Amanda's grave. He grew increasingly impatient, however, as several months passed and Karen seemed to become more depressed and preoccupied with thoughts about Amanda, instead of less.

When she was showering one morning, getting ready to visit Amanda's grave, Karen inadvertently ran her hand across her right breast. A surge of terror flashed through her mind and body as her fingers touched what felt like a small lump. Karen began probing her breast, pushing the tissue around and trying to determine if what she felt was really a lump or natural tissue. But she couldn't be sure. Was this a lump? Did she have breast cancer just as Amanda did? Karen's thoughts began to race:

> I couldn't bear to go through the horrible treatments that Amanda had. And what point is there, anyway, if you are going to die? I can't stand the idea of wasting away in misery the way she did. I can't put my husband and kids through this.

Fleeting thoughts of ending her life had occurred to Karen since Amanda's death, but she hadn't seriously entertained carrying them out. Now her mind locked on the idea of taking her own life before cancer did, and before she and her family would have to endure months of agonizing treatments and eventual death. Karen knew the sensible thing to do was to see a doctor about this lump, but she believed that as soon as cancer was diagnosed, she would lose control over her life. She would be at the mercy of the doctors and tests and hospitals. And that would be unbearable. By the time she had finished her shower, Karen had convinced herself she had breast cancer and was going to die. She was also convinced she was going to commit suicide.

Fortunately, just as she was stepping out of the shower, Karen's husband walked into the bathroom. The instant she saw him, she broke into tears. Eventually he pried out of her the reason for her tears, and he immediately called their physician. An exam and biopsy were done within twenty-four hours, and they showed no evidence of breast cancer.

The fortuitous intervention of her husband was lucky for Karen. If her overthinking had gone much further, she might have acted on her suicidal thoughts. Short of suicide, overthinking can contribute to prolonged, severe grief reactions that greatly impair the health and well-being of bereaved people.

The Bereavement Coping Project also provided powerful evidence that overthinking can severely impair people's relationships. Psychologist Christopher Davis of Carleton University and I examined the changes in close relationships that overthinkers and nonoverthinkers experienced over the eighteen months following their loss.[4] The overthinkers actually reached out to others for support and encouragement more than the nonoverthinkers did. After all, they had a great deal on their minds, as Karen did, and wanted to share their thoughts and feelings with others. But the problem with American society is that we have strong norms for how long and how much you should talk about your grief, and these norms aren't generous or realistic for bereaved people. For overthinkers, whose feelings and thoughts about their loss linger much longer than those of nonoverthinkers, the social time clock for "getting over" loss is really punishing. People become tired, even annoyed, with overthinkers for continuing to talk about their loss. They may simply withdraw, or if they can't withdraw, they may eventually blow up at the overthinker, expressing anger and frustration rather than sympathy and concern. Laura, a thirty-six-year-old woman whose father had died and whose mother was dying after a prolonged illness, said:

> I think the stress that it puts on a marital relationship is great. My husband has never experienced the death of a parent, or the illness of a parent, so he's not really good with compassion. He doesn't have the foggiest idea. He says, "Well, it's been six months. You should be over this by now." I felt invalidated by him along the way quite a bit.[5]

We found that overthinkers reported receiving significantly less emotional support from other people after their loss, compared to nonoverthinkers. Overthinkers also reported a lot more "social friction"—out-and-out conflict between them and their friends and family members. Karen's husband grew impatient when Karen continued to overthink and be depressed over Amanda's death many months after it occurred. Some family members and friends are much harsher, becoming derisive and abandoning the grieving overthinker.

You might be saying to yourself, "Well, no wonder these people were upset and overthinking. Their friends and family members were being so unkind to them." We did find that experiencing lots of social friction and too little emotional support from others fed overthinking—people with low social support became stronger overthinkers over time. But overthinking also fed social friction and withdrawal of support: The overthinkers lost more and more social support over time.

The Other Curse of Womanhood

There is a startling difference in women's and men's mental health. Women are twice as likely as men to develop depression, both mild and severe. This two-to-one difference has been found in a wide range of studies in the United States and Europe, and in most cultures of the world.

As soon as people hear this fact, they begin generating explanations for it, as you may have. Some people say it's women's hormones that cause so much depression. Others say it's women's lack of power in society. Still others say it's something about women's personalities.

I've been studying the causes of women's depressions for over twenty years now, and there's one thing I am sure of—there is no one single reason women are more prone to depression than men. Indeed, there are *too many* reasons. Many different biological, social, and psychological factors come together to make women twice as likely to be depressed as men.

Overthinking is one of those factors. This was most apparent in my Women and Depression study, which consisted of interviews with about 1,300 women and men from all walks of life, ranging in age from twenty-five to seventy-five. These people were randomly chosen from communities in the San Francisco Bay Area and invited to participate in our study. We asked people about everything from their jobs and marriages to their outlooks on life to the traumas they had experienced to their medical histories. Of course, we also asked people about their tendency to overthink.

Women were significantly more likely than the men in the study to say they overthink when they feel sad or anxious or depressed.[6] The women were also more likely than the men to be depressed. When we looked at the extent to which overthinking and several other factors we measured in this study contributed to women's higher rates of depression, we found that overthinking was one of the biggest contributors (in a statistical sense). It certainly wasn't the only contributor. Women also had more traumas in their past, such as sexual abuse, that contributed to their higher rate of depression. Women also faced more chronic situations that made them feel powerless, such as poverty or job discrimination, which also contributed to their higher rate of depression. But overthinking accounted for a big chunk of the difference between women's and men's rates of depression.

Thought Pollution

What makes overthinking so bad for us? You'd think that pondering the causes of your emotions would be a good thing. After all, that's what so many of the pop psych books written since the 1960s have recommended. And that seems to be what we go into therapy to do.

The problem with overthinking is that it doesn't uncover the deepest and truest meanings and realities of your life. It doesn't give you clarity and insight into your past or solutions to your current problems. Instead, it pollutes your thinking with negativity to the point where you are defeated before you begin; immobilized and demoralized, you sink deeper and deeper into depression.

I've studied the effects of overthinking in a number of controlled laboratory studies, conducted with Jannay Morrow of Vassar College, Sonja Lyubomirsky of the University of California, Riverside, and Andrew Ward of Swarthmore College. We created a way to make people overthink in the laboratory by asking them to focus on their emotions and how their lives are going, with statements such as:

> Think about your level of motivation right now.
> Think about your goals for the future.
> Think about how happy or sad you feel right now.
> Think about your relationship with your family.

You'll notice that these statements don't explicitly ask people to think about their negative memories and feelings. We wanted the statements to be neutral so we could look at how this form of thinking would affect the moods of people who were relatively happy as well as those who were already somewhat depressed. We suspected that this overthinking task would have little effect on the moods of nondepressed people because it was so neutral, and because thinking about yourself is not an

inherently depressing thing to do. But for the already-depressed people
in our studies, we suspected that this overthinking task would lead them
to be more sad and blue and pessimistic, because their depressed moods
were already making them think in more depressed ways.

We also designed a distraction task, which involved statements that
drew people's attention away from their emotions and self-evaluations,
such as:

> Think about a cool breeze blowing on a warm day.
> Think about a plane flying slowly overhead.
> Think about the shape of the Statue of Liberty.
> Think about the layout of your local mall.

Again, these were emotionally neutral statements, so we expected they
would have little effect on the moods of depressed people. But because
they would distract the depressed people away from their ongoing concerns, we hoped they would have some positive effect on their moods,
however short term.

Our expectations for the effects of the overthinking and distraction
tasks were confirmed. Sad people became more sad after doing the overthinking task for 8 to 10 minutes, whereas the sad people who did the
distraction task for the same amount of time became significantly less
sad and depressed. On the other hand, the people who weren't sad when
the study began showed no mood changes in response to either the overthinking or distraction tasks.[7]

We then went on to explore the effects of overthinking and distraction on thinking. In a long series of studies, we invited depressed and
nondepressed people to come to our lab, where they were randomly
assigned to do either the overthinking or distraction task for 8 minutes. Then we asked them to do a new task that would indicate what
kind of thoughts they were having about the past, the present, or the
future.

In a set of studies focusing on people's thoughts about the past, we
found that when depressed people overthought, they tended to generate
more negative memories from their past than depressed people we distracted from their overthinkings or the nondepressed people in the

study.[8] In real life, this means that when you overthink your sadness and concerns, your mind travels down only the dark and dreary memory lanes to those times in your life that have been marked by failure, loss, and disappointment. You can remember in detail the embarrassments and pain you've suffered––being laughed at by other kids, being criticized in front of coworkers, feeling unloved by your parents. These sad memories flood your consciousness, making you even more depressed. They also seem to justify your current depression—of course you're depressed, from all the pains you've suffered in the past. Your mind, however, is systematically ignoring your positive memories of the past. It's as if there are road blocks on the bright and cheery memory lanes preventing your mind from traveling down those paths to equally valid experiences. As a result, your perspective on your past is greatly unbalanced toward the negative.

It's not just the past that is polluted by overthinking. We also found that depressed people who were overthinkers were more hopeless about their future than depressed people who had been distracted or the non-depressed people.[9] Overthinking made depressed people believe it's unlikely that good things—like having a long and successful marriage or relationship, finding a great job and being a success in a career, living a long and healthy life—would happen to them in the future. But they thought it was highly likely that the bad things of life (illness, financial troubles, broken relationships) would happen to them. Expecting only bad things to happen in the future can make you hopeless, and hopelessness is a powerful contributor to long-lasting depression.

Depressive overthinking also clouds your vision of the here and now. We asked the participants in our studies to talk about how their lives were going recently. Depressed people who overthought were more critical of themselves, saw more problems in their lives, and felt more hopeless and out of control about those problems, compared to the depressed people who had been distracted or the two nondepressed groups.[10] For example, the depressed people in the overthinking group said things like:

> Nothing in my life is going the way I want it to right now. I'm
> overwhelmed by school and I'm feeling really lonely. I keep getting

advice from my friends about what I should do, but none of them really understand.

In contrast, depressed people in the distraction group said things like:

I'm really frustrated with some things in my life right now. My grades are lower than they should be—I'm smarter than that. My mom suggested I get a tutor, and maybe that's the solution. I feel really lucky that she's willing to help me pay for it. I'm sure I'll pull my grades up with a little help.

There was no reason to think that the depressed people in the over-thinking group actually were living worse lives than those in the other groups, because everyone in the study was randomly assigned to be in either the overthinking or distraction conditions. Instead, overthinking made depressed people more pessimistic and self-critical about their current lives.

Many people say they get into cycles of overthinking because they are trying to understand and solve their life problems. How can you ever overcome these problems if you don't think about them? Unfortunately, overthinking while you are depressed probably makes you a lousy problem-solver. We had depressed and nondepressed people do the overthinking or distraction task, and then we presented them with some hypothetical problems that are actually very typical in the lives of depressed people. For example, one of the problems was: "Your friends don't seem to want to be with you anymore." Then we asked them how they would go about solving problems such as these. The depressed people who had been overthinking generated solutions that were of significantly lower quality than the other three groups of participants.[11] For example, when asked what they would do if a friend avoided them, the depressed overthinkers responded with solutions like, "I guess I'd just avoid them, too." In contrast, the depressed people who had been distracted from their overthinking generated solutions such as, "I'd ask the person I was closest to in that group what I was doing that made people avoid me." Overthinking also makes depressed people generate poorer solutions to the problems they are actually having in their lives.[12]

Even if they come up with a decent solution to their problem, over-thinkers have more trouble initiating it. We found that overthinkers feel less certain about any solution they generate, and want more informa-tion and time to ponder before committing to a decision, compared to people who don't overthink when they are depressed.[13] As a result, over-thinkers will stay stuck in self-perpetuating cycles of doubt and indeci-sion, never quite sure about the right thing to do.

Overthinkers not only get stuck on big problems, but overthinking seems to sap their motivation to take even little steps toward solving their problems. We presented the participants in one of our experimen-tal studies with a list of small things they might do to make themselves feel better and more in control of their lives, such as going to dinner with friends or playing a favorite sport. We asked each of the partici-pants how useful they thought each activity would be in lifting their mood, and found that everyone, whether depressed or not, and whether in the overthinking or distraction groups, thought these activities would be very helpful. Then we asked them how willing and motivated they would be to engage in each activity if they had the opportunity. The depressed people who had been overthinking were considerably less willing to engage in these activities than the other groups, even though they had said moments before that the activities would help lift their moods.[14] In other words, the depressed overthinkers couldn't muster the motivation even to do those things they could intellectually acknowl-edge would be helpful to them.

So overthinking makes you more negative in your thinking about your past, your present, and your future. It interferes with your ability to come up with good solutions to your problems and saps your confidence and motivation in implementing any solution you do consider. And as I mentioned earlier, overthinkers seem to lose social support more quickly after a loss or trauma than nonoverthinkers. No wonder overthinkers are more likely to be depressed than nonoverthinkers.

It is important to note that overthinking is equally toxic for women and men. In all our studies overthinking is as likely to lead to depression, negative thinking, and poor problem solving in men as in women. Women, however, are more likely than men to fall into the trap of over-thinking and thus to experience its dangerous consequences.

Depression isn't the only outcome of overthinking. Shortly after I moved to teach at the University of Michigan, a graduate student named Cheryl Rusting came to see me about some ideas she had about overthinking and anger. She thought that if overthinking amplified the effects of depressed mood on thinking, it ought to do the same thing for an angry mood. That is, the more you overthink when you are angry, the angrier you get and the more reasons you can think of to be angry. Cheryl tested her ideas in experiments in which she actually made people angry—by having them recall the angriest experience in their recent past, or to imagine themselves in a situation that would make most people angry (being cheated out of a good grade in a course). Then she had people overthink or distracted them, using similar tasks to those that Sonja and I used in our depression studies. Cheryl found that people who overthought when they were angry grew much angrier, while people who were distracted after becoming angry did not.[15] She also found that overthinking flamed angry thoughts. After making people angry and then having them overthink or distracting them, Cheryl presented them with emotionally ambiguous situations, such as "An older person is talking with a younger person," and asked them to generate a story about each situation. People who had been overthinking generated stories that were more negative and angry than people who had been distracted from their anger.

There are some differences between the kinds of thoughts fanned by angry overthinking and those fueled by depressive overthinking. Angry thoughts tend to focus on injustices we feel we have suffered and blaming others for those injustices. So when we are angry, we have thoughts like, I can't believe she did that to me! I'm going to get her back for that! When we are depressed, our thoughts are more likely to focus on our own faults and mistakes, and a sense of loss and failure. The reality is, however, that our thoughts and moods are seldom only angry or only depressed or only anxious. We bounce back and forth between these moods and their related thoughts, and often our feelings are a jumble of different moods. All the while, overthinking can amplify all the thoughts activated by our different moods, making us overwhelmed with questions about whether others are to blame or we are to blame for our predicaments, and whether we should take retribution against others or just withdraw in defeat.

If overthinking makes us sadder, more anxious and angry, damages our relationships, derails our careers, and incapacitates our problem solving, then why do we do it? In the next chapter, I explore four historical shifts that have inflated our tendency to overthink in recent generations, and the reasons why women are so much more prone to ruminate than men.

2

If It Hurts So Much, Why Do We Do It?

Amy doesn't know just how she gets into these states. Her day might start off perfectly fine, as she drives her SUV down the highway toward her job as a paralegal in a major law firm. Amy likes her job, and even likes the attorneys she works with, who are always working on important cases that involve huge sums of money. Dressed in her usual conservative black skirt and smart blouse, Amy walks into her office and drops last evening's work down on her desk. Instantly, her eyes catch the yellow note lying in the middle of her work space. "Amy, please see me at 10 A.M. Stu." Stu is Stuart Wayman, Amy's supervisor and one of the partners in the firm. Amy likes and respects Stu, but being called into his massive, dark office sends shivers down her spine. "What's going on?" she asks herself, and her overthinking begins. In the hour between 9 and 10 A.M., Amy's moody ruminations cover a wide expanse of territory:

> Why didn't he tell me what he wants to talk to me about? When he wants me to research something, he usually leaves me detailed instructions in an e-mail. My stomach is churning. If he gives me bad news, I know I'll break down and cry. Then what kind of reference will I get from him when I have to apply for another job? How am I going to tell my family about this? My sister keeps harassing me to go to law school and become a real lawyer myself. She has no idea. She never really did listen to me, even when we were growing up. I'm feeling light-headed. Just watch me faint

and make a fool of myself. If I was in better physical shape I could handle stress like this more. But I'm just too lazy to go to the gym. I can't stand being around all those skinny young girls in their tight workout clothes anyway. I just can't play that game. Which is another reason I have no social life.

At 10 A.M., Amy tiptoes into Stu's office, quivering. Stu begins ominously with, "Amy, I have something I need to talk with you about." Amy's mind is racing and she can hardly hear what Stu is saying. He continues, "We've got that big case in Chicago next month, and I have to stay there for the duration. You're the best paralegal in the firm, and I would love to have your help. But I hate to ask you to live out of a suitcase for perhaps a month straight. Would you be willing to go? We'll compensate you well, of course."

Amy's anxious ruminations have clogged her ears and mind to the point that she's not sure what Stu's just said. She's pretty sure she didn't get fired, and she thinks he's asked her to go with him to Chicago. But the details escaped her. Amy manages to stammer, "Uh, sure Stu, whatever you need." He goes on to discuss when they will leave and to make a list of documents they must be sure to bring with them.

When Amy gets back to her desk, she commences with chaotic overthinking:

> What an idiot I am! How do I let myself get so crazy and scared? There's no way I can become an attorney. I can't handle any level of stress! Why did Stu pick me to go? I think he said I was a good paralegal, but does he have other motives? I've heard he and his wife are having problems. Oh man, if he puts the moves on me, I won't be able to cope. I'm really pissed at him for putting me in this position. But I'm pissed at me, too, for being such a mess. Why do I do this to myself?!

Why, indeed, do we sink into self-destructive overthinking? And why are women more prone than men to get into this state? Recent research suggests there are multiple answers to these questions. One focuses on the brain. The way the brain is organized makes it quite easy to overthink, and for some people, overthinking may become hard-wired into the brain over time. Also, social circumstances can push us into overthinking.

Historical changes over recent decades in our self-concepts, values, and ways of coping have encouraged more overthinking in both men and women. And for women, lack of social power and dependence on others contributes even more to overthinking.

Your Overthinking Brain

The organization of our brain sets us up for overthinking. Each little thought and memory we hold in our mind does not sit there isolated and independent from other thoughts. Instead, our thoughts are woven together in intricate networks of associations. There may be one network or node that has to do with your family. Another may have to do with your job. Still another may have to do with your weight and appearance.

Many of these nodes are connected to each other. Thoughts about your family may be connected to thoughts about your weight, because weight problems run in your family or your mother always chided you for being chubby. Thoughts about your job may be connected to thoughts about your children because you are always feeling guilty for either focusing on your job and ignoring your children, or shirking your job responsibilities because you want to spend time with your children.

One result of all these interconnections is that thoughts about one issue in your life can trigger thoughts about issues that are connected through these networks. Sometimes the connections are obvious—as when your thoughts about your weight immediately trigger thoughts about your mother's snide comments. Other times, you may not be consciously aware of the connections. For example, your thoughts about your weight may be connected to your thoughts about your job, because both have to do with your image of yourself. So when you get a job performance evaluation that is less than what you expected, you may be surprised to find yourself thinking about how fat you feel.

Stanford University psychologist Gordon Bower discovered over twenty years ago that our network of thoughts about different issues in our lives is also connected through our moods and emotions.[1] Usually, the things that happen to us cause us to feel either a happy or unhappy emotion. Every time your mother called you chubby, you felt humiliated and sad. Each time you got a good performance evaluation at work, you felt proud and happy. Situations that have aroused negative moods tend to be connected in one network of memories, while situations that have aroused positive moods tend to be connected in a different network. As a result, when you are in a bad mood of some type—depressed, anxious, just altogether upset—your bad mood tends to trigger a cascade of thoughts associated with your mood. These thoughts may have nothing to do with the incident that put you in a bad mood in the first place, as when a poor job performance causes you to think about your aunt who died last year.

This intricate organization of the brain into interconnected networks of memories, thoughts, and feelings greatly increases our efficiency of thinking. It's what helps us see similarities and connections between issues. For example, when you realize that your spouse is grumpy on Tuesdays, when he must meet with his supervisor, and Saturdays, when he visits his father in a nursing home, you may deduce that his supervisor somehow reminds him of issues he has with his father.

But our spiderweb of a brain also makes it easy to overthink. In particular, the fact that negative mood connects negative thoughts and memories, *even when these thoughts and memories have nothing else to do with one another,* sets us up for overthinking. When you are in a bad mood for any reason, your mood activates—literally lights up—those nodes of your brain that hold negative memories from the past and negative ways of thinking. This makes them highly accessible: it's easier to get there with your conscious thoughts. This is why it is easier to think of negative things when you are in a bad mood than when you are in a good mood.

It is also easier to see interconnections between the bad things in your life when you are in a bad mood. Amy, the paralegal we met earlier, saw connections between her fear of getting fired, her sister's behavior when they were children, her dislike of the gym, and her concerns about her social life. There was a logical string of associations we could follow in Amy's overthinkings. But her ability to jump so quickly from one concern or memory to another is due, in part, to her negative mood that activated all those negative nodes in her brain, making it easy for them to enter her conscious thoughts.

Amy's bouts of overthinking, like most, begin with a surge of negative emotion triggered by some recent event. Then Amy turned inward to ask herself what was happening. Her negative mood activated the nodes of negativity in her brain, which then gave her all kinds of compelling answers to her questions—she was going to get fired, she can't handle stress, her boss might make a pass at her.

Unfortunately, the more often we fall into overthinking, the easier it becomes to overthink. When you are overthinking on top of a bad mood, you are exercising your networks of negative thoughts and memories, strengthening the connections between them. You ask why you are feeling so bad, and your brain dishes out a cascade of good reasons— it's that argument you had with your spouse last week, it's your dissatisfaction with your job, it's your concerns about your weight, it's your lousy relationship with your mother. You ask what's going to happen to you in the future, and your overthinking brain gives you little to hope for. You think of some way you could solve some of your problems and your brain raises all kinds of "yeah, but . . ." counterarguments based on things that have gone wrong in the past. As you exercise your negative mood networks through overthinking, the intricate connections among all these pessimistic thoughts and memories become stronger. Even more thoughts connected to feelings of sadness, shame, anxiety, and anger come to the forefront. You can become so flooded that you feel confused and bewildered, overwhelmed by this sea of problems that seem so big and real. Your mood sinks deeper and deeper.

In the meantime, the interconnections between your nodes of negativity get stronger. Then, the next time you get into a negative mood for some reason, these negative brain nodes and the connections between them are even more easily activated than the last time, making you more consciously aware of and drawn to them.

This was demonstrated in an important study by psychologists Jeanne Miranda of Georgetown University and Jacquelyn Persons of the San Francisco Bay Area Center for Cognitive Therapy.[2] They invited a group of forty-three women to participate in an experiment. Half of them were randomly assigned to read sad sentences such as, "I feel sad and tired," and "I feel depressed." Reading these sentences typically puts people into a mildly depressed mood, and it did in this experiment. The other half of the participants read sentences that put them into a happy mood. Then both groups filled out a questionnaire that assessed how negative their thinking was at the moment. The women who had been put into the mildly sad mood were more negative in their thinking on the questionnaire than the women who had been put into the happy mood. More important, the sad mood increased negative thinking much more among the women who had experienced episodes of depression in their past than among women who did not have a history of depression. In other words, the women who had experienced depression in the past had a network of negative thoughts and attitudes that was easily activated by the sad mood during the experiment.

Most of us have at least some negative memories from our past, worries about the future, or concerns about our present lurking in our brains. Most of the time we are probably not conscious of these negative memories and thoughts. But when a negative mood comes over us—even if it's only because it's a dreary day or because we drank too much wine at dinner last night—it's easier to recall those negative memories or dredge up those negative worries and concerns and begin overthinking. And the more often we overthink on these negative nodes, the more likely they are to pop up the next time a negative mood comes over us.

Obviously, some of us are much more likely to fall into overthinking than others. How do we account for the differences among people in the tendency to overthink? Here, brain research is only beginning to give us answers. Psychologist Richard Davidson of the University of Wisconsin has been investigating what he calls "affective neuroscience," the ways the brain processes emotion.[3] Using sophisticated neuroimaging technology (such as positron emission tomography, or PET), he has found that negative emotion activates the right side of a part of the brain called the prefrontal cortex, more than it does the left side of this area of the brain. The prefrontal cortex is involved in emotion regulation—our conscious and automatic attempts to channel and control our emotions adaptively. Damage or miswiring of the prefrontal cortex could lead a person to have maladaptive emotion-regulation strategies, such as overthinking, and to be prone to depression. Two other areas of the brain, the amygdala and the hippocampus, which are involved in learning and remembering about emotional situations and cues, may be damaged in people prone to depression and overthinking. In particular, people whose amygdalas are overactive may be biased toward paying excessive attention to

negative information in the environment, which would promote rumination. Over the next decade, work by scientists such as Davidson may
uncover important clues as to the brain origins of overthinking.

Other clues as to why some people are more prone to overthink than
others have come from the community-based studies I have conducted
over the years. These studies suggest that a tendency to overthink may
not just be the result of a miswired brain. It may also be a by-product of
important historical shifts in our culture.

The Overthinking Generation

Overthinking is a disease of the young and middle-aged. In our study of
1,300 people randomly chosen from the community (described in chapter 1), 73 percent of the young adults and 52 percent of the middle-aged
adults could be classified as overthinkers: they knew exactly what we
meant by overthinking and could vividly describe bouts of it. Take, for
example, Christie, a blue-eyed, twenty-six-year-old executive who wore
perfectly pressed business casuals. Christie had ridden along on the mete-
oric rise in dot-com businesses in 2000, and as a result she was wealthy
beyond her wildest dreams as a college computer major. She had a beautiful house in Silicon Valley, drove a Lexus, and ate out almost every night
in the better restaurants in town. Yet, when Christie wasn't consumed
with some programming problem, or in a fast-paced meeting trying to
push her idea for a new software product, she slid into overthinking. She
described how she would sit staring at her computer screen, looking as if
she was working, when she was really entertaining thoughts like:

> The guy I dated last weekend was such a bore. I can't believe he
> thought I'd be interested in endless stories about his golf game.
> Am I just picking the wrong guys to date? Or is there something
> wrong with me that I'm turned off by most of my dates?

As she continued fretting, Christie's thoughts turned to her work:

> Maybe it's because they see me as a computer geek. The money
> I'm making in this business doesn't make up for my lack of social

life. I'm not even interested in this job half the time anyway. It's
like nothing is going right in my work or my social life.

As thoughts like these swirled around in Christie's head, her heart
would get heavier and heavier, and the world would look more and more
bleak. The thoughts wouldn't end until Christie was interrupted by one
of her coworkers or until she had become so upset and overwhelmed
that she just got up and went home, where she usually resumed overthinking.

Yet, the older adults in our study—those over sixty-five—had a lot of
trouble understanding what we meant by overthinking. Only about 20
percent of these people could be classified as overthinkers. When we
asked them if they ever found themselves thinking for long periods of
time about how sad or anxious or angry they felt, or why something
wasn't going their way, many of them gave us a puzzled look and said,
"Well, maybe every once in a while, but not usually. That wouldn't be a
helpful thing to do, would it?"

Others immediately gave us their remedy for rumination. A short,
pert seventy-year-old named Phyllis, her hair crafted into a lovely silver
chignon and wearing a flowery cotton housedress, poured the interviewer a cup of tea and sat down in her faux velvet easy chair, ready to
start the interview. Phyllis's husband had died many years previously,
leaving her with their small, run-down house and only a little money.
Phyllis had been forced to go to work at the age of sixty, just so she could
pay for groceries and blood pressure medications. Phyllis viewed going
to work as an opportunity, however, and not a burden, because it took
her out of the house, introduced her to new people, and let her learn
new skills. When the interviewer asked Phyllis if she ever found herself
overthinking, she leaned forward slowly, handed the interviewer another
homemade oatmeal cookie, and said with a sympathetic smile, "Oh
honey, let me tell you what to do when you get into that state. You say a
quick prayer to the Lord and hand over your worry to Him, then you get
busy with something useful around the house."

Our conversations with older adults led me to believe that few of
them had ever done much overthinking, despite confronting tremendous hardships in their lives. As they moved through their adult years,
every day they faced difficult situations that would devastate most of us

younger folk—they did backbreaking labor to put food on the table, they lost children to dreaded diseases, they sent their sons off to war. Some people were defeated by these events, but most dealt with adversity with dignity and strength. They did what they could given their circumstances, drew close to friends who could support them, and used their values and faith to understand and cope.

But over the last few generations there seems to have been a growing epidemic of overthinking in place of coping. This is paralleled by a historic upsurge in depression, anxiety, and uncontrolled anger. For example, research by Gerald Klerman and Myrna Weissman of Columbia University has shown that recent generations are extraordinarily more prone to serious depressions than previous generations.[4] Fewer than 20 percent of people born before 1915 have ever had an episode of serious depression at any time in their lives. In contrast, over 40 percent of people born after 1955 will have an episode of depression serious enough to meet a psychiatric diagnosis at some point in their lives. Many more people will experience at least mild episodes of depression.

We can hope that as the baby boomers and Gen-Xers grow up, we'll gain wisdom about how to cope with adversities that will confront us and be less prone to depression than we have been in our younger adult years. We can also hope that our children will not continue the historical trend toward more and more overthinking. Sadly, studies I've done with children as young as twelve suggest that many youths, especially girls, do worry and overthink, about anything and everything. In one study, we asked 615 children ranging in age from twelve to sixteen to look at a list of possible "worries" they might have and tell us how often they worried about each issue.[5] These children were not seeking treatment for any psychological problems—they were just your average kids in middle school and high school. The girls worried more than the boys about almost every issue we asked them about, including their physical appearance, their relationships with their friends, being safe, personal problems, problems their friends were having, problems in their families, being liked by other kids, and what kind of person they were. The only worry that boys reported more often than girls was about succeeding at sports or other extracurricular activities. The kinds of concerns that girls report as worries—relationships, self-image, the problems of their friends and family members—are not easily fixed and can provide a lot of fuel for overthinking.

Causes of Current Overthinking

What accounts for the historical shift toward more and more overthinking? I believe there are at least four cultural trends involved.

1. *The Vacuum of Values*

First, we have many choices these days, but there is a vacuum of values that guide these choices. We can choose what profession to pursue, whether to marry, and whether to have children. These choices free us to do what we think is best for us, rather than what we are told to do by our parents, our religion, or societal norms. But how do we decide what is best for us?

Previous generations may never have questioned the value systems that led them to make the choices they made, but we question everything: religion, patriotism, humanism. Pop culture tells us to value being richer, more successful, more beautiful, and more popular than the next person. But what it means today to be a success is a moving target—we may think we've achieved success but then we're told we're not doing quite enough. We get a promotion at work and come home feeling good about it, only to see a story in the newspaper about a twenty-something college dropout who started his own company and is now a billionaire. So we brood. We go over all our possible choices, trying to discern which one is best for us but not knowing how to define "best." We desperately want advice from others but we get confusing and conflicting opinions. We question our motives, our desires, our ability to make judgments. We second-guess the choices we've made, asking ourselves how we could have made the bad ones, worrying that we will make more poor choices in the future.

We can probably never return to the consensus of beliefs that characterized previous generations. Indeed, many of us would not want to return to a set of strict rules for our behavior and choices imposed by other people in the community. But a vacuum of values is fertile space for overthinking.

There is hope, however. I believe that buried in the muck of most people's moody ruminations is a set of values they hold dear, that they would be willing and happy to base their decisions and choices upon. The problem is that these values can be almost impossible to see when they are obscured by the negativity and chaos caused by overthinking. When this negativity and chaos can be cleared away, however, those core values shine, illuminating answers to our most troubling questions.

2. *The Entitlement Obsession*

We have also developed an extraordinary sense of entitlement. We feel entitled to have lots of money and a dream job, to have a consistently fulfilling relationship, to have our opinions listened to and respected by others, and to feel good most of the time. When these expectations are violated, as they inevitably are, we do not easily accept it as a normal part of life and instead begin overthinking about why we are not getting what we deserve. Sometimes our ruminations focus on what is wrong with the world that it is not providing us with what we want, and sometimes our overthinking focuses on what is wrong with us that we can't accomplish our goals: "Why is my employer holding me back and not giving me the promotion I deserve?" "What am I doing wrong that my boyfriend can't get an erection?" "Why does no one seem to care what I think?" The result is rage, anxiety, sadness, negativity, and impulsive acts that damage ourselves and others.

Our obsession with entitlement can be summarized in the following beliefs:

> I deserve whatever I want.
> No one else has the right to make me feel bad.
> Anyone who makes me feel bad should be punished, publicly if possible, so everyone else will know I'm right.

The entitlement obsession is manifested in the explosion of blame and confrontation that today characterizes our courts, popular media, and the simplest activities of our everyday lives. The smallest conflict between neighbors often ends up in court, with both litigants feeling entitled to retribution against the other. A dozen nationwide talk shows on television, such as the *Jerry Springer Show* and thousands of local radio shows, are devoted to people airing the wrongs others have committed and claiming the status of victim. Even a disputed call by a referee at a children's soccer game can result in a fistfight between parents who feel they and their children are entitled to justice and success.

The entitlement obsession can lead to abundant overthinking: Why am I not progressing in my job? Why am I not rich? Why haven't I benefited from the economic boom of the last ten years? We answer these questions, based on our sense of entitlement, by continuing to overthink even more: Maybe it's because my boss is sabotaging my career for fear I will take his job. Maybe it's because my parents wouldn't pay for me to attend an Ivy League college. Maybe it's because my family responsibilities are holding me back. Maybe it's because I'm not as smart as everyone else.

Any one of these answers could have an element of truth. One problem with an overdeveloped sense of entitlement is that it keeps our focus on how we are not getting what we deserve rather than on what steps we can take to deal more effectively with our problems—and on how well things may actually be going. The second problem is that it puts us in an adversarial relationship with everyone in our lives. A third problem is that many of us simply begin to doubt whether we really deserve the very things we thought we had wanted.

Olivia's story fits this pattern. You'd never know Olivia suffers from bulimia by her looks. She carries her 130 pounds on her 5'4" frame well, always dressing nicely in public, letting her beautiful, long blond hair flow softly down her back. But at least once a day, Olivia binges, usually on a combination of sweets (Pepperidge Farm cookies are her favorites) and salty foods (especially Nacho Cheese Doritos). Olivia doesn't stop bingeing until her stomach hurts or all her food is gone. Then she promptly goes into the bathroom, sticks her finger down her throat, and throws it all up with an efficiency that comes with practice.

Olivia's bingeing and purging regularly take up two or three hours per day. She used to be able to confine it to the evening hours, but a few months ago she began bingeing during the day. She'd binge frantically over her lunch hour, often returning to her job as a receptionist in a real estate office well beyond 1:00 P.M., when she was supposed to be at her desk. Then she'd spend forty-five minutes in the bathroom, throwing up and cleaning up any mess. Her long absences from her desk caused her to get fired. Since then, Olivia has just stayed home alone in her apartment.

All day long the TV is on, usually turned to one of those confess-all talk shows in which people blame all their troubles on the misdeeds of others. Inspired by the people on these programs, Olivia has begun to go over each of her relationships with her family members and friends, dissecting and comparing her relationships with others'. She hasn't found any one event or person responsible for her predicament, but she is sure that, like the people on the talk shows, something about her past is causing her current problems. Was she sexually abused as a child? Olivia can't remember any incidents, but therapists on these talk shows said that people often repressed childhood abuse. Maybe she was not sexually abused, but emotionally abused? Olivia goes over and over things her parents had said to her as a child or an adult. They *seemed* supportive, but what did they *really* feel toward her? Certainly her mother didn't seem to understand why Olivia just stayed alone in her apartment and did not try to do anything to overcome her problems. Surely there was some critical experience or relationship in Olivia's life that was to blame for her unhappiness and bulimia. The talk shows made it clear that if you just dig deep enough into your history, you can find your personal villains.

One day, in a frustrating phone conversation with her mother about her bulimia, Olivia began yelling that she was sure her problems were her mother's fault for not being as supportive and emotionally expressive as Olivia needed her to be. Olivia's mother was devastated by the accusation and quickly got off the phone. Olivia felt good for a while—relieved and triumphant—but then began to worry about her outburst and inability to pinpoint exactly what it was that her mother had done to cause her problems. Maybe her problems weren't her mother's fault. Maybe Olivia was just a failure, defective in some way, and she'd never be happy.

Even when we can identify the villains in our lives, we are not always able to express our rage at them, or when we do it doesn't always help us feel better. Catharsis often only feels good in the moment, and then—despite the strong sense we had that we deserved to release our distress and be heard—we are back to overthinking, trying to understand why we are still in pain and who is at fault. Catharsis can also create its own troubles—we blow up at our boss and get fired, we tell off our parents and they don't speak to us for months, we accuse our spouse of wrongdoing and communication breaks down. This gives us more to ruminate about.

Tragically, Olivia is now trapped in her overthinking with no exit in sight. The quality of her life has spiraled down to an all-time low. Is the only alternative to swallow her pain and deny the traumas she has experienced? Definitely not. People like Olivia can learn to break free of overthinking, move to higher ground, and then evaluate the causes of their unhappiness more accurately and thoroughly. This then leads people to develop and implement more effective strategies for overcoming the causes of their unhappiness.

3. The Compulsive Need for Quick Fixes

The third societal shift leading to more overthinking is our compulsive need for quick fixes. If we're down or blue or upset, then there must be some quick fix. Change our job, change our relationships, stop talking to our parents. Sometimes these are the right choices, but if they are done as quick fixes for dissatisfaction, they tend to accumulate into a string of failures that gives us more to overthink about. Sometimes we try to get our minds off our concerns through frenetic activity, taking up yet another sport or signing up for another class. Taking breaks from your worries is a healthy first step to breaking their grip. But, as I will discuss throughout this book, breaking the grip of overthinking is just the first step. The second, equally important step is finding your higher ground, evaluating the causes of your dissatisfaction in effective ways that lead to positive change and reduce the likelihood that you will have more to overthink about in the future.

A quick fix that has been around for a long time is binge drinking. Overthinkers are twice as likely as nonoverthinkers to binge on alcohol on a regular basis.[6] And overthinkers say they drink to forget their worries and feel more self-confident. Getting drunk can help some people forget their worries for a while. But for other people, perhaps especially overthinkers, alcohol may actually narrow their attention on their worries, a phenomenon that psychologists Claude Steele of Stanford University and Robert Josephs of the University of Texas call alcohol myopia.[7] It's as if the alcohol sharpens your awareness and perception of your worries, making them seem even bigger and worse than they were before. Finally, frequent binge drinking can obviously create new problems for people to worry about. I have found that 25 percent of overthinkers show at least one sign of alcohol abuse—such as drinking so often that they miss work—compared to about 8 percent of nonoverthinkers.

A more modern quick fix that Americans are increasingly turning to is prescription medication. Prozac and other drugs known as serotonin reuptake inhibitors have been lifesavers for people with serious depressive and anxiety disorders. Many people taking these drugs aren't suffering from severe depression or anxiety, however. They are people who will go to their doctor with complaints about finding life stressful. Often they will directly ask their doctors to prescribe Prozac, Zoloft, or a similar drug. Other times their physician will prescribe the drug, with good intentions, but without a psychiatric evaluation to determine if the drug is necessary. Unfortunately, there is little evidence that the serotonin reuptake inhibitors are helpful to people facing the daily stresses of life. So these people are left with their stressors, and with their ruminations about these stressors, feeling as if nothing can help.

To overcome overthinking, you must put aside any desire for quick fixes and do the slow, difficult work of identifying the true problems in your life and designing long-term solutions to these problems. Only then can you prevent new bouts of overthinking from hobbling you again.

4. Our Belly-Button Culture

One of the predominant themes of popular psychology and culture since the 1960s has been the importance of self-awareness and expression of emotions. This can be seen in the catchphrases of the culture ("Get in touch with your emotions." "Express your inner child."), the lyrics of popular songs, and the prescriptions of popular psychology books.

But many of us have taken this self-awareness too far. In the fourth cultural trend, we have become a belly-button culture, chronically staring at our own navels, analyzing every twist and turn of our emotions. We become totally self-absorbed in pondering the meaning of a twinge of sadness, a slight rush of anxiety, a fit of pique. We award even minor mood swings with great significance and peer into our moods to discern their message. Sometimes our mood swings do hold messages. But they can also be the result of completely inconsequential events—a bad night's sleep, the day's weather, getting stuck in traffic on the way to work. Psychologist Norbert Schwarz found that he could significantly change people's ratings of their own moods by arranging for them to "find" a quarter on the floor of an experiment room before they made their mood ratings.[8]

We also hyperanalyze the events in our lives. A friend makes a rude remark and we may spend hours wondering what this *really* means about his character. The boss is irritable one morning and we dissect every word he said, trying to determine what it means for us. Our lover is disinterested in sex for a while and we assume it has meaning for our attractiveness or the future of our relationship. Again, the friend could be a bum, the boss could be out to get you, and the lover may be bored. But we seldom consider simpler explanations—the friend had one of those momentary lapses we all have; the boss confronted his own traffic jam on the way to work; the lover is distracted by stresses at work. Instead, we imbue these events with great significance and become hypervigilant for further signs of trouble. This is great fuel for overthinking.

· · ·

These four cultural shifts in the last few decades help to explain the epidemic of overthinking and depression in younger generations. They do not fully explain why women are so prone to overthinking, however. Here again, our community-based studies are providing some clues into the origins of women's overthinking. I discuss these studies in the next chapter.

3

Women's Unique Vulnerabilities

It is sometimes assumed that women's greater vulnerability to overthinking, compared to men, is due to some biological difference between women and men—for example, women's hormones, or the organization of women's brains. Future research may provide some evidence for these assumptions, but right now the evidence is pointing toward social and psychological roots to women's overthinking.[1]

Women May Have More to Overthink

Women's status in society has changed remarkably in the last fifty years. No longer confined to a narrow range of occupations, women are becoming visible at the top levels of many professions, and demanding salaries that equal men's. In their relationships with men, many women expect respect and equal sharing of domestic chores.

But we still have a long way to go. Women still earn only 74 cents for every dollar men earn, and the wage gap is particularly great among low-income workers.[2] Although women may be asking for more "help" from men with housework and child care, they often don't get what they need. Our studies suggest that the majority of married, working mothers still carry the lioness's share of the load around the house. And although women are pursuing more prestigious and lucrative professions than ever before, many say they do not feel their male partners sufficiently value or respect their work.[3]

These chronic strains—the grinding annoyances and burdens that come with women's lower social power—appear to contribute to women's tendency to overthink. Our research has shown that people who have more chronic strains—and these are more likely to be women than men—are significantly more likely to overthink.[4]

These chronic strains may convince some women that there is little they can do to control their lives, which is why they overthink. Yet, I suspect that most women under chronic strain hold out some hope that there is something they can do to improve their situation and thus do not become fully hopeless and helpless. Instead, they search for some understanding of why their lives are not going as they wish, why they feel frustrated and distressed so much of the time, what they can do to convince their partners to share in the work of the home and child care (happily), and how they might be better appreciated by their partners and families.

The answers to these questions are unfortunately not always obvious to women. Psychologist Faye Crosby of the University of California, Santa Cruz, has found that many women who, by objective standards, are in unequal and unsupportive relationships or are being directly discriminated against in the workplace, do not—perhaps cannot—acknowledge that they are being victimized.[5] Even when they acknowledge their victimization, women often do not have the resources to break away from that victimization. If a woman does not want to break away from an unequal relationship, but just wants to improve that relationship, it means changing the attitudes of her partner and the patterns of exchange between her and her partner, which may be entrenched. Thus, many women under chronic strain may retain a moderate sense of mastery, but may overthink the causes of their situation, their feelings about the situation, and what they should do about it. This overthinking then contributes to depressive symptoms.

The painful, often traumatic, experiences that women suffer because we still lack equal power and status with men are great fuel for overthinking. One trauma that women suffer much more often than men is sexual abuse. We can quibble about the actual rates of sexual abuse in modern society, but it is clear from research by psychologists such as

Mary Koss that women are at least twice as likely as men to be the victims of severe sexual abuse such as rape and incest.[6] In my research, I have found that women (and men) who have suffered sexual abuse are much more likely to fall into bouts of overthinking.[7] These traumas violate our basic assumptions about the world as a place where bad things happen to other people. If the perpetrator of the trauma was a family member or friend, these experiences can shatter the survivor's sense of trust and security with others. As a result, survivors are also left with ruminations about why they suffered their traumas.

A twenty-two-year-old incest survivor named Carole was particularly prone to overthinking. Carole had escaped the perpetrator of her abuse, her father, when she was sixteen by running away to live with Martin, a guy she met at a party. Martin was no prince, however, and occasionally beat Carole until her beautiful black skin was swollen and red with bruises. After one especially vicious beating, Carole ended up in the emergency room of the hospital with a concussion and one eye swollen completely shut.

Wendy, an advocate from the Women's Health Center, spotted Carole (along with that evening's other victims of abuse) and encouraged her to seek shelter in a secret home for battered women and runaway teenagers. Because she had nowhere else to go when she was discharged, Carole went to the shelter. There she found, for perhaps the first time in her life, people who seemed to genuinely care for her. They gave her clean clothes and decent food. More important, they believed her stories. Over the next few weeks, they helped Carole find a job and a cheap and safe place to live.

But Carole never followed through with her promise to Wendy to call a counselor to talk about her incest experiences. For one thing, Carole didn't believe she could afford counseling. She also believed she could just forget the incest and her beatings by Martin, and get on with her life. She trudged through the next six years, doing well enough in her job to be promoted and save enough money to get a nicer apartment.

But whenever she was home alone, overthinking would intrude. Sometimes the thoughts were directly about her past traumas—flashbacks to specific incidents or questions about why these things had to happen to her. Often, however, her overthinking did not seem directly related to her abuse:

I'll never get a better job, I'm just a loser. I can't even hold a conversation with the customers in the store. They look me directly
in the eye and I just get overwhelmed. I can't get promoted any
further if I can't get my act together. I'm pathetic. I'm so damned
lonely, too. But there's no one I want to be with. The only place
that feels halfway good is here at home alone.

Carole's immobilization probably has a lot to do with the issues of
trust and self-worth that can be so difficult for trauma survivors. Her
overthinking takes her down the paths to self-loathing, but she has
trouble recognizing its connection to her abuse experiences because she
works so hard to block those out.

Women suffer many other conditions in addition to sexual trauma
because of our lack of social power. Psychologist Deborah Belle of
Boston University has shown that women are much more likely than
men to live in poverty.[8] Poverty brings with it an increased risk of a
number of severe stressors, including exposure to crime and violence,
the illness and death of children, and physical or sexual assault. Poverty
also brings many chronic, uncontrollable, negative life conditions,
including inadequate housing, dangerous neighborhoods, and financial
uncertainties. This gives poor women plenty to overthink; indeed, my
research indicates that poverty among women is connected to their tendency to overthink.[9]

The first step to breaking free from oppressive situations and beginning the process of healing from past traumas is to move out of overthinking. Only then can women move into productive self-reflection
and action that overcomes their circumstances and helps them redefine
their sense of self.

Women's Self-Definitions
Fuel Overthinking

One of the biggest and most consistent personality differences between
women and men is in how they relate to other people.[10] Women are
much more likely than men to define themselves in terms of their
relationships—I am the daughter of Catherine and John, the wife of

Richard, the mother of Michael. Women also build social networks that are broader and deeper than men's. We know more people at a deep emotional level and we are more attuned to the emotions of others than are men.

Women's broad and deep emotional networks provide a wonderful richness to our lives and are an important foundation of support in times of need. Unfortunately, they also give us more people to ruminate about. Harvard University sociologist Ron Kessler has found that women are more likely than men to be emotionally affected by traumatic events in the lives of others.[11] When a friend or family member is severely ill or injured, or is facing some other major stressor, women are more likely than men to feel sad and blue, and to worry about these people.

Perhaps more important, psychologist Vicki Helgeson of Carnegie Mellon University has found that women are more likely than men to cross a line between being emotionally connected with others and being emotionally overinvolved with others.[12] These women base their self-esteem and well-being too much on what others think of them and how their relationships are going. This leaves them chronically concerned and anxious about the implications of even the slightest change within their relationships. It also leads women to make bad choices in their lives in an effort to keep other people happy. My research shows that the tendency to become emotionally overinvolved with others contributes to chronic overthinking in women.[13]

A good example is a lanky, vivacious twenty-nine-year-old physical therapist named Denise. All it takes for Denise to begin overthinking is for her husband, Mark, to wake up on the wrong side of the bed. He is definitely not a morning person and, especially when he has had trouble sleeping the night before, tends to be grumpy in the morning. He'll sulk around in his sloppy robe not talking to anyone, his dark hair sticking every which way, as he sips coffee from his National Public Radio mug. At the breakfast table he has been known to snap at the kids unnecessarily for their table manners.

Denise, on the other hand, loves the mornings and feels best then. She wakes up at 5:30, does three miles on her treadmill, and after a quick shower goes cheerfully to breakfast. As soon as she enters the kitchen and detects that Mark is grumpy, Denise's mind begins to race:

Did I do something last night to make him upset? I don't remember anything. But I'm so sleepy at nighttime maybe I can't remember what I did. Did the kids do something awful? I wonder if he's worried about work. Oh, I don't want to raise anything about work—I can't stand it that he's unhappy there.

Eventually, Denise will meekly ask Mark what's wrong. If he's really grumpy, he'll bark, "Nothing!" But usually he recognizes he's just in his morning mood and tells her so. Denise never believes this is the full truth, however, and always wonders what's really bothering Mark. Sometimes she'll pester him, trying to pry out of him why he's upset. Particularly on those mornings when nothing is really bothering Mark except the fact that it's morning, Denise's persistent questions and suggestions of what might be wrong annoy him. If he can hold it together he'll just walk away from her, saying he has to get dressed. Sometimes, however, he blows up at her, telling her to leave him alone and stop creating a mountain out of a molehill.

Of course, this just gives Denise more to overthink. She can spend the rest of the day worrying about what is wrong with Mark and kicking herself for handling the morning altercation badly.

The answer for women is obviously not to become cold and uncaring toward others. But those of us who define ourselves too much in terms of our relationships can find a more solid base for our self-concepts so we are not constantly at the mercy of the inevitable ups and downs of these relationships. We can only do this, however, once we recognize our tendency to fall into overthinking and develop strategies for breaking free.

Is Overthinking Normal for Women?

Maybe women overthink more than men simply because they are more emotional. Even preschool children will tell you that girls experience and express emotion more than boys, and this belief holds among adults of all age groups. This is one cultural myth that might actually have some truth, at least for some emotions. Psychologist Lisa Feldman Barrett

of Boston College has found that not only do women say they experience more emotion than men do, but direct observations of women and
men from many age groups and geographical areas confirm that women
articulate and express emotion more than men do. Feldman Barrett and
her colleagues asked participants in seven different locations and occupations around the United States and in Germany to describe how they
would feel, and how another person would feel, in each of twenty scenarios.[14] For example, one scenario was: "You and your best friend are in
the same line of work. There is a prize given annually to the best performance of the year. The two of you work hard to win the prize. One
night the winner is announced—your friend. How would you feel? How
would your friend feel?" The participants wrote out their answers to
these questions and the researchers analyzed the responses in terms of
the amount of emotion expressed. Across all seven groups, women
demonstrated greater awareness of their own emotions and the emotions of the other people in the scenarios than men did.

Is emotional awareness something women are born with? Well, possibly, but there is also reason to believe that, from an early age, women
are trained to pay more attention to their emotions than men. Research
by developmental psychologists such as Eleanor Maccoby of Stanford
University and Judith Dunn of the Institute of Psychology in London
has shown that one powerful difference in the ways parents treat their
daughters and sons is that they pay attention to and support the expression of sadness and anxiety in girls, but discourage it in boys. Many the-
orists have argued that discouraging the expression of negative emotions
is unhealthy for boys because they learn to deny and repress their feelings of sadness and fear.[15] This is no doubt true to some extent.

But there is increasing reason to believe that parents don't do their
daughters much good by massaging their negative moods. Some parents
excessively reinforce their daughters' expressions of sadness and anxiety,
for example, by encouraging them to talk about these feelings and pointing out all the reasons why their daughters should feel anxious or sad
and *not* helping them think through ways of changing their difficult situations or cope better.[16] In addition, some parents talk a great deal about
their own feelings of sadness or anxiety, expressing a sense of helplessness and hopelessness. And most important, they talk this way more in
front of their daughters than their sons. Girls get these messages pretty

clearly: unhappiness is all around and there is little you can do about it except focus on it.

In our studies, we've asked women and men how controllable negative emotions such as sadness and anxiety are. The women were significantly more likely than the men to say that these emotions are uncontrollable—there's little you can do about them.[17] Unfortunately, when you simply let your negative emotions and the thoughts associated with them run, you're soon into a bout of overthinking. In our study, the more a person thought negative emotions were uncontrollable, the more likely she or he was to be an overthinker.

Many women also engage in tit-for-tat overthinking. They sit and emote with each other, rather than encouraging each other toward active management of the emotions or active problem solving. When friends just stoke the fires of each other's negative ruminations, they may feel understood and validated, but still overwhelmed and unable to do anything about the problems they face. Such was the case with Helen and Betsy. Helen is a single, thirty-eight-year-old woman living in Chicago who for the last six years has been stuck in a dead-end job as a gate agent for a major airline. Every morning she dresses for work and feels a cold, heavy dread in her mind and her body as she contemplates another day with her rigid boss, her self-centered work colleagues, and the hostile customers. Every morning she thinks about what she'd rather be doing—shopping, traveling, anything more interesting than her job. And every morning she just puts on her uniform and plods out the door to drive to O'Hare Airport.

Why doesn't Helen just find another job? This is a question she asks herself constantly. Her inner dialogues around this question go something like this:

> I should start looking for another job. That takes so much energy. I don't have any energy. Or any motivation. I feel like a lump. I don't have the technical skills to get a better job. I should go back to school. School takes money. I don't have any money because I'm in this dumb job and it pays nothing. I guess I could borrow some money. What do I have as collateral for a bank loan? There's always my parents. Yeah, right, like I could ask them for anything. They'd just hold it over me every time I saw them. Just like they criticize me for not being married or having

kids yet. They're probably right—my life is pathetic. I'm so tired, and sick and tired of this whole thing.

Helen's thoughts spin on and on, and often don't stop until they are interrupted by some external event—traffic coming to a sudden halt, the phone ringing, someone approaching her at work. The distraction from her thoughts helps to lift her mood a bit, but as soon as she's got a little thinking time on her hands, she sinks right back into her inner dialogue.

Sometimes she calls up her friend Betsy, because she knows Betsy will listen and sympathize with Helen's concerns. By the end of these calls with Betsy, though, Helen often feels even worse. All Betsy can ever seem to say in response to Helen's complaints is, "Uh-huh. Gosh, that's hard." Betsy seems to feel the situation is as hopeless as Helen thinks it is. If Betsy does suggest something Helen might do to overcome some of her problems, like contact a local employment agency, Helen tells Betsy all the reasons why Betsy's suggestion won't work, and often accuses Betsy of not truly understanding her situation. Betsy immediately retreats, feeling guilty, and lapses back into "Uh-huh" and "Wow" answers to everything Helen says. At the end of the day, all Helen has the energy to do is to go home, microwave some food, retreat into her TV shows, and eventually go to sleep.

Friends can be important antidotes to overthinking, and in chapter 4 I discuss how to work with friends to overcome your tendencies to overthink. Women may have to work harder than men to avoid falling into overthinking parties together, in the false belief that this is how women are supposed to support one another.

There's Hope

I've given you lots of reasons for overthinking in this chapter. There's hope, however, and a great deal of it! The remainder of *Women Who Think Too Much* gives you concrete strategies for overcoming overthinking and leading a more productive and happy life. The first step is to break the hold of overthinking on your brain.

Part II

Strategies for Overcoming Overthinking

Overthinking can have a strong grip on you, but you can overcome it. In Part II, I describe the three phases of conquering overthinking: breaking free of its grip, moving to higher ground and gaining a new perspective, and avoiding future traps by building your resources.

4

Breaking Free

Breaking free from overthinking can be tough—it involves bootstrapping yourself out of self-defeating thoughts even though they have a firm grip on you. But breaking free is absolutely critical if these morbid meditations are not going to pull you deeper and deeper into emotional quicksand, eventually smothering your spirit.

In this chapter, I offer several suggestions for breaking free. Some will resonate with you, some will not. Try them, adapt them to suit your situation. If you find yourself saying, "I just can't get the motivation to do anything" or "None of these things will help me," realize that your over-thinking and your mood are making you feel this way. Dozens of studies of interventions with seriously distressed people, pioneered by psychologists such as Peter Lewinsohn of the Oregon Research Institute, have found that breaking the cycle of overthinking and passivity is a critical first step to relief and recovery. If you try some of these techniques, I'm sure you'll experience a sense of relief in your mind and your body.

Understand That Overthinking
Is Not Your Friend

When people are in the midst of overthinking, they often have the sense that they are onto something important about their lives: "I've stripped

off the rose-colored glasses. I'm finally facing how bad my life really is."
We discovered this in one of the experiments I did with Sonja Lyubomirsky of the University of California, Riverside.[1] When depressed people
spent just eight minutes overthinking, they felt exceedingly insightful
about themselves and their relationships with others. "Now I realize
how bad my marriage really is!" "I can see I'll never be promoted in this
job!" "I'm just being realistic—there's no way I'll make it through school!"
"My childhood was such a mess, I'll never completely get over it!"

Were the overthinkers correct about their insightfulness? No. Overthinking doesn't strip off your rose-colored glasses and make you see life
more clearly. Instead, it gives you tunnel vision that can only focus on
what's wrong in your life. It makes everything look dismal and gray and
overwhelming. It drains your motivation to do anything positive and
cripples your thinking about solutions to your problems.

Still, the sense that you are gaining important new insights can
make breaking free from overthinking very difficult. It seems wrong to
put aside the compelling issues you are pondering, just because the
overthinking is making you feel bad. You feel deeply justified in your
anger and sadness—you deserve to be furious, you have a right to be
depressed. You do indeed have a right to your feelings. But overthinking
only fans them into a huge fire that gets out of your control. You may
sink into a depression that you can't pull out of. You may lash out in
anger in ways you'll later regret.

Before you can use any of the other strategies in this chapter, you first
have to recognize that overthinking is not your friend. It is not giving
you deep insights. Instead, it is stealing away your power over your own
thoughts and feelings. It is lying to you and seducing you into thinking
and doing things that are not in your favor.

If you find yourself in a fierce bout of overthinking, you might try
something as corny as saying, "Overthinking, you are not my friend! You
are hurting me! Go away!" If you have small children, think about how
you've taught them to be assertive when other children are bothering
them, and say the same things to your overthinking: "I don't like that! I
want you to stop!" Then implement one of the other strategies in this
chapter to get further distance from your overthinking.

Give It a Rest

One of the simplest but most important strategies for freeing yourself from overthinking is to give your brain a rest by engaging in pleasant distractions. In my research, I have found that giving people positive distractions from their overthinking for just eight minutes is remarkably effective in lifting their moods and breaking their cycle of repetitive thought.[2]

Even more important, we have found that breaking the hold of overthinking by having people focus on pleasant distractions improves their thinking, making them more positive and balanced and less negative and biased. And it improves their problem-solving skills, making them better able to think of solutions to their problems and more energized to carry out these solutions. So although pleasant distractions may provide only short-term relief from overthinking and negative moods, they set the stage for longer-term relief by improving people's abilities to overcome the problems that they are overthinking about.

Janice, an attractive African-American thirty-nine-year-old homemaker living in Decatur, Illinois, had a tendency to sit at her kitchen table in the morning after her kids left for school, sipping coffee and morbidly ruminating about everything that had happened in recent days. After just a half hour of this, she felt overwhelmed and defeated, unable to think clearly about how to have an impact on problems in her life, such as her son's poor grades in math, or her elderly mother's inability to care for herself. She eventually learned, however, that taking breaks from her thoughts by doing household chores or cooking up something elaborate made her much more effective in dealing with the stresses in her life:

> I only have so much mental energy. If I can get very focused on something, like making bread or pastries, and if I'm very focused on what I'm physically doing, it leaves little room for me to get stuck on my problems.

Everyone can find his or her own personal way or tool that distracts them from overthinking. One of the favorite distractions of the people who've participated in my studies is exercise. Whether it's jogging, rowing, tennis, racquetball, or some other sport, exercise provides a biochemical boost to your brain and a healthy distraction from overthinking. Make sure to choose an exercise that is right for your body (you may want to talk with your doctor before starting anything new). Sports that require all your attention—like a challenging squash match or a technically difficult mountain climb—will do a better job of distracting you from overthinking than sports you can do automatically and with little concentration. Longtime runners often find they can go on autopilot and overthink fiercely while running. If you've been doing a solo sport like running or swimming for a long time, you may need to change your routine frequently to keep your mind as well as your body active.

Hobbies, such as glass-blowing, gardening, model construction, or painting can be great distractions. Losing yourself in the activity is the key. Try something fresh that requires you to build new skills. Both hobbies and exercise can give you a sense of accomplishment and identity that shores you up and prevents you from falling back into overthinking.

Some people can immerse themselves in a book or movie to break up overthinking. Others find work to be both a great distraction and a source of self-esteem. Playing with your children can take your mind away from your ruminations and ground you in what's important in your life. If you don't have children, play with a pet—run with your dog, buy your cat a new toy.

Helping other people is a great distraction, as well as an important expression of your values. Volunteer to serve soup in a homeless shelter. Help an environmental group clean up a park. Take meals to an elderly person who can't leave her home. Your concerns can be seen in a different light after you've spent some time with the less fortunate or have exercised your values through community action.

Distractions free you from overthinking by breaking the connections between the nodes of negativity in your brain, much like you might cut the telephone lines linking homes in a neighborhood. If these nodes of negativity can't communicate with each other, they don't feed on each other to amplify your negative mood and give you more to overthink.

Obviously, it's not healthy to avoid thinking about our concerns all the time by engaging in constant diversions. Much of the psychology research since Freud's time has focused on people who chronically deny or avoid their negative feelings, and it's clear this is not a good thing to do. But I'm concerned with people on the other end of the spectrum who spend too much time thinking about their negative emotions and concerns, and thus spiral downward into uncontrolled depression, anxiety, and anger. For those folks, an occasional distraction is a useful tool to halt the downward spiral and set them on the road to more effectively cope with their problems.

There are unhealthy ways to distract yourself. Some people, especially women, find themselves binge eating in an attempt to distract themselves. The eating feels good at first, but it can feel very bad later. Physically, you may feel bloated and sick. Emotionally, you'll probably feel angry at yourself, depressed, out of control. In the end, the binge will just give you more about which to overthink.

Some women try to drown their concerns in alcohol. This can work in the short term but typically backfires in the long term. Alcohol acts as a depressant on the central nervous system, and it brings your mood down, which can then activate more negative thoughts. Alcohol can cause you to be more self-absorbed, and that certainly doesn't discourage overthinking. And problems related to frequent alcohol use give you much more to be concerned about. As I discussed in chapter 1, people who are overthinkers are more prone to binge drinking and to having social problems related to alcohol use (like the loss of a job).

Such was the case for Paula, a twenty-eight-year-old real estate agent. Paula's bouts of overthinking usually centered around her ex-husband, Vince, a true jerk whom Paula divorced after she discovered he was cheating on her with a good friend of theirs. Paula and Vince had been working hard to earn enough money for a house, and Paula had hoped to go back to school to earn her master's degree once they were more comfortable financially. That day never happened, in part because Vince had spent their money on toys—a speedboat for the summer, expensive ski equipment for the winter, and memberships in a golf club, a health club, and a vacation time-share. "Relax, have some fun, don't be so uptight," he would say to Paula when she complained about his expenditures.

When Paula discovered Vince's infidelity, she was devastated, although not entirely surprised. He begged her to forgive him and stay with him, but she was so angry and hurt that she filed for divorce as quickly as she could and refused to discuss reconciliation with Vince. That was two years ago. Since the divorce was finalized, Paula has had many doubts about whether she did the right thing. It's clear that Vince was trouble, and she deserved to protect herself. She just can't shake the questions that haunt her late at night, or when she's alone during the day:

> How could I not have known that Vince was cheating? It was so obvious in retrospect. Maybe if I hadn't been so blindsided by this, everything wouldn't have fallen apart so quickly. I hate him for what he's done to my life. We were going to have a good life, a nice house, some kids, a comfortable life. We were having fun, even if we couldn't entirely afford it. And now I have nothing. No husband, no house, no kids. I'll never be able to afford to go to school on my own. Why wouldn't I work with him, to see if we could put the marriage back together?

Often, when she's stuck in these thoughts, with her mood sinking quickly, Paula will pour herself a glass of wine from the bottle that is always ready for her in her refrigerator. She tries to confine her drinking to the nighttime hours. But because she has a lot of flexibility in her schedule, she can sometimes stop home during the day to have a drink and "wind down." The alcohol doesn't relax her much, however. Instead, she often ends up sitting on her couch for a few hours, drinking several glasses of wine and railing at herself and Vince for the breakup of their marriage.

In the last six months, her daytime drinking has increased so much that most days of the week she has at least a couple of drinks, even when she has to show a house or meet with a client later in the day. She's switched from wine to vodka tonics for her daytime drinks ever since a client commented that she "must have had a fun working lunch" after smelling alcohol on her breath at two o'clock in the afternoon. A couple of times in the last six months, Paula has missed important meetings with clients when she simply forgot them or fell asleep after drinking in her apartment for a few hours. Her sales have declined quite dramatically and her boss has noticed. Paula is caught in a mixture of overthinking, anger, depression, and alcohol, and she's sinking fast.

Paula needs to pull out of her self-blame and her unresolved anger at Vince, and reconstruct her life without him. She won't be able to do so, however, until she stops using alcohol to drown her thoughts. Alcohol is not only a lousy distraction from overthinking but a great contributor to it.

There are many safe and positive distractions, however, that can help you break free temporarily from overthinking. Work to find those that will lift your spirits, free your mind, and give you a quick sense of control and gratification.

Get Up and Get Moving

In my research, we've found that distractions that involve concentration and activity are most effective at breaking up overthinking. For example, Jannay Morrow and I did a study in which we gave depressed people two kinds of distraction tasks: one that required they get up and move around the room, and another they could do while sitting quietly at a desk.[3] The active distraction did a better job of reducing their depressed mood and their overthinking. Why? There may be some biochemical effect of activity that has a positive effect on mood and thinking—the release of brain chemicals such as norepinephrine or serotonin. It's also just harder to lapse back into overthinking if you're actively moving about and really concentrating on what you're doing.

It can be especially important to get up and move about if you find yourself ruminating in the middle of the night. If you have been lying in bed overthinking for more than 15 or 20 minutes, get up and leave the room. Don't fall into the trap of thinking that if you just lie there another few minutes, you'll be able to shut off your concerns and fall asleep. And especially don't fall into the trap of thinking you're gaining great insights into your problems by thinking them through during the night. The thinking we do in the middle of the night rarely holds any special benefits, and often is fraught with anxiety and fear. Plus, if you lose a lot of sleep during the night, you'll be tired the next day, which will undermine your ability to cope and to think straight. Get up and go someplace quiet, such as your living room, and do some recreational reading. Don't do work and don't read anything distressing. When you begin to feel tired, try going back to bed.

If there are places that tend to trigger overthinking for you, such as your office, you might try changing the look of the place. For example, if I walk into my office and see disorganized piles of papers all over my desk, I often feel overwhelmed and begin to worry about having too much work to do. Organizing my desk and getting rid of extraneous paper seem to quell those concerns. I don't know whether it's the sense of taking control, the physical moving around, or changing the appearance of my office that helps—probably it's all of these. But you may be able to reduce your overthinking in a specific place by changing its look.

Sometimes you may simply have to leave the premises if you find yourself ferociously overthinking. Take a walk, go for a drive, go out for lunch. The key is to do something pleasant that will remove you for a bit from the direct stimulus for your overthinking and act as a distraction.

Join the Thought Police

Sometimes we are in a situation in which it's difficult to find a distraction from our overthinking or to get up and move around. Consider, for example, Carolyn, an attractive forty-year-old executive in a Wall Street investment firm who found herself sitting through a deadly boring presentation. The guy giving the talk was standing there in his black wool suit and power tie, which perfectly matched the black wool suits and power ties of all the other men in the room. The presenter was spouting ivory-tower nonsense about where the markets were going. Carolyn was sure this guy had never put in his time on the trading floor of the stock exchange or in any other front-line investment job.

As she sat there, Carolyn began ruminating about an argument she had with her boyfriend Ned last night. They had been lounging on the leather couch in her spacious apartment, watching a movie. Ned wasn't really watching the movie. Instead, he kept staring at Carolyn. She was especially attractive that night, dressed in black leggings and a simple, slightly tight T-shirt, her black hair hanging loosely around her face. Ned began to initiate some intimacy with Carolyn, but Carolyn told him she was really tired and didn't want to have sex. Ned pouted for a couple of hours while they watched the movie. Carolyn could tell he was upset with her, but instead of being sympathetic, she got mad at him and accused him of being selfish. He counterattacked by accusing her of not having enough sex drive. He got up and went home instead of staying the night. Carolyn was awake half the night, steaming about the argument and worrying about any long-term damage to her relationship with Ned.

As she was overthinking her argument with Ned, Carolyn started worrying that what Ned had said was true—she really didn't have enough sex drive. After all, she hadn't initiated sex with Ned for a couple of weeks, and she truly couldn't have cared less about sex last night. The more she thought about this, the more inadequate she felt. She started thinking about how her mother had said she lost all interest in sex in her forties. Was there something genetic going on here? Was Carolyn becoming frigid like her mother?

Carolyn realized she had to get hold of these thoughts, but the meeting she was in sure wasn't working as a distraction. She usually stopped her tendency to overthink by going to the gym or by reading a good book, but she couldn't do such things in this meeting. So she yelled, "Stop!"—not out loud, of course, but in her mind. That interrupted her thoughts for a moment. When they started creeping in again, she yelled, "Stop!" again in her mind. On the paper in front of her, she drew a stop sign and printed STOP in bold letters on it. Interrupting her overthinking like this gave her the opportunity to look around the room and find some way of diverting her attention. She decided to actually listen to the guy giving the presentation, and to write down on her paper counterarguments to everything he said. This proved to be quite engrossing and Carolyn was able to avoid ruminating about Ned for the remainder of the meeting.

Everyone has the ability to create her own inner "Stop!" sign and thereby call a halt to negative spiraling. Some people actually buy a little stop sign from a toy store and put it in their desk or purse, so they can pull it out whenever they need to play "thought police." Others draw their own stop sign and tape it to the inside of their desk or the wall of their office.

Maybe saying "Stop!" won't work for you, but some other word or phrase will. Try "No!" or "Don't go there!" or "Done!" Think about what would halt your thoughts in their tracks. This will stop your overthinking only for a short time, but with hope long enough to allow you to intervene with yourself in other ways that will have a longer-term effect.

Don't Let the Thoughts Win

If you can interrupt your overthinking for a few moments, your mind will have enough time to consider more complicated phrases or concepts that can help you get even more distance from your concerns. If you are going over and over some conflict with another person in rant-and-rave overthinking, you might say to yourself, "I'm not going to let them win by taking over my thoughts!" Back this up with thoughts about how, if you continue to overthink, those other people will have won the battle by making you miserable. Getting some distance from angry overthinking doesn't mean you've conceded your position or given into others' demands. It simply means you aren't going to let them take over your thoughts and wreck your mood. After you've gotten some distance from the conflict, you can reconsider it with much more brainpower available to find good resolutions to the conflict.

Kay's thoughts were screaming about a letter she had received this morning about her lawn mowing. Kay had been mowing her lawn on Saturday mornings for the last four years with no complaints from any of her neighbors. She always waited until at least 11 A.M. to begin mowing so she didn't wake anyone up, and she was done within a half hour. She liked getting the exercise, and she was proud of how well her lawn had come in, given the sandy soil in her area.

Then this morning she had received an officious letter from the executive board of her homeowners association saying there had been "complaints" about her lawn mowing, and was told that she should only mow it between Monday and Friday during the period of 9 A.M. to 5 P.M. Of course, Kay couldn't do this because she worked during those hours. To comply with the demand she would have to hire a lawn service, and she did not feel like going to that expense.

> Why didn't my neighbors come talk to me if they had a problem
> with my lawn mowing? How dare they tell me when I can mow

my own lawn! These stuck-up bastards! They need to get a life! Going around snooping on their neighbors! Just because they don't have to work for a living during the week!

Kay was probably justified in at least some of her thoughts, but they literally took over her mind for a couple of hours, keeping her from concentrating on her work and tying her stomach in knots. She thought of all kinds of things she'd like to say to her neighbors, and ways she'd like to pay them back by telling on them to the board. In the meantime, her body felt worse, her mood became worse, and her day was being taken over.

So Kay first yelled, "Stop it!" to herself. Then she told herself she did not want these people to own her thoughts. She would figure out some way to fight this, but she couldn't do it when she was seething. For now, she wanted to feel better and she wanted to reclaim ownership of her mind.

After her brain had a rest from her overthinking for a few hours, it occurred to Kay to consult the by-laws of the association to see if the board had any right to force her to stop mowing her lawn on weekends. A quick reading made it unclear what rights she had to contest the board's ruling, so she showed the by-laws to an attorney friend of hers that evening at her son's softball game. He said he thought she could probably get away with a letter to the board saying she had consulted her attorney and was assured that she had every right to mow her lawn on weekends. Kay followed her friend's advice. The board hasn't bothered her since.

If your overthinking is about a situation, you can tell yourself, "I'm not going to let this situation take over my life!" or some other phrase that helps you get back in control. The point is not to let your overthinking take over and rule your consciousness, but to make clear decisions about when and how you will think about a situation that is bothering you.

Put It in Your Date Book

When you feel that you just can't toss aside the compelling issues you are worrying about, you can gain some control by scheduling overthinking hours—times that you set aside to do nothing but think. Then you can say to yourself, "I'm not avoiding my problems, I'm just scheduling quiet time to think about them rather than trying to evaluate them now, when I have other things I have to attend to." This can set you free from your overthinking for enough time to turn your attention to necessary tasks—your job, caring for your child, getting some sleep.

People often discover that once their scheduled hour arrives, the issues they were thinking about somehow don't seem so real. When they were engaged in life-of-their-own overthinking earlier in the day they may have felt absolutely sure that they were wasting their lives, or that their relationship with their child was a mess. When they entertained their rant-and-rave overthinking, they were sure they had been victimized and could think of many ways they wanted to strike back at their victimizers. But when they return to these issues in their thinking hour, their problems often seem smaller and less overwhelming. Their victimizers seem more human and the need for retribution less clear. This is because breaking free of overthinking earlier in the day allowed their mood to lift and their thoughts to clear, so that they could have a more balanced perspective on their concerns once their thinking hour arrived.

If you do schedule a thinking hour, don't make it for just before you go to bed. You don't want to have all those distressing thoughts in your mind as you try to go to sleep. Try to make your overthinking hour for a time when you are likely to feel relatively good and can sit down quietly on your own or with a trusted friend to think through your concerns. If you find yourself ferociously overthinking during your thinking hour, you might need to take breaks from it for short periods so that you don't fall into a deep, deep hole of despair. If you think it's likely you will fall into this hole, it's especially important to have some help during your thinking hour from a confidant or perhaps a therapist.

Hand It Over

Remember Phyllis, the pert seventy-year-old described in chapter 1, who told one of our interviewers to hand over her worries to the Lord and get on with life? One of the surprises from my research is that, despite how nonreligious our society claims to be these days, 40 percent of the people we interviewed in our community-based studies said that they turn to prayer or spiritual meditation to break free from their distress and overthinking.[4] Even people who did not subscribe to any particular religion said they would often utter a little prayer for support and help when they were feeling overwhelmed by worry. Many people have a sense that they are connected to some greater purpose or power that can guide them in times of need, even if they are not a member of any official religion.

If you aren't comfortable praying or are an atheist, you might consider taking up meditation. There are many forms of meditation. University of Washington psychologist Alan Marlatt, who teaches his clients meditation as a way of overcoming addictions and compulsive behaviors, describes the two basic kinds, concentrative meditation and insight meditation.[5] In concentrative meditation, you intently focus your attention on the moment and perhaps on a phrase or image that you hold in your mind, while you let your overthinking fall away naturally. You relax your body, letting go of tension and regulating your breathing. You might focus on each breath, feeling its coolness as it enters your nostrils and its warmth as it leaves. If troubling thoughts enter your mind, you gently pull your attention back to your breathing or your image or phrase. After ten minutes or so, you will feel your body deeply relaxed and your mind less burdened.

In insight meditation, or what psychologist John Teasdale of the Medical Research Council in England calls mindfulness meditation, you let yourself be keenly aware of any thoughts, images, physical sensations, or feelings as they occur moment to moment.[6] Rather than battling with these thoughts and sensations, you accept them with the attitude of a detached observer. You lovingly watch them pass by, not evaluating them but noting that they occurred. The goal is to develop the ability to engage in "mental disidentification," in which your thoughts no longer control you, nor do they make up your sense of self. Rather, your thoughts are something you observe dispassionately.

If you don't want to take a class on meditation or see a therapist who teaches meditation, you can consult one of the how-to books on the topic, such as Paul Wilson's *Instant Calm* (Plume Books, 1995). This book is full of quick techniques that can help you break loose of negative thoughts and calm your mind. Even taking three deep breaths and concentrating only on the feelings of air going in and out of your lungs can temporarily break an overthinking cycle. Another helpful book, one of the original books on relaxation techniques, is Herbert Benson's *The Relaxation Response* (Plume, 1975).

This may all seem like mystical hooey to you. Or you may feel that your problems are so great that something simple like meditation can't begin to make a dent in them. Research by psychologists Alan Marlatt, John Teasdale, and J. Kabat-Zinn finds, however, that meditation can help people who suffer from serious psychological problems such as severe depression, panic attacks, obsessive compulsive disorder, eating disorders, or drug addiction to gain more control over their feelings, thoughts, and behaviors.[7] Meditation is also helpful to many sufferers of physical diseases, such as chronic pain or cardiovascular disease. You don't have to believe in Eastern religions, or any religion, to gain benefits from the practice of meditation.

How does meditation work? There are several theories, but frankly we don't really know. The relaxation that comes with meditation can counteract the tension of anxiety, anger, and depression. Being released from these feelings for a while can free up overthinking and convince you that you truly can feel better. Some research suggests that meditation changes the balance of activity across the two hemispheres of our brain and that might contribute to its beneficial effects. John Teasdale suggests that learning to gain distance from negative thoughts through meditation helps people feel that they are controlling their thoughts rather than their thoughts controlling them. This frees them to discard or overcome self-defeating ways of thinking and to attack their problems with greater self-confidence and self-love.

Lean on Others

One of the most popular ways of breaking free from overthinking for the people in our studies has been to talk with a trusted family member or friend. Ninety percent of the people we interviewed said they talk out their overthinking with others at least sometime, and 57 percent said they often or always talk with others to break their overthinking cycles.[8]

Talking with another person can help to overcome negative ruminations if that person makes you feel accepted and understood, and also helps you sort out your thoughts and move to higher ground, into problem solving. For example, a friend might ask you to explain more about the situation that triggered your bad mood. She might agree with you that you were the victim in this situation. Then she might help you think of good responses to this situation and help you gain the confidence to carry through with whatever seems best.

Talking with others about your overthinking can backfire, though. Friends can just fan the flames of your concerns by sitting and emoting with you but not helping you gain perspective on your problems. The key is to learn to recognize when you are overthinking with friends and to directly ask them to help you pull out of your circular thoughts and move to where you can more effectively evaluate your concerns and possible solutions.

Terri knew she needed to talk with someone. She and her husband, Joe, had had a terrible fight at breakfast, which culminated with Joe saying he wanted a divorce. It was clear their marriage had been in trouble for months, but Joe's declaration still stunned Terri. As she drove her minivan around town that morning running errands, her mind was reeling with what Joe had said and the contents of all the other fights they had had in the last few months. She nearly back-ended another car because she was paying more attention to the echoes in her head than her driving. So she drove over to Sue's house.

Sue and Terri had been friends since high school. They were both class "intellectuals," more involved in the literary club than the athletic teams. Both had gone to prestigious colleges, and both had returned to their hometown after college. Sue had chosen to stay at home with her children, and Terri was pursuing a career as an accountant. They weren't the best of buddies, but Terri knew that if she needed someone who would calm her down and help her think clearly, Sue was the best person to seek out.

As soon as she opened her front door, Sue could see that Terri was distraught. She invited her in and made a fresh pot of coffee. Terri took a deep breath and said, "Joe wants a divorce. What am I going to do? I don't want things to go on as they have, but I don't want to lose this marriage either! I can't think! I feel so helpless!"

Sue told Terri to take a deep breath and a sip of coffee. Then she had her go through what had happened that morning and what Terri saw as the major problems in her marriage. Sue mostly listened, but if Terri began to beat herself up for "ruining the marriage," or expressed complete helplessness and hopelessness, Sue had her take another breath, slow down, and try to stick with concrete details. They talked for the next few hours. By the end, Terri was feeling much calmer, and certainly affirmed and supported by Sue. And Sue had helped Terri decide how she was going to respond to Joe in the short term—that she would write him a note and say she wanted to work with him to see if they could save their marriage. Then Sue helped Terri find the phone number of a marriage counselor that another friend of theirs had used and had said was very helpful. Terri left Sue's house unsure that she could save her marriage, but feeling back in control enough that she could get through the day and face Joe that evening.

If you want a friend to help you get past overthinking and back into control, you might say something like, "I'm feeling really stuck and helpless and I don't know what to do. I'd like you to help me think through some things I might be able to do to begin to get more control over some of my problems." If, even after asking directly for this kind of help from a friend, your friend is still just uh-huhing you or your friend begins engaging in tit-for-tat worrying ("Oh, something like that happened to me, let me tell you about it."), you may need to find another friend to talk with. Look for friends like Sue, who seem to be quite good at dealing with the stresses in their lives—who can admit that they get stressed but don't seem to get totally overwhelmed by their anxieties and concerns.

Commit It to Paper

As an alternative to talking with others, many people find it useful to commit their thoughts to paper. Translating your fears into sentences or phrases puts some limits and structure around them. Rather than swirling uncontrollably in your head, these concerns become contained in little marks on a paper. Writing them down can give you a sense of control over them—they don't control you, you control them by putting them into words and transferring them to paper or a computer screen.

Some people say that writing is like purging the brain, giving them a tremendous sense of relief. Judi, a fifty-year-old secretary who frequently ruminates about her grown children's welfare, told us:

> Just having to write it out, let it out, and then go, it's in God's hands now. But allowing myself to emote, to me, is the best coping strategy and part of that to me is writing it out, letting myself intellectually acknowledge what my feelings are. Then once I do that, it helps. It's purging, that's what I call it.

Seeing your overthinking on paper can also help you sort it out. Some of the thoughts may seem patently ridiculous as soon as you see them written down. Others may stand out as capturing the heart of your concerns. If you write them down, take a break from them for a while, then go back to consider them, you are even more likely to be able to sort out the core concerns from the irrational ones.

Research by James Pennebaker of the University of Texas at Austin shows that writing about our deepest thoughts and feelings and about experiences in our past actually improves our physical health, as well as our emotional health.[9] But Pennebaker finds that writing is only helpful if people move out of overthinking and into understanding and problem solving. We can't simply repeat our negative thoughts and feelings over and over on paper, we must begin to challenge these thoughts to sort out the life-of-their-own overthinking from the realistic concerns, and generate actions we can take in positive response to these thoughts.

At first, just write down your worries and fears and thoughts of failure and anger, then leave them there and go do something else. They will still be there when you return, and you will see them with a much clearer eye and mind.

Seek Your Bliss and Use It

When we interviewed people who were caring for a dying loved one, we asked them lots of questions about how they were coping with the stress of caregiving and the imminent death of someone they loved dearly.

Several gave answers similar to the following quote from Letitia, a serene thirty-seven-year-old African-American woman whose forty-five-year-old sister, Annie, was dying of brain cancer:

> Every day I find something nice to do for myself. It might be as simple as eating a York Peppermint Patty. I make it a point to look up at the sky and notice its beauty every day. I think back on something fun Annie and I did in the past, like the time we went shopping together and Annie found that perfect skinny black dress. Just something little—something that pulls in a little joy in the midst of all the bad feelings and worries.

Groundbreaking new research shows that actively looking for ways to infuse stressful situations with momentary positive emotions improves not only psychological well-being but also problem solving and physical health. Psychologist Susan Folkman of the University of California, San Francisco, has called these *positive emotions strategies*.[10] She found that men who lost their partners to AIDS showed more rapid decreases in depressive symptoms if they actively tried to infuse positive emotions into their lives.

Similarly, in our bereavement research, we have found that people who, like Letitia, find ways to bring moments of positive emotions into the experience of caregiving and loss fare better over time. We asked people how often they used four specific types of positive emotions strategies:

1. I tried to remember the positive times with my loved one.
2. I told myself things that helped me feel better.
3. I looked for positive aspects of the situation"
4. I used my sense of humor.

People who said they were actively using these positive emotions strategies to cope with caregiving and loss adjusted faster to their loss over time, regardless of how depressed they were at the time of the loss.

In her "broaden and build" theory of positive emotions, Barbara Fredrickson of the University of Michigan has argued that using positive emotions to cope with negative mood not only helps you to repair your mood but also improves your thinking, leading you to respond to challenges in the environment and take new initiatives more easily.[11] Experimental studies show that helping distressed people experience momentary positive emotions (by showing them amusing film clips) helps their bodies and their minds to recover faster from stress. This suggests that positive emotions may also reduce the negative effects of chronic stress on your body's physiological systems.

A fascinating study of Catholic nuns lends support to the notion that positive emotions are good for your physical health. Researchers Deborah Danner, David Snowdon, and Wallace Friesen of the University of Kentucky were able to obtain short autobiographies of 180 nuns from two convents in the United States, written shortly after the sisters took their final vows sometime between 1931 and 1943, when they were between the ages of eighteen and thirty-two.[12] They rated each of these biographies for the amount of positive emotions a sister expressed in writing about her life. Then they related the positive content of the autobiographies to a definitive measure of health—whether or not a sister had died by the year 2000. It's important to note that the sisters all had relatively the same amount of education, access to health care, and socioeconomic status. The sisters' tendency to express positive emotions was strongly related to their longevity. The sisters who expressed the least amount of positive emotion in their early-life biographies were 2.5 times more likely to have died by the year 2000 than the sisters who expressed the greatest amount of positive emotion in their autobiographies. In addition, low positive emotion sisters died an average of ten years earlier than the high positive emotion sisters.

Making use of positive emotions can help you to cope better with life in general. People have lots of ways of infusing positive emotions into the moment. Here are just a few ideas:

> Get your hair done.
> Get a massage.
> Take a bubble bath.
> Play with small children.
> Watch a funny movie.
> Tell some jokes.
> Go for a walk in a beautiful place.

Look through photograph books of loved ones.
Turn on your favorite music—loud.
Play an instrument.

Positive emotions can open up your thinking so that as you quiet your overthinking and move to higher ground, you will be more open-minded and creative in understanding your problems and finding good solutions for them.

A Quick Reference Guide

We've covered a lot of strategies in this chapter. Here's a quick summary of them:

Strategy	Description	Example
Understand that over-thinking is not your friend.	Realize overthinking is not giving you insight, but clouding your vision.	Say to yourself, "Overthinking, you are not my friend! You are hurting me! Go away!"
Give it a rest.	Use positive distractions to take your attention away from your overthinkings for a while.	Read an engrossing book. Indulge in your favorite hobby. Help someone else.
Get up and get moving.	Engage in physical activity as a distraction; temporarily leave a situation that is triggering your overthinking.	Get out of bed and read something pleasant when overthinking at night. Take a walk if you are ferociously overthinking at work.
Join the thought police.	Tell yourself firmly to stop overthinking for the moment.	Silently yell "Stop!" to yourself. Keep a toy stop sign on your desk.

Don't let the thoughts win.	Tell yourself you won't let your thoughts control you.	Realize that the other guy wins the battle if you continue to overthink about a conflict.
Put it in your date book.	Put off overthinking until a scheduled thinking hour.	Tell yourself, "I will wait until 6 P.M. to overthink so I can focus on my work now."
Hand it over.	Pray for help with your overthinking or take up meditation.	Ask God's help with your concerns. Learn meditation to get distance from your overthinking.
Lean on others.	Talk with others about what you are overthinking.	Seek a friend who handles stress well and ask for help in sorting out your concerns.
Commit it to paper.	Write down your thoughts.	Keep a computer diary of your overthinking.
Seek your bliss and use it.	Seek out activities that bring positive emotions.	Get a massage. Play your favorite music. Watch a funny movie.

These techniques will help you break free of your overthinking in the short term. They can't solve the problems you are overthinking, however. To do that, you need to move to higher ground and attack your problems effectively. Chapter 5 focuses on how you can do this.

5

Moving to Higher Ground

Once you break free of overthinking, it is very tempting to avoid thinking about your problems altogether, not wanting to deal with issues that make you sad or anxious or angry. This is particularly true if you've grown accustomed to quick fixes for your feelings: "Hey, I don't feel bad anymore. I don't want to think about that stuff again!" But problems that are not solved only come back to haunt you, giving you more and more to overthink. Thus, once you've broken free, it is critical to embrace your problems and begin to solve them. In this chapter, I describe the strategies that will enable you to make clear decisions and take action to improve your life.

Adjust Your Focus

The *distorted lens effect* of overthinking makes us see our troubles only from the most hopeless perspective. We peer intently at the most negative interpretations of our situation and the problems we foresee in overcoming it. Meanwhile, more positive viewpoints are blocked out. As a result, we are held back from doing what we can to deal effectively with the situation.

The only way to fix distorted lenses is to get new lenses that adjust our focus so that we have a more realistic and hopeful outlook on our situation. The first step in this process is simply to decide to change your outlook by saying to yourself, "I have the right to choose how I look upon this situation, and I am going to exercise that right." By taking this powerful stand, you will feel more in control of the situation and less at the mercy of your overthinking. You will become free to think more clearly about the situation and make better decisions about how to respond to it.

Some of us don't feel we have enough courage or self-confidence to choose how we want to view a situation or problem. How can I know what's right? How can I just ignore what others say and take my own stand? Indeed, some people are born with a stronger sense of self than others. But courage and self-confidence are muscles that grow with exercise. Deciding to adjust your focus and choose your own perspective instead of letting it be chosen for you builds emotional strength so that it comes more easily and naturally the next time round.

Consider the powerful perspective-shifting experience of Lori, an energetic thirty-eight-year-old nurse with short, straight brown hair and sparkling blue eyes. Lori is mother to eight-year-old Andrew, who shares Lori's blue eyes and her husband's curly blond hair. Andrew's greatest passion in life is soccer and he has been playing on the same team of little boys since he was in kindergarten. He is pretty good, but the most important thing to Lori is that Andrew loves the game, loves the exercise, and loves his teammates. The boys bumble around on the playing field, occasionally scoring goals, but mostly just trying not to trip over the ball and each other. This year, the parent who had been coaching Andrew's soccer team moved to another city, so the team was left with no coach. Lori had played soccer through high school and college, and so was drafted by the other parents to be coach. She really didn't want to—she'd never coached children this age, and generally didn't like to be at the center of attention. But Andrew begged her, and the team needed her, so she agreed. She bought several books on how to coach young children, attended a couple of Saturday morning workshops on coaching, and began working with the team.

Lori's coaching proved to be very good, and the boys won all but one game in their spring season while still having a great time playing together. In fact, they beat the other teams in their league by such wide margins that they didn't find the games very challenging. Lori thought the boys were ready to play in the more competitive league in town and proposed this to the other parents. Most parents agreed and were eager to have their boys face more challenging teams and build their soccer skills.

A few parents, however, did not agree. They worried that their children would be left behind in a tougher league, although during the spring season Lori had worked very closely with these boys and their skills had improved considerably. One of these parents, Mitch, began calling other parents on the team, urging them not to let their boys move into the new league with Lori's team. He accused Lori of being "hypercompetitive" and "only caring about winning." He also claimed that, if they moved to the new league, Lori would play only Andrew and the strongest boys, and would bench the boys with weaker skills.

Lori got wind of these phone calls through some of the parents. For several nights, she was up for hours, rant-and-rave overthinking what was happening behind her back.

> How could Mitch say such things? How could he believe what he's saying—there isn't any evidence for them, is there? What should I do—confront Mitch? I hate confrontations. Besides, what would I say? His accusations are so ridiculous. I could tell him he's making a fool of himself. I could say he's only worried about his own kid, he doesn't care about the team. Maybe I should call up all the other parents and tell them my side of the story. I don't want to look defensive, though, because that will make it seem like Mitch might be right. What can I do? He's tearing this team apart!

After about a week of this, Lori realized she was letting Mitch and this crazy situation make her feel that she was the helpless victim of a conspiracy. She knew she had to break free of this perspective and adjust her focus or this situation would tear her up. First, she decided she would confine her thoughts about this situation to a certain time of the day—her own personal worry hour. When her concerns popped up again at three in the morning, she put them aside, saying it was not time for her worry hour and she would deal with these thoughts when that time came later in the day. When her worry hour began, she decided she had to adjust her focus on this situation rather than letting herself feel victimized. Lori decided that the only sensible perspective was that Mitch was being ridiculous, but if he wanted his son not to play on a more competitive team, that was fine with Lori. Furthermore, if other parents wanted to pull their sons from Lori's team, it was their right. She would do what she knew was right for these boys and move on. Lori began sleeping soundly again at night and moved her team into the higher league with the full backing of most of the other parents.

Once Lori broke the grip of her overthinking by relegating it to her worry hour, she moved to higher ground, to a healthier way of dealing with her situation, and was able to adjust her focus rather than letting Mitch impose his contrarian perspective on her. If Lori had continued to let Mitch's accusations and the doubts they created in her shape her vision, she would have continued to ruminate about the situation. She might have given up and abandoned the team altogether to avoid the controversy. Or she might have caved in and left the boys in the lower league, even though she knew that was not best for them.

When you purposefully adjust your focus, you actively choose your perspective. You shift your gaze from negative perspectives and see a more adaptive view of the situation.

To summarize, Lori adjusted her focus and successfully solved her problem by:

- Limiting her overthinking to a certain hour each day.
- Actively deciding to not look at the situation from a victim's perspective.
- Deliberately filtering out Mitch's ridiculous remarks.
- Believing in her own vision of the situation.
- Making the firm decision to take responsibility for her decisions and actions.

Feel Your Pain and Then Move On

It is ironic in this age of entitlement that we often overthink whether we are justified in feeling certain emotions. Is it okay to feel angry? What right do I have to be depressed? What's wrong with me that I'm so anxious? Women are especially prone to questioning whether we have a right to feel angry. For forty years now, the women's movement has told us that we do have this right, and, at least on the surface, we believe we do. But deep down inside, many of us get queasy when we exercise this right because it means violating interpersonal rules that many of us hold without even realizing it: we should never make another person upset, and everyone must like us. This ambivalence shows up as overthinking after the times when we've exercised our right to be angry. Something happens, we blow up, and for days afterward, we overthink whether it was okay to blow up.

The first step in breaking the grip of these thoughts is to accept that you have an emotion—period—without trying to build an airtight case that your emotions are justified. Another key to controlling these brood-ings is to recognize that your emotions don't have to dictate your actions. You can accept that you are angry, sad, or anxious. But you are free to choose the best response to your situation, the response that sat-isfies your objectives for that situation rather than the knee-jerk response motivated by your emotion.

I will illustrate with Rhonda's story. A soft-spoken fifty-year-old author of high school science books, Rhonda is a modest woman, not taken to boasting or making demands on others. She is very proud of her work, however, particularly her textbook *General Science*, which is now in its sixth edition. Recently she was corresponding by e-mail with a young editor named Hannah who was working with her on the revisions of *General Science* for its upcoming seventh edition. Rhonda had been annoyed for months about how her publishing company was handling this book—decisions would be made, and then unmade for no apparent reason. They kept coming back to ask her to do things that would nor-mally have been their responsibility. Then Hannah was given the task of telling Rhonda that the company wanted her to retype all her references in a different style from the way she had submitted them months before. Rhonda does all her own typing—she doesn't have a secretary—so this would mean hours of tedious work that she thought was completely unnecessary. She blew her stack in an e-mail to Hannah, saying this was the most unpleasant experience she had ever had around any book she had written, and accusing the company of trying to get her to act as sec-retary and printer as well as author. Then she started to overthink.

Was I being arrogant and unreasonable about doing this work? What right do they have asking me to retype all the references? I've never been asked to do such things before! They have been a total pain in the neck this entire process! I should tell the publisher this and demand an apology. But what if he doesn't apologize? What if he defends this process? Will I be able to come up with enough examples to convince him I am right?

To stop this torrent of thoughts, Rhonda first tried simply to brush it off. This failed because she would immediately think, "But I don't have to say I'm wrong when I'm not wrong!"

Instead, she first had to embrace the fact that she was mad and she had a right to be mad. When she accepted her own emotions, she freed herself to think more clearly about the action she had taken. Even though she was really angry, she realized that it probably wasn't the best choice to blow up at Hannah. Her higher goal was to get her book published, not to get mired in arguments. By realizing this, Rhonda stopped herself from falling into ceaseless overthinking and was able to take direct and immediate action to improve her situation. Once she apologized for blowing up, and explained to Hannah more calmly why she was upset, Hannah acknowledged that she also thought Rhonda had been asked to do a lot of unnecessary tasks and worked with her to find ways to get the tasks done without Rhonda having to do them all herself.

If Rhonda had continued to question her initial angry response rather than accept her anger, her relationship with Hannah might never have been repaired. Hannah might have sought retaliation against Rhonda, sabotaging her book project, or pushing her into even more clerical tasks. Once she accepted her emotions, Rhonda had a clearer head to choose an appropriate response that was honest but also was in line with her goal of working with Hannah to see her book through publication.

Keep It Simple (At Least Initially)

When we are consumed with life-of-their-own overthinking, we see problems in our lives that don't really exist, or at least aren't as big as we make them out to be. These life-of-their-own thoughts are especially likely to sprout and grow when we are upset but we don't know why. Nothing particular has happened to make us upset, and we can't identify a cause or good reason for our feelings, at least initially. But as we over-think, we begin to find all sorts of reasons—our jobs, our relationships, our health.

Sometimes, the reason we feel bad is amazingly simple. It may be you are menstruating. You may not have gotten enough sleep, or been drink-ing too much. It may be something in your diet. Or it may be some event that is unusual and isolated but nonetheless made you feel bad—your boss was grouchy or your child flunked a test. But instead of recognizing these simple explanations for our mood, we stare at our navels until much more dramatic and complex reasons come to mind—the demise of our marriage, the failure of our career, the poverty of our soul.

When you are in a bad mood for no apparent reason and begin to ruminate about all the possible causes of it, consider the simple ones first. Did you have anything to drink recently? Could you be hungry or tired? Is it that time of the month? If the answer to any of these is possi-bly yes, you need to be especially careful about letting your thoughts run rampant. You may need to take a nap, eat a bite, or get busy with some-thing other than your overthinking for a while. Your real problems will still be there when you come back, but the ones that are the figments of your overthinking will be gone, or at least a lot smaller than they were before.

Stop Comparing Yourself

We all have a tendency to compare ourselves to others. Social compari-son is drummed into us from an early age. Parents will say openly that one of their children is smarter, more athletic, or more outgoing than another. Beginning in elementary school, the grades we get on exams may be on a "curve," so that our performance is meaningful only in rela-tion to the other children's performance. In high school, college, and professional school, lots of opportunities—scholarships, entrance to elite schools, a place on the varsity team—are dependent on us outper-forming other students. We tend to know our rank compared to others on dozens of dimensions—our salaries, our status in the company, our competitiveness as a tennis player.

Intriguing new work by Sonja Lyubomirsky of the University of California, Riverside, shows fundamental differences in the ways happy and unhappy people use social comparison.[1] Unhappy people engage in social comparison a lot. They are more attuned to their status compared to others and worry more about how they are doing. And their moods are more affected by information about their status. How they compare to others is even more important to unhappy overthinkers than how they actually performed. For example, in one lab study, Sonja had college students try to solve difficult puzzles and then gave them feedback about how they did and how another student in the experiment did. The unhappy students felt *worse* when they got an *excellent* evaluation but another student got an *even better* evaluation than they did when they got a poor evaluation but the other student got an even poorer evaluation. In other words, the unhappy students' opinions of themselves depended more on how they compared to other students than on how they actually performed.

On the other hand, happy people largely ignore social comparison information. Instead their views of themselves are based on more stable internal standards they hold. If they meet their own internal standards, then they are happy. If they don't, they are less happy, but go into action either to make themselves feel better or to improve their future performance.

The moral here is obviously to avoid comparing yourself to others. This is tough at times, particularly given all the training we've had in ranking ourselves in the pack. A sense of entitlement feeds social comparison—if someone else has something we don't, or is being treated better than we are, then our entitlement obsession leads us to overthink about why we're not getting what we deserve. And if we live in a vacuum of values, we have trouble identifying our internal standards and are more vulnerable to judging ourselves in comparison to the standards of modern culture.

If you find yourself overthinking about how you compare to others, step back and ask yourself, "What does it really matter? Do I want to care about this? So what if that other person has something I don't—can I be satisfied with what I have? What are my ultimate goals here?"

Stop Waiting to Be Rescued

We've all seen movie after movie in which the beautiful woman is in a precarious position, about to be swallowed by the dinosaur, or to be attacked by the bad guy, or to continue on in a miserable existence alone, when the handsome male star bursts upon the scene to rescue her. This is nice stuff for fantasies. But it doesn't happen often in real life. Meanwhile, too many women are waiting around to be rescued. We don't have to face the jaws of a dinosaur very often these days, and hope we won't find ourselves held captive by the bank robbers. Some women are trapped by bad guys—husbands or boyfriends who beat them, a social system that makes it impossible for them to get the education and good job they need while single-parenting their children. But many of us feel trapped by unseen forces—a sense of boredom and mediocrity, regrets over choices we've made in the past, a nagging sense that things could be better. We overthink, ponder, and worry. And we engage in the "if onlys . . ."

> If only I could lose a few pounds, then I could find a boyfriend. If
> only I could get a better job, then I'd be happy. If only I'd meet a
> guy . . . If only the phone would ring . . .

Waiting around to be rescued from your unhappiness is guaranteed to prolong your unhappiness. You basically have two choices: learn to like your current circumstances or change them. If you are in an oppressive situation—in particular, an abusive relationship—making a change is critical. You may need help, such as a social worker or women's advocate who will help you to safety and make you aware of your options for a new life. But please, don't wait around to be rescued if there is any way you can seek help.

If you're in less dire circumstances, there are likely to be a number of options. Learning to like our current circumstances may be the most mature option. We've become so accustomed to quick fixes that it's easy to believe that a quick change in circumstances—a new job, a new lover, getting pregnant again—is always the way to go. But it's important to weigh the costs of these changes as well as the potential benefits, and be realistic about whether a change is the best option. Perhaps finding ways to be satisfied with what you have now, or to make more incremental changes rather than huge changes, is the most appropriate pathway to personal growth. If you are bored in your job, rather than resolving to leave it, consider ways you might change the job to make it more challenging. If you are bored with your lover, rather than looking around for another, examine your own behavior in the relationship to see if there are ways you could make it more exciting. If you are dissatisfied with your family life, rather than believing another child will solve everything, try out some new rituals and activities that may bring your family closer together and into deeper relationships.

If a change in your circumstances is needed to improve your life, you are the one who must make that change. The next several strategies will help you begin that process.

Let Them Flow

When you have concrete problems you must solve, it is helpful to do some old-fashioned brainstorming to begin generating solutions. Rather than thinking of something you might do to overcome a problem and then immediately dissecting and analyzing it until you're sure it won't work, let your ideas flow, writing them down, typing them into your computer, voicing them to a friend or a tape recorder as you go. It's a good idea to let dumb ideas as well as good ones flow. Then you can go back and evaluate the pros and cons of each solution.

As a caseworker for the Los Angeles County welfare department, forty-three-year-old Doreen is deeply dedicated to helping others and is very committed to her work. The work is stressful, however. By the end of the day, Doreen often feels a combination of anger at the clients who aren't motivated to help themselves and pity for the clients who aren't able to help themselves but are still being shoved off the welfare rolls. She tries to leave her stress at work, but lately it has come home with her in the form of irritability with her husband, Frank, and two children. On several evenings, Doreen has either exploded at one of her kids for something minor, like not turning off the television when she called him for dinner, or has secluded herself in the den all evening, trying not to blow up at the million things she found annoying around the house.

On Saturday, Doreen broke free from her overthinking by talking with her priest about them. The priest was sympathetic but encouraged Doreen to do something to overcome her stress and control her behavior. Doreen went home and brainstormed a list of possible actions:

1. Quit my job.
2. Go to half-time.
3. Get my kids to be less irritating.
4. Ask Frank to control the kids more.
5. Find a less stressful job.
6. Find some way to release the stress before I get home.

Then Doreen began to evaluate the items on her list. She knew numbers 1 and 2 were impossible. She couldn't just quit or go half-time—the family needed her full-time income. She jumped down to number 5 on the list—find a less stressful job. There were lots of advertisements in the paper for jobs in service businesses, such as for store managers. But when Doreen contemplated such a job, she felt a deep sense of loss. Even though her job as a welfare caseworker was extremely frustrating at times, she got tremendous gratification when she helped a client find the services he needed to improve his life. Doreen's job was embedded in her deeply held religious conviction that we are on this earth to serve the less fortunate. She didn't want to manage a store. She wanted to continue helping people, and she wanted to do it in this job. Unless welfare rules and other social policies changed drastically, which wasn't likely to happen soon, any job serving the underprivileged was likely to be stressful.

So this meant that her solution probably needed to focus on ways she could manage the stress better at home. Solutions number 3 and 4 on her list—getting her kids to change or her husband to control them— were the solutions she often thought about when she was overthinking her situation. Doreen would slip into thoughts like, "I work so hard for other people and to feed this family, I deserve some peace and quiet.

Those kids have to behave better. There's no discipline in this household." Now that she had broken the grip of her overthinking and was standing on higher ground in the bright light and cool breezes of clear thinking, Doreen knew that her kids and Frank were not the problem. She made a mental note to herself to remember these truths the next time she found herself overthinking.

Doreen began considering whether there was any way to implement solution number 6 on her list. Her drive home certainly didn't give her much stress relief. She fought traffic on the Los Angeles freeways for at least an hour each night. While she was driving, she listened to an all-news radio station. Stories about how politicians were spending money on boondoggle projects just increased Doreen's ire and sense of hopelessness about where society was going.

Doreen decided to talk with Frank about her behavior and her desire to unload some of her stress before she got home. Frank was greatly relieved that Doreen was taking responsibility for her behavior. He threw out a few ideas for Doreen: Listen to soothing music on CDs rather than the all-news radio show on the way home; leave work a little bit early and stop at the "Y" to work out before coming home; and they could develop a signal Frank could use to let Doreen know she was being irritable. When he used it Doreen could take a brisk walk around the block to let off steam. Doreen thought these were great ideas. Even more so, she was touched that Frank wanted to work with her to help her. This gave her even more motivation to find good solutions for her stress.

Like Doreen, you can generate a range of possible solutions for your problems, evaluate them, and identify potentially effective ones, if you first break the grip of your overthinking and rise above it.

Raise Your Sights

Our overthinking often revolves around the details of a situation—he said, she said, I should have said, and so on. Doreen could have gotten lost in the details of who was to blame for her stress—her son shouldn't have turned his Nintendo game on when Doreen wanted to watch the baseball game; Frank didn't remember that Doreen had an evening meeting and thus he was supposed to make supper for the kids; Doreen had worked for a month to get a drug-abusing client into a rehabilitation program only to have the client refuse to go at the last minute.

Instead, Doreen chose to look above the details and fix her gaze on her deeper desire to serve other people and therefore fulfill her religious convictions. This freed her from overthinking the minutiae of her stress to focus on possible solutions. Some of us don't have religious beliefs that guide us, but most of us still have values. They may have been drowned out by entitlement values or the values of pop culture, but research by psychologists Abigail Stewart of the University of Michigan and Dan McAdams of Northwestern University shows that most of us, especially as we grow older, have a desire to improve the lives of others and leave a legacy of positive change in our world.[2] How we live out that desire will depend on our individual talents and resources.

Our higher values provide powerful tools for evaluating how we should handle the difficult situations we face. When we have broken the hold of our overthinking and have moved to higher ground, we are free to connect with and affirm those beliefs. Then they can provide answers to some of the thorny questions we were overthinking about, as well as guideposts for effective change in our lives.

How do you connect with these higher values? Spend quiet time alone, not overthinking but asking yourself questions such as, "What's really important to me? Why? What would I like my legacy to be when I'm gone? What would I like people to say about me now?" Think about those people you admire in your life and in the larger society—not movie stars or wealthy people but those people who have contributed to the lives of others, to the earth, or to the arts and culture in impressive ways. What values do they embody? Read biographies and autobiographies of such people to get a sense of their motivations. If a religious or spiritual group, or a community organization, appeals to you, investigate it further. You're not looking for a set of values that someone will hand to you on a platter. You're looking for those values that resonate with you, that touch you as true and lasting, and that you'd be willing to base some of your life choices on.

Just Do Something (Small)

Once you've got a plan for overcoming a problem, it can seem overwhelming to implement it. The sense that you must fix your problem immediately, completely, and finally may leave you feeling utterly immobilized. Many times, by focusing on doing something small, you can break through these feelings of immobilization. Just as every dollar to a worthy cause counts, doing some small activity that could make a dent in your problems may help enormously to break the cycle of overthinking.

Charlene was at a loss as to what to do when she was laid off from her job at the automobile manufacturing plant. She knew the chances of the job returning were slim because the company was probably folding, and that all the good jobs in her area were at high-tech firms. At age fifty-five, and with only a high school degree and no computer skills, she couldn't see how she could land a high-tech job. Charlene spent a few days overthinking how unfair it was that she was laid off after thirty-five years of service, and that all the younger employees could find new jobs. She just sat around the house, with the TV blaring in the background, filling up on junk food and soda. She soon tired of this, however, and decided she had to do something, anything, about her job situation. Charlene logged onto the Internet and found the home page for her city's chamber of commerce. There she saw an item about the local junior college's courses on computer programming. She decided to look at the Web site for the junior college, although she doubted there was anything there for her. To her surprise she found herself fascinated by the course descriptions. She also discovered that the junior college had a tuition assistance program for unemployed, middle-aged people trying to change careers. Her mood was lifted more than it had been since the layoff.

Doing something small toward solving our problem often is a foot-in-the-door technique. That small effort makes it easier to get the other foot, and eventually our whole body, in the door. Little victories accumulate until soon we begin to see the end to a problem, and how to get there. The increased energy and motivation we get from little victories can help us to weather other setbacks that come along.

Go with It

Another factor that can plunge us into overthinking instead of moving into action is a desire for certainty that our actions are going to be effective. In a study, we asked a group of chronic overthinkers and a group of nonoverthinkers to develop strategies for dealing with a difficult local problem, the lack of adequate housing for undergraduates on our university campus.[3] Both groups came up with plans. But the overthinkers were much less certain than the nonoverthinkers about the wisdom of their plans. They were more reluctant to commit to the plans or to reveal the plans to others. They kept saying they needed more time to think and more information before they could settle on a plan. People who were not overthinkers were able to accept that what they planned to do might not work, but that it was better to give it their best shot than to do nothing.

Sarah's situation shows just how immobilizing uncertainty can be. A new family crisis had brought Sarah, a forty-nine-year-old homemaker, and her forty-six-year-old sister, Joyce, to an impasse. Their eighty-two-year-old mother had fallen and broken her hip, and their eighty-nine-year-old father was too frail to care for her. Sarah and Joyce had always approached life differently. Careful and methodical, Sarah usually had her life quite under control, with her family's activities scheduled weeks in advance. Sarah's house was always clean, her short blond hair was always perfectly styled, and Sarah's neighbors knew she could always be counted on in a pinch. Joyce was the wild one. Joyce had chosen to be a travel agent so that she could go to exotic places and move from one agency to another when she got bored. Every time Sarah saw her sister, Joyce had a new hairdo, sometimes tinged an iridescent shade of purple or green.

Both women deeply loved their parents. Somehow their parents had been able to appreciate and nurture the distinct differences of each daughter, even though Sarah and Joyce could hardly stand each other as they were growing up. Now the sisters were faced with what to do about their parents' care. They had talked a few times on the phone, but these conversations usually ended in a shouting match about past wrongs the sisters had committed against each other. After one of these conversations, Sarah would spend hours in rant-and-rave overthinking, going over what she said and what Joyce said, thinking about how upset she was, thinking about how insensitive her sister was, wondering why she said certain things, and so on. Sarah knew she had to talk again with Joyce, and often rehearsed in her head what she would say. Sometimes the words came out reasonable and calm, but sometimes they came out bitter and accusatory. Sarah didn't really know if she should talk with her sister. What if she couldn't say what she really meant? What if her sister started yelling at her? Sarah avoided calling Joyce for days, meanwhile growing more frustrated with her and guilty that her parents' needs still weren't being properly met.

Eventually Sarah decided she had to do something—even if it risked alienating her sister even further. She thought that a good way to unleash herself from uncertainty and move forward would be to write out a script for what she wanted to say to Joyce. She tried hard to raise her sights and focus beyond the details of her past interactions with Joyce and on to her higher aims of resolving the problems of her parents' care. She rehearsed the script in front of a mirror. This helped her recognize where her thoughts and words got jumbled. She revised the script in these places. She also recognized that some of the things she wanted to say to Joyce would probably only cause conflict rather than resolve anything. She could see her own face tightening up in the mirror as she said these things. She revised the script further and practiced it more.

Sarah also came up with a reward she was going to give herself when her conversation with Joyce was done—a box of Godiva chocolates. Sarah arranged to meet Joyce and carried through with her script. To Sarah's surprise Joyce seemed relieved that Sarah had come up with some concrete ideas for dealing with their parents' care. The two of them parted smiling.

Sarah would have still been overthinking her family if she had not decided to banish uncertainty and go with it—by trying to engage Joyce in problem solving. It's important to note that Sarah put a lot of thought into exactly what she wanted to do with Joyce. She didn't just act impulsively. Instead, once she came up with her best plan, she put aside her uncertainty and moved forward.

Lower Your Expectations

Monica is a bright, high-energy twenty-seven-year-old with vibrant brown eyes and long black hair. She has worked hard to land her job as an assistant professor in one of the most prestigious sociology departments in the country. She paid her way through college working as a waitress because her parents, who immigrated from Guatemala, couldn't afford the tuition. Monica's grades in college were stellar, and she earned the respect of her professors, so their letters of recommendation for her were glowing. As a result, she landed a full scholarship to graduate school. Monica continued to excel there, through a combination of intelligence and diligence, and had several job offers when she graduated.

Monica felt she was adjusting well to the stresses of her first year as an assistant professor. The senior faculty was generally supportive, not loading her with too much teaching or administrative work. Several of the graduate students seemed interested in working with Monica; in particular, one named Belinda, who was in her fourth year of the Ph.D. program. Belinda had come to Monica with complaints that none of the senior professors let her pursue her own ideas, but instead expected Belinda to help them get their work done. Monica knew this often happened. She liked Belinda—they were very similar in age and Belinda was fun to sit around and chat with. So Monica agreed when Belinda asked if Monica would become her advisor.

Within a few weeks, however, the relationship between Monica and Belinda had grown tense. Monica gave Belinda some readings she thought were pertinent to Belinda's research interests, and suggested she do some preliminary analyses on a data set that Monica handed over to her. Two weeks passed before Monica saw Belinda again, and Belinda had not made any progress on the readings or the data analysis. When Monica asked why, Belinda informed her that she had taken a short vacation because the opportunity for a cheap flight to St. Thomas had arisen. This was despite the fact it was in the middle of the semester and Belinda had to submit her thesis proposal by the end of the semester or she would be in poor standing in the Ph.D. program. Monica suggested that Belinda needed to focus on getting her work done. Belinda bristled and suggested that Monica was beginning to sound like the senior faculty, and soon Monica too would have no life outside of the department.

Over the next few weeks of delays and excuses by Belinda, Monica found herself overthinking this situation:

> Why is Belinda sabotaging herself? Why can't I motivate her? Am I going to be able to work with graduate students well? Was Belinda right that I'm too concerned about work and productivity? I'm certainly working harder than ever before. I don't want to become a workaholic. But why can't she see that it's critical for her to get some work done this semester?

Fortunately, Monica chose to talk with Ellen, a senior faculty member who was about twenty years older than Monica, and very supportive, warm, and wise. Monica went on and on about not understanding Belinda and feeling guilty that she couldn't help Belinda more. Ellen paused and then said slowly, "You know, most students are not like you. I'm not just talking about intelligence. Most students don't understand that it takes much more than intelligence to be successful—it takes hard work, the willingness to learn from others' work, and persistence. You know that, Monica, but Belinda doesn't know that, and she may never know that." Ellen's words helped Monica move above her overthinking and accept that she could not turn Belinda into a success if Belinda refused to learn from her. Monica decided to have a frank talk with Belinda about what she expected from her if she was going to continue working with her. After this talk, Belinda seemed disappointed and bitter, but Monica knew she had taken a stand that was healthier for her and potentially more helpful to Belinda.

So many of the questions we ask in our rant-and-rave overthinking are about other people's behavior: How could your child grow up to be a Democrat when your family has been Republican for generations? How could your employer think you'd be willing to lie in the company's annual report to the government? Sometimes the only answer to such questions is Ellen's answer to Monica: Many people are not like you. Accepting this can free us from trying to understand how other people's behavior fits our own expectations—it simply doesn't. This freedom can then help us make more clear-headed decisions about what, if anything, we should do in response to their behavior.

Forgive and Move On

How could they do that to me? is one of the most frequent questions asked in overthinking. How could your parents have raised you the way they did? How could your family have treated you so? How could friends have abandoned you? How could your teacher or your boss or your lover have betrayed you?

If we could look into the hearts and souls of the people who have wronged us and understand what caused them to behave as they did, we might get some relief from our overthinking and emotional pain. This sometimes happens in the course of psychotherapy as people analyze their past and come to understand how they came to be the way they are and what the motivations of others might have been. It can also happen when we confront others about the wrongs they have inflicted upon us, and we are able to have a deep conversation about what happened and why.

But often we can never know the hearts and souls of others, and even if we do know, we may never accept their behavior. For example, Fran came to understand that her father was an alcoholic and when he beat her it was usually when he was drunk. But this understanding did not answer Fran's overthinking:

> Why couldn't he have gotten some help to overcome his alcoholism? Why did this have to happen to me? How am I ever going to get over this?

The only thing that eventually helped Fran overcome ruminations about her father's behavior was to forgive him for his bad treatment of her. She acknowledged that her father's behavior was reprehensible, unbelievable, something that many people wouldn't forgive. But she needed to forgive him and move on.

Forgiving others for their wrongs does not fit with the entitlement obsession that has developed in our culture in the last couple of decades. According to the entitlement obsession, we have a right to have things go our way, and when they don't we have a right to take public retribution against those who have offended us. Forgiving others means giving up this right to retribution. This is tough for many of us emotionally, because we've been drilled over our lifetimes not to give in, not to let go, not to back off. Particularly if the wrong committed against us was egregious—we were sexually assaulted, we were neglected, we were unlawfully fired—forgiving the wrongdoers can seem impossible.

A critical first step is to realize that forgiving others for their actions does not mean you condone those actions or deem them acceptable. It also doesn't mean that the wrongdoer should not be held accountable for the actions. You may still want to press charges, file a lawsuit, or simply confront the wrongdoer. But, according to psychologist Michael McCullough of Southern Methodist University, forgiving means letting go of the desire for revenge for the sake of revenge and pulling away from the hold that anger and hatred have on your heart and mind.[4]

Another powerful trigger for overthinking is our own feelings of guilt and shame, so sometimes we need to forgive *ourselves*. Modern society gives us endless reasons to feel contrite and embarrassed about the things we have done to others and the choices we have made.

> How could I have said such horrible things to my child? Am I ruining my children by working full-time while trying to raise them? My elderly parents want to see me more often—how can I stay away for months at a time? What if they die?

Understanding why you behave the way you do can help you to avoid behaving in the same way in the future. But understanding yourself doesn't always bring relief from your guilty overthinking, just as understanding why other people mistreated you doesn't always bring relief from overthinking grounded in anger. You may understand why you yelled at your child, but still feel guilty for allowing yourself to do so. You may understand that you need to work, but still feel guilty every time your child or parent demands more of your time. Here's where forgiveness comes in. If we can forgive ourselves, we can move on to action, rather than remaining mired in overthinking. When we forgive, we let go of our desire for revenge and retribution, and focus on recovery and repair. We then arrive on higher ground where we have the mind space to think of ways to prevent our work stress from spilling over at home. We have the energy and creativity to balance time at work and time with children and parents. And we are less likely to allow our guilty feelings to be transformed into anger against those who are making us feel guilty.

Important new research suggests that forgiving others not only improves our mental health, it also improves our physical health. Psychologists Charlotte vanOyen Witvliet, Thomas Ludwig, and Kelly Vander Laan of Hope College conducted a study in which people were asked to identify a particular person they blamed for mistreating, offending, or hurting them and to describe what that person had done.[5] Then half the participants were randomly assigned to imagine taking a forgiving stance toward their offender, trying to understand and empathize with the offender, and then granting the offender forgiveness. The other half of the participants were randomly assigned to imagine taking an unforgiving stance toward the offender, rehearsing in their minds the offense that had been committed, and harboring a grudge against the offender. The researchers took a variety of physiological measures that indicated anxiety, tension, and heart functioning, including the participants' heart rate and blood pressure. The results showed that heart rate, blood pressure, and other indicators of stress increased more substantially when people imagined being unforgiving than when they imagined being forgiving. The researchers suggested that people who are chronically unforgiving may experience chronic cardiovascular hyperactivity and chronic physiological arousal. In turn, chronic arousal is tied to increased risk for cardiovascular disease and immune system problems.

The good news is that people can become more forgiving, and this can have positive effects on their health. For example, psychologist Carl Thoreson of Stanford University, working with men who had experienced at least one heart attack, found that helping these men let go of blame, hostility, and anger by becoming more forgiving of others improved their coronary health.[6]

Listen for Other People's Voices

Often our worries are not our own, but the voices of other people telling us what we should be doing, thinking, feeling. I'm not talking about the kind of voices heard by people who suffer from schizophrenia. Instead, these voices sound like our own thoughts and ideas: You should speak up more and stop being so shy! You'll never get ahead if you don't lose some weight!

Often the voices that women hear tell us that we must be nice to everyone, we must ensure that everyone is happy, and we must keep our relationships at any cost. When someone in our life is upset, we are prone to think: What did I do wrong? How can I fix this? We twist ourselves into a knot, trying to make our partners, children, parents, coworkers happy. We kick ourselves for twisting ourselves into knots, then turn right around and do it again.

Much of the time, the concerns that are other people's voices come in the form of what Stanford University psychiatrist David Burns has dubbed "the tyranny of the shoulds."[7] You should be a better mother. You should be more attractive. You should be more successful. You should get more education. You should not watch television. You should not take a mental health day and go shopping. A woman I worked with in therapy once said, "I should myself in the foot all the time."

How do you escape "should" overthinking? When you hear yourself begin saying, "I should . . ." try to stop and ask yourself, "Who says?" Who says you shouldn't take a mental health day? Your dad who drove you to work hard all the time, and who doesn't give you credit for the work you do? Who says you should be more attractive? Companies trying to sell you their remedies for nonattractiveness? Who says you should get more education? Your snooty brother who has spent most of his life in school because he likes it there?

Sometimes it's not easy to identify the source of the voices. They can be so ingrained in us, so much a part of our self-concept, that we don't even realize where they come from. Psychotherapy can help to uncover the origins of your voices and the situations that trigger them. This insight will only take you so far, however. To move to higher ground above these voices, you need to challenge them, and to pick and choose which ones you want to listen to.

A Quick Reference Guide

Here is your quick guide to the strategies discussed in this chapter for moving to higher ground:

Strategy	Description	Example
Adjust your focus.	Move your focus away from the distorted lenses of overthinking to a healthier perspective on your situation.	Marie refused to believe the cruel criticisms her boss gave her and viewed his grouchiness as due to his impending divorce.
Feel your pain and move on.	Accept your negative emotion but don't be ruled by it.	Brenda accepted that she was depressed about losing her job, but vowed to begin job seeking anyway.
Keep it simple (at least initially).	Look for simple reasons for your distress first.	Carla was tempted to overthink her anxiety, but looked at the calendar and realized it could be PMS.
Stop comparing yourself.	Try not to judge yourself based on how others are doing or what they have.	Willa Jean decided that rather than always comparing her salary to her sister's, she'd determine what salary she thought was appropriate for her job.

Stop waiting to be rescued.	Rather than waiting for others to change your situation, change it yourself or accept it.	Aisha stopped waiting for marriage to improve her finances and improved them herself by going back to school and finishing her degree.
Let them flow.	Brainstorm possible solutions to your problems.	Aisha first made a list of all the ways she might increase her income before deciding to go back to school.
Raise your sights.	Connect with your higher values to evaluate possible solutions to your problems.	Patti thought about how her grandmother, whom she respected greatly, would handle her current marital problems.
Just do something (small).	Take some small action to begin overcoming your problems.	Stevie called a family therapist for an appointment to talk about her son's school problems.
Go with it.	Move forward in implementing a solution to your problem despite feeling uncertain.	Paulina began the new diet her doctor prescribed, even though she wasn't sure it would help her lose weight.
Lower your expectations.	Realize that other people don't always share your values or standards.	Gilda accepted that her daughter may never be as good at math as she is.

Strategy	Description	Example
Forgive and move on.	Try to forgive others who have wronged you so you can let go of overthinking their offense.	Nicole forgave her mother for being emotionally cold and distant and gave up trying to change her.
Listen for other people's voices.	Recognize when your overthinking is the result of others telling you how you should be feeling, acting, or thinking.	When Vonda heard herself saying she should do something, she asked herself, "Who says? Is that what I want?"

These strategies will help you begin to solve the concrete problems you are overthinking today. But what about tomorrow? How can you keep yourself from falling into overthinking new problems that arise? Chapter 6 gives you strategies for avoiding future traps of overthinking by being proactive in reshaping your life, your attitudes, and your future.

6

Avoiding Future Traps

As our lives unfold and new challenges and dilemmas confront us, there is always the risk that we will fall back into overthinking. We may have turned off the inner voice of doubt and worry for a time. But then, with a single life event—a disappointing evaluation at work, a conflict with a friend, the death of a loved one—the voice returns, and we slip back into the quicksand. In this chapter you'll learn how to avoid plunging back into overthinking.

Don't Go There

We can often identify themes in our concerns and the situations that trigger them. For one person it might be interpersonal conflict. You just can't stand it when other people are upset with you, so any conflict has the potential of sending you back into overthinking. For another person it might be lack of achievement. You have high goals for yourself and any setback can lead you to ruminate about whether you have what it takes to achieve your goals.

You can't completely avoid your weak spots—everyday life brings constant conflicts, failures, and rejections. But there are ways you can structure things to reduce the chances that life's perennial challenges will consistently push you back into the quagmire of overthinking.

Marla was an excellent technician who worked in the research lab of a major pharmaceutical company. She had been working there for eight years, since she finished her master's degree in biology. Now, at age thirty-three, she was being told that she could move into a supervisory position in the lab, where she would have new responsibilities and a heftier salary. Marla was well liked by her coworkers. She was tall and athletic, always the captain of the company baseball team. She had a great sense of humor and drew funny political cartoons, which she posted on the bulletin board in the cafeteria. Marla was also an expert technician and loved the challenge of setting up experiments and solving technical problems.

Marla was not at all sure she would be a good supervisor, however. Though she was comfortable arguing with other scientists in the lab about the proper way to set up an experiment—that was her territory and she was confident in her opinions—she knew that being a supervisor also meant doing performance evaluations of the other technicians and negotiating their salaries, areas rife with just the sorts of conflicts Marla despised most. She cringed at the thought of any of her coworkers arguing with her about their evaluations and their salaries. She also dreaded the prospect of having to argue with upper management about resources the lab needed, or assignments they would be given. Marla was given two weeks to decide if she wanted the supervisor's job, and she spent most of the two weeks ruminating about what she would do and say in these kinds of thorny managerial situations.

At the end of the two weeks, Marla decided not to put herself in a new role that was sure to lead to constant overthinking. She turned down the supervisor's job, but negotiated to have a wider range of technical responsibilities for the lab. She was splendidly happy with her new responsibilities, and relieved that she had not walked into her own personal overthinking pit.

It is not always a good idea to avoid the sources of your ruminations. Sometimes avoidance can mean giving up important opportunities that you really do want to pursue. But there are some places you may just not want to go because the potential payoffs are not as great as the likelihood that you will plunge into chronic overthinking.

Plug the Holes

If Marla wanted to take the supervisor's job, but still felt uncertain about her ability to handle the interpersonal conflicts that come with such a job, then what should she do? If she simply took the job and fell into chronic overthinking, she'd be unhappy and potentially ineffective in the position. A better idea would be for Marla to learn the managerial skills she felt she lacked, so that she could have both the job and the peace of mind she desired.

Once we've pulled out of the muck of overthinking and made it to higher ground, we're in a good position to see our weaknesses clearly and do something about them. Often this will involve getting help from experts who can help us overcome those weaknesses. You might have to take some courses to improve your job-related skills or to acquire a degree needed to move into a new career. If your weaknesses include bad habits, such as drinking too much or binge-eating, it is a good idea to see a therapist who can help you develop more adaptive coping skills. Therapists can also help you learn anger control or assertiveness. If your weaknesses involve your relationship with your children, you might want to talk with a therapist who specializes in family therapy and can help you learn how to deal more effectively and lovingly with your children. If your overthinking is full of spiritual questions, you might need to talk with a religious counselor who can help you come to some peace on these questions.

A critical strategy for preventing falls from higher ground is to carry through with your plans, asking for help from others, so that the main sources or targets of your concerns are completely overcome. We cannot succumb to the satisfaction of a quick fix, which we may have when we initially get some control over our overthinking. We can't just put out the small fires and think that chronic problems won't pop back up again. We need to do the long, hard work of plugging the holes in our character and our skills that lead us into the muck over and over again.

Let Go of Unhealthy Goals

You may have goals that you've been striving for all your life that are setting you up for nothing but pain and overthinking. It can be difficult to recognize such goals, as well as to give them up. Sometimes they serve as our self-definition. But letting go of unhealthy goals is often essential to avoiding returns to chronic overthinking.

In my first few years as an assistant professor at Stanford, my husband and I lived in the undergraduate dormitories as sort of faculty den parents while we saved to buy a house. There I met dozens of bright young first-year students who, from the first day they arrived, were absolutely sure that they were going to be premed majors and eventually become physicians. They couldn't be convinced to be open-minded about their options, to explore the wonderful variety of courses and opportunities that Stanford offered. No, it was medical school or nothing.

Then first-year biology and physics hit. Half of the premed students flunked the courses, and many of those who survived got grades they were not happy with. Eventually, many of these students were forced to give up their dreams of becoming a physician and explore other careers. Perhaps the saddest cases, however, were the students who did well in their premed courses but had no business being in premed because their hearts weren't in it. Often these students came from families in which there were strong expectations that they become a physician.

This was true of Trin, a thin, beautiful Vietnamese-American woman with shimmering black hair and a shy smile. Trin arrived on move-in day at the dorm and announced amid the chaos that she was going to become a neurologist. It had been her dream since serving as a research assistant to a neurosurgeon in her hometown. The determination in Trin's eyes when she spoke of her goal made most of us back away from arguing that she should keep an open mind about her long-term future, given that it was her first day of college.

Trin drew much of her great strength of spirit from her family. The family had settled in the upper Midwest after escaping from Vietnam in the 1970s among the "boat people." As Vietnam fell to the Communists, the family, including baby Trin and her six older brothers, packed into small boats and headed out to sea. All their material goods had been hastily sold, the money converted into gold which was sewn into pockets in the parents' clothes. Far away from shore, the boat sank in heavy seas. Trin's parents were forced to shed their coats, and thus their gold, to avoid sinking and drowning. Miraculously, a fishing trawler was nearby and saved the family from peril. Several months and several refugee camps later, Trin and her family arrived in the United States, and were "adopted" by a church in the Midwest. There they slowly rebuilt their lives, the father finding work as a janitor, then a retail clerk, and finally a store manager. From her preschool years, Trin's intelligence shone, but she had to fight for her father's attention and respect, as the youngest and only daughter in the family.

Then Trin was admitted to Stanford. This, coupled with her experience working with the neurosurgeon, crystallized a dream she had of becoming a famous neurologist—wealthy, internationally respected for her work, perhaps eventually a professor at a major university. Trin didn't see any connection between this goal and her lifelong pursuit of her father's love. Instead, it was a rational choice of careers, based on her abilities and interests.

Trin certainly had the ability. She sailed through the biology, chemistry, and physics courses required of premeds in the first few years. But those of us who knew her well always wondered if she had the desire. Although she could ace any class she took, Trin never seemed to have the intrinsic passion for her work that you like to see in anyone devoted to such an ambitious goal. The only time her eyes lit up was when she attended one of the poetry-reading sessions we occasionally held in the dorms, or a lecture by a visiting faculty member on the history of pioneer women in the American Southwest. If by some chance Trin didn't get the highest grade on an exam, she would come back to the dorm and overthink:

> How could I have been so stupid? Why didn't I study the chapter on quantum mechanics more? I let myself get distracted—I'm going to have to move out of the dorms so I can be alone and quiet to get my studying done. But then I'll have to cook for myself and that will take time away from my work. I've got to get moved to a quieter dorm, out on the edge of campus away from all the noise and activity.

Then in Trin's junior year of college, tragedy struck. Her father was killed in an automobile accident while driving home from work. Any loving child would be stunned and overwhelmed when they unexpectedly lose a parent. Trin, however, was not only taken by grief, she became a rudderless boat. She left school, not officially dropping out of class, just disappearing. She lost all sense of motivation to continue her studies or much of anything else about her life. She just hung out at her boyfriend's apartment, occasionally taking walks or watching a little television, much of the time staring out the window.

It was six months after her father's death when I next saw Trin. She was even thinner than before, and she had cut her hair short. Her eyes, though, were what I noticed first. Gone was that look of steely determination, that "don't get in my way, I'm going to class" attitude. Instead there was a softness, a depth, which I had seen only on those rare occasions when Trin was sitting quietly listening to classical music or reading a book of poetry instead of her biology textbook. I asked her what happened.

"I just floated for a couple of months. Thankfully, Sean"—her boyfriend—"kept me from self-destructing. I even thought of committing suicide a few times. I kept seeing my father, hearing him, when he wasn't there. He was trying to tell me something, but I couldn't understand, I was so scared. I thought I was losing my mind." At this point, tears began running silently down her cheek. "Then, several weeks ago, when I was asleep, I heard my father calling me: 'Trin, Trin, here, listen to me, daughter. Follow your heart. Follow your heart.' I couldn't tell if it was a dream or what, I just knew I heard him, and I knew he said, 'Follow your heart.' But what did that mean? I lay awake the rest of the night, listening for his voice, asking him what he meant. But I heard nothing more, except the echo of his words, 'Follow your heart.'

"I spent a lot of time walking in the hills, still listening for my father. I was no longer seeing him or hearing him everywhere—it was as if he had spoken what he needed to tell me, and now he was really gone. I wanted him back, I wanted to ask him questions. But that was his way. He spoke something once, and only once, then he moved on. What was in my heart? I kept asking myself. No clear answers came, except one—it wasn't medicine. Medicine wasn't in my heart. 'How could that be?' I asked myself, I've been driven toward medicine ever since high school. I'm very good at it. I could make a brilliant physician. But it was not in my heart. When I first realized this, I thought, 'I've lost my father, now I've also lost my calling, my career.'

"But instead of feeling empty and grieved, I felt a tremendous relief. It was as if something that had been holding me by the back of my neck for years had suddenly let go. My father had let go. He hadn't been the one holding on to me, exactly; it was what I thought he wanted of me, what I thought I had to do for him. And now he's gone. So my reason for pursuing medicine is gone."

I had always viewed Trin as a mature young woman, but now I stood gaping in awe of her insight and growth. "What," I asked, "is going to replace medicine?"

"I don't know yet," she responded. "I'm coming back to school to find out. I've dropped the premed major and have declared an English major. My mother and brothers think I've lost my mind. But I think I've found it."

Trin eventually graduated from Stanford with a bachelor's and a master's degree in American literature, and went on to graduate school. Her other accomplishment, though, was in letting go of a goal that was not truly hers but was running every aspect of her life—the goal of becoming a doctor. She could have achieved the goal. But because it wasn't in her heart, achieving it would not have given her rich and abiding pleasure.

Several psychologists have argued that the main reason people get stuck in overthinking is that they can't let go of impossible or unhealthy goals.[1] Often these goals are core aspects of our self-definition. Jennifer Crocker of the University of Michigan calls these "contingencies of self-worth."[2] We set up these contingencies that we must meet in order to feel good about ourselves—we have to achieve a certain salary level or look like the models in the fashion magazines. The trouble comes when the contingencies, or goals, we set for ourselves lead us to engage in self-destructive behavior or are impossible to reach. Perhaps your goal for your weight is unrealistically low, yet you continue to starve yourself until you do damage to your body. Crocker has found that women whose contingencies of self-worth have to do with achieving extreme thinness are more vulnerable to developing eating disorders.

Perhaps your marriage is failing, but you just can't let go of your vision of yourself as happily married to a successful person, with lovely kids and a nice home. So you overthink:

> I've got to save this marriage. Maybe if I lose a little weight, then Jerry will find me attractive again. But it seems like nothing I do makes him happy anymore. He's cheating on me, I know it. What am I going to do if he leaves me? I can't stand this!

Women often hang on to impossible goals in relationships, including the goal of making everyone around them happy. If anyone is upset, even a friend, we share the pain, try to fix it, and in the meantime overthink about it. If someone gets mad at us, even a store clerk, we feel responsible and overthink about our behavior. Fundamentally, we have to let go of the goal that all our relationships and encounters with other people will be positive, and that we will never be the source of another person's pain. It's just not possible, and it creates a lot of misery in our lives.

Sometimes we feel locked into certain goals as the only solution to bigger problems we have. You have to save the marriage because you are poor and you need his income to feed your kids. You have to stay in this job you hate because you have no job skills and could lose your home if you become unemployed. Because women are more likely to live in poverty, take responsibility for their children, and have less education or advanced job skills, they often do have fewer alternatives to sticking with unhealthy situations. But overthinking blocks our view of the alternatives that do exist for our current dilemmas. When we're overthinking, we can't see ways of obtaining more public assistance or getting job training that could increase our options and free us from the nasty situation we currently live in. So even when we get stuck in impossible goals because of the circumstances in which we live, escaping from overthinking is critical. Then we may be able to see how to let go of these goals and create more options for our lives.

How can you know if your goals are healthy? Psychologists have identified a number of characteristics of healthy goals—goals held and achieved by happy people. First, as with Trin, your goals need to come from you, not from your family, friends, or other external sources. As discussed in chapter 5, it can be important to recognize when you are saying to yourself, "I should . . ." and to ask yourself "Who says?" If the answer is anyone but you, you may want to question whether this goal is one *you* want to pursue or just one you think other people will be happy if you pursue.

Second, if you are to avoid overthinking, your goals need to be realistic and feasible. Constantly striving for impossible goals—getting into a size 6 dress, changing your mother's personality, never upsetting your spouse or partner—is guaranteed to lead to overthinking. Ease up on your goals so they become more reasonable. Try for a size 10 dress. Resolve to find ways not to let your mother's personality bother you so much. Realize that conflict in a partnership or marriage is normal and often healthy. In studying "successful aging"—how older people successfully cope with the decreases in physical capacities and opportunities that come with old age—psychologists Paul and Margret Baltes of the Max Planck Institute and the Frei University of Berlin found that the happiest elders were those who adapted their goals to fit the reality of their circumstances.[3] A lifelong runner had to give up jogging because of joint problems, but she developed an alternative set of less strenuous physical exercises to keep herself healthy and active. An avid gardener could no longer take care of the community vegetable garden, so she planted her favorite vegetables in a ten-by-ten-foot plot just outside her back door. Of course, you don't want to give up a goal just because someone else says it's unrealistic. Many of the most successful people in the world have been told that their goals and hopes and dreams were impossible, that they should give them up. Talking with a variety of friends and family members whose opinions you trust, and maybe with a neutral party such as a therapist, can be helpful in sorting out which of your goals are realistic (even if highly ambitious) and which are not.

Third, try to recognize when you have conflicting goals and to resolve that conflict at least somewhat. Women who work and have children are old hands at conflicting goals. They want to pursue their career but they want to raise healthy children. Working on one goal always seems to undermine the other one. So we overthink:

> I'm never going to get tenure if I don't get more papers written and published. There never seems to be enough time. Already

this week, I've lost two days of work because Alex had an ear infection. How can I be so hardhearted about my kid? There he was, in pain and miserable, and all I could think about was the grant deadline next week. I don't spend enough time with him. And when I do, I'm tired and distracted. I'm going to miss out on his childhood.

Some women choose to abandon important goals because they conflict with other important goals. They may decide not to have children so they can pursue a career, or they may drop out of the fast track to devote more time to their children. These can be positive choices for some women. But even when we actively make choices such as these, we are prone to overthink our regrets, or messages from others that we didn't make the right choice:

> I thought I wanted to be a full-time mom. I'm not sure that was the right decision, though. It just doesn't come naturally to me. I have such a hard time thinking of things to do with the kids all day. My sister thought I was crazy giving up my management job when the baby was born. She doesn't know what to say to me now. She probably just thinks I'm not worth talking to anymore.

Dropping one of a set of conflicting goals can help reduce overthinking, but it's not guaranteed to. Another strategy is to lower your expectations for each goal to make it more likely you'll find ways to accomplish both goals in their reduced version. Say you want to be a tenured professor and a good mother, but striving for both is driving you crazy. Maybe you could give up your goal of getting tenure at the best university in the country and settle for tenure at a respectable university where the standards are not quite so high. And maybe you could give up your goal of having four children, as your mother did, and settle for one or two.

Fourth, in your goal-setting, strive to achieve success rather than to avoid failure. Developmental psychologist Carol Dweck of Columbia University has produced a fascinating series of studies that differentiate children whose goal is to achieve success from children whose goal is to avoid failure.[4] The children who want to achieve success attempt more challenging tasks, are more creative and adventurous, and bounce back easily after failure. The children who want to avoid failure stick to the tasks they already know how to do rather than trying new and possibly more interesting tasks. They become despondent and self-blaming when they fail. And they overthink when things don't go their way.

Similarly if we are always focused on avoiding failure instead of achieving success, every little setback can become a focus for overthinking:

> I can't believe I even applied for that new management position in the company. I should have known I didn't have a chance. I should just stick with my current job, even though I hate it. At least it's safe. What does the boss think of me now? I exposed how weak my training is compared to the others. Now even this job may not be safe!

If we are more concerned with achieving success than avoiding failure, we can handle setbacks as inevitable glitches on the road to our ultimate goals. We are less likely to be vigilant for signs that the ax is about to fall, the worst is about to happen. Even if the worst does happen, we are in a better psychological position to pick ourselves up, regain our focus, and move on.

Be Gentle with Yourself

In chapter 4 I described exciting new work by Susan Folkman of the University of California, San Francisco, that demonstrated that people who purposefully create opportunities to experience positive emotions even while they are coping with extremely stressful circumstances, such as the terminal illness of a loved one, fare better both emotionally and physically over time. I also cited Barbara Fredrickson of the University of Michigan who suggests that positive emotions broaden our perspectives, making us more creative in solving our problems. Actively cultivating positive emotional experiences can have both short-term benefits, giving us a boost to our mood, and long-term benefits by helping us overcome the obstacles in our lives and probably by reducing overthinking.

Consider Debby, a twenty-nine-year-old auburn-haired homemaker who grew up with a bitter and supercritical mother. Debby had always vowed she would be a better mother to her own children. All during her pregnancy, however, she worried about whether she would be capable of being a good parent, given that she had had such a bad role model. The pregnancy went well, and Debby was blessed with a beautiful baby boy whom she named Thomas. Debby devoted herself to Thomas's care, and his development was healthy and normal. But whenever there was the slightest difficulty with Thomas, such as trouble sleeping because of teething, Debby was flooded with overthinking about her adequacy as a mother and her anger at her own mother.

> I'm a failure at this, just like my mother said I would be. He's going to grow up to be a neurotic with me acting like this. Why did I have to be saddled with such a horrible mother? Why couldn't she have just given us up for adoption rather than wrecking my self-esteem like this?

On Thomas's first birthday, Debby decided these broodings had to stop. She was making herself miserable, being vigilant for signs that Thomas was not well or happy, and beating herself up when something was slightly wrong. Debby decided to play to her strengths rather than dwell on her possible weaknesses. Debby first broke the hold of her negative thoughts by talking them through with her sister, Patty, who was a few years older and had gotten emotional distance from their mother years before. Patty sympathized with Debby's concerns, but helped her dismiss them as a product of their mother's bitterness rather than Debby's incompetence as a mother. Patty encouraged Debby to find activities that she was good at and enjoyed, and together they brainstormed some possibilities. "You're a great athlete and terrific with your hands," Patty told Debby, who felt encouraged by her sister and distracted from her concerns. Within just days, Debby found a tennis program at a club (that also has a child care facility for Thomas) and enrolled in a sculpting class at a nearby community college.

Although overthinking her mothering skills was under control, Debby knew that falling back into overthinking was a risk for her. So she made plans for what she would do when she felt herself sinking. First, she wrote down the things she could do to experience positive emotion and to break free of overthinking—she regularly played tennis, worked on her sculpture, and called Patty to talk. She made a pact with herself to try at least one of these things when she felt herself sliding into rumination. Then she wrote down some of the important things she had learned once she had broken free and moved to higher ground—that her insecurities have *nothing* to do with her own competencies, that everyone else thinks she is a great mother, that she'll never change her own mother or win her acceptance so she won't try anymore, and that she may not always know exactly what to do every time Thomas has a problem, but she will try her best. Whenever Debby felt the pull of overthinking, she used this list to remind herself of her strengths, and she engaged in one of the activities that made her feel better.

Debby cultivated positive emotions in her life in two ways. First, she found some new activities that she enjoyed. Second, she found ways to talk back to her fears and concerns and remind herself of her personal strengths. These strategies helped her to stop beating herself up and begin to be more gentle with herself, building the kind of positive life and self-concept that she hoped to give to her son, Thomas.

It's important to build positive emotional experiences into your everyday life on a regular basis, not to wait until you are distressed and overthinking, when it can be hard to think of doing anything positive. Perhaps you can make a daily practice of exercise, meditation, a hobby, a walk in the woods—whatever reliably makes you feel uplifted. Particularly if your daily schedule is currently a grind—you do the same thing all day every day, or you are frenetically on the go and under pressure all day— to purposely set aside even a few minutes each day to do something happy and nice for yourself is critical. The very fact that you are regularly doing something good for yourself can make you feel better and more in control. Having more periods of positive emotion will also give you more opportunities to think creatively about changes you might want to make in your life or about ways you can cope with ongoing stressors.

Find Your Story

So often our overthinking is an attempt to understand our story—how we got to where we are, why we are the kind of person we are, why certain things have happened to us. Women seem to need an explanation— a narrative, as some psychologists are calling it these days—for why their lives have unfolded the way they did. This is particularly true when our lives don't seem to be working out too well. We need to know why our kids have turned to drugs, or why we always seem to dislike our boss, or why we can't seem to stay in a stable relationship.

Certainly a critical step to overcoming our problems is to understand their causes. And searching for the story behind our predicament can be functional, but it can also be dysfunctional, because it can lead to over-thinking. Constantly asking yourself "why" questions but being unable to settle on answers to them is fundamental to overthinking. We found this in our study of bereavement.[5] People who couldn't answer for them-selves, Why did my loved one die? were considerably more likely to remain depressed for many months after the death. In contrast, people who were able to come up with some answer to this question tended to stop overthinking and find some relief from their grief-related depres-sion within a couple of months after the death. It didn't really matter how they answered the question—they could give an existentialist answer ("You are born and you die. That's just how it works."), a reli-gious answer ("It was part of God's plan.") or even a scientific answer ("She smoked three packs a day. She got lung cancer and died."). As long as they could answer the question somehow, it seemed to help them.

So a strategy for combating your overthinking over the long term is to try to find a story that answers your deepest "why" questions in a satisfy-ing way. "But," you might say, "that's what I've been trying to do all along!" If you've been searching for answers to your "why" questions, and it's only been leading you into overthinking, it's probably time to get some help. Psychotherapy can be useful here. Psychotherapist Jerome Frank suggested that one thing all psychotherapies have in common is that they give us a story, a way of understanding our feelings and our lives, which gives us a sense of insight and coherency.[6] The specific story that different psychotherapies will promote will vary. A psychodynamic therapist will help you explore conflicts and experiences in your early life that led you to become who you are. A cognitive therapist will help you identify unhealthy ways of thinking that are driving your emotions and your behaviors. The story that one psychotherapist suggests may make more sense than the story another psychotherapist suggests, and you may have to try more than one psychotherapist to find the story that seems right to you. But fundamentally, psychotherapy is about understanding our own stories. In addition, each psychotherapy offers a set of prescriptions for how to make changes so that your life story improves.

Many people these days are turning to biology to understand their stories. The popularity of biological explanations for our psychological troubles is based in part on the rapid advances in biological psychiatry in finding genetic and biochemical factors that influence our moods and personalities. I also think that our passion for biological explanations for everything about us is part of our obsession with the quick fix. If my son drinks too much, it must be because my Uncle Sid was an alcoholic and my son has inherited his genes. If I'm depressed, it must be because the chemicals in my brain are out of balance. This is true in some cases. In others, such simple biological answers can allow us to avoid the painful realities and choices in our lives that we'd rather not face. Instead, all we have to do is to take some medication and everything will be fine.

There are many other places we turn to in order to find our stories. Some of us find satisfaction in the stories offered by religion, either traditional religion or more New Age spiritualism. Some of us take academic courses, read books, and do research to investigate the many possible explanations for what we've experienced. Or simply talking with friends and family members about your "why" questions can help you answer them. You might discover that a sibling shares the same anxieties and weaknesses you feel you have but has never shared this with you. He has come to his own story of how these concerns developed over time, and you might find elements of his story to be true for your life as well.

Whatever story you settle upon, it is important to realize that things are seldom as simple as we might want to make them out to be. We may be able to identify key experiences in our past that contributed to our personalities. We may have good evidence that we carry a genetic disposition for depression or other psychological problems. But we human beings are complex biological and psychological systems, and we live in even more complex social systems. As the writer E. B. White once said, "There's no limit to how complicated things can get, on account of one thing always leading to another." If we remain too rigidly fixed on one simple explanation of who we are, then when evidence that contradicts this explanation arises we can be plunged back into overthinking. We need to recognize the complexity of the human system and embrace it, viewing it as providing multiple opportunities for change. For example, if you believe your depression is largely biological, but your medications aren't working, remaining open to complexity will allow you to consider that psychotherapy might also be helpful to you. Similarly, if you believe your depression is rooted in your childhood experiences, but after years of psychotherapy you are still having mood swings, you may need medication in addition to psychotherapy to gain control over your moods.

Broaden Your Base

Odds are high that your overthinking bouts happen most often around those parts of your life that are most important to you and that form a big part of your concept of yourself. When our concept of ourselves is based on just one role in life—for example, as mother or as career person—we are especially vulnerable to overthinking. In such cases, it becomes critical that things always go well in this role, because it's all we have. If your total view of yourself is based on your role as a mother, then when problems arise in this role—your child develops behavior problems or you find yourself frequently irritable with your children—they threaten your entire self-concept. As a result, you'll be hypervigilant for trouble in this role, you'll be devastated when trouble arises, and you'll have no other sources of self-esteem and satisfaction to turn to for relief and support.

Sheila thought she had attained everything she wanted in her life. At thirty-one, she was happily married to a successful lawyer, she had two beautiful, healthy children, and she had a lovely home in the nicest suburb of a large southern city. Sheila had finished college before she married Dale, and had spent some time applying her business degree in a position as a marketing manager for a small software firm. Once she had their first child, Christine, Sheila quit her job to become a full-time mom. Sheila was totally devoted to Christine and loved being able to give her her full attention. The baby shared Sheila's bright blue eyes, and probably was going to be blond, like Sheila, once she had any hair at all. Eighteen months later, baby Mark was born, and Sheila had her hands full raising two rambunctious small children.

Dale worked long hours, so Sheila and the kids rarely spent much time with him. When Sheila quit her job, the small network of friends she had developed fell away, and she had been so busy with the children that she hadn't developed many other friendships. So Sheila felt somewhat isolated and lonely. "But," she told herself, "I've got the kids, and I can barely keep up with them, so I don't really have time to see friends anyway."

Even though she was always chasing after one of the children, or reading them a story, or feeding them, or playing with them in the park, Sheila had plenty of time to think. Sometimes this thinking evolved into overthinking:

> Am I doing the right things for my kids? Should I get them involved in a preschool? I keep reading that early cognitive development is so important to their success in school. But I really want them with me all day. What will I do if they are in some nursery school? I can read to them. But what about interactions with other kids? Do they get enough just playing here in the park? My mom never put me in any nursery schools. Maybe that's the reason I'm kind of shy. Maybe if I wasn't so shy, I'd be more comfortable in finding playmates for my kids.

When Christine was three, Sheila took her for the usual yearly exam with the pediatrician, and her peaceful, content life with the children was blown apart. The pediatrician detected a heart murmur in Christine. This led the pediatrician to take Christine's blood pressure, and she discovered the child's pressure was highly elevated. She recommended that Christine be seen by a pediatric cardiologist. As Sheila drove home from the doctor's visit, her mind was racing:

> What does this mean? What's wrong with my baby? Why didn't they detect it before? Why didn't I notice something was wrong? What are they going to have to do? Oh, I can't cope with this, I can't stand this.

As usual, Dale didn't get home until nine that night. By that time Sheila was frantic with worry and enraged at him for not being there when she needed him. She blew up at him for being late as soon as he came in the door, even though he had left a message on their answering machine earlier saying he was going to be late. Then she dumped the news about Christine's heart murmur and blood pressure in a mixture of anger and fear. Dale tried to be soothing and assure Sheila that everything would be all right. She didn't take much comfort from his assurances. All night, Sheila was up worrying and overthinking about Christine, and then Mark:

> What if there's something wrong with Mark and they just haven't discovered it yet? I can't believe I didn't know there was something wrong with Christine! What kind of mother am I that I couldn't tell my own child's heart wasn't working right? Should I insist that he also be seen by the cardiologist? Is what Christine has genetic? Which of us gave it to her? There aren't any heart problems in my family. What if they want to do surgery on Christine? I won't be able to deal with that. I can't face the image of my daughter all cut up and in pain.

These worried thoughts and gruesome images kept Sheila awake all night, and the next day she was completely strung out. Her overthinking bouts continued through the days and nights until Christine's appointment with the cardiologist finally arrived two weeks later. He listened to Christine's heart and confirmed the murmur. Sheila thought she was going to cry. The cardiologist was trying to tell Sheila that murmurs can be caused by a host of factors and are not necessarily cause for alarm. Sheila was barely able to listen, however, because the gruesome images of Christine in surgery came popping back into her head. Then the cardiologist took Christine's blood pressure and found it to be normal. "What!" Sheila burst out. "I thought it was supposed to be high." The cardiologist replied that blood pressures are notoriously fickle, subject to all sorts of conditions, including the stress of seeing your pediatrician—the person who gives you shots. The cardiologist waited a while, then took Christine's blood pressure again, and again found it to be normal. The visit ended with the cardiologist recommending that he see Christine again in a couple of months to check her murmur and blood pressure.

Sheila went home exhausted and confused. Should she get a second opinion? Should she call the cardiologist back and ask him to repeat what he said about the murmur so she was sure she understood it? What should she do?

She called her mother. Sheila hadn't told her mother about Christine's murmur yet—she had not wanted to worry her until the heart problems had been confirmed by the cardiologist. Before her mother even finished saying hello, Sheila began spilling out the details of the visit with the pediatrician and then the cardiologist, and all her fears and worries about Christine.

Her mother finally said, "Sheila, girl, get a grip. Calm down. You've got yourself whipped into a total frenzy about this. Now, let's go through this again slowly." When Sheila got to the part where the cardiologist said that murmurs didn't necessarily mean anything was seriously wrong, her mother pointed out that this was very encouraging. She also pointed out that the hospital where the cardiologist worked was one of the best pediatric hospitals in the country, so there was reason to believe this guy was good. After a while, Sheila felt much calmer and more clear-headed than she had felt since before seeing the pediatrician.

Then her mother asked, "Sheila, why didn't you call me about this earlier?" When Sheila said she hadn't wanted to worry her, her mother said, "Girl, you've got yourself so hidden away in that pretty house with those pretty kids you've lost your perspective. The people who love you want to support you. And you need to find more people to talk to, and more things to do, other than stay at home with your kids all day long. If they do eventually find that something's wrong with Christine, you are not going to be able to cope with it and be there for your daughter if you are holed up, all by yourself, with only your kids and your worries to think about."

At first, Sheila was furious at her mother for saying this, for not being entirely supportive in this time of need. Soon, however, she realized her mother was right. She had become so isolated she had no one to talk to except the kids and Dale, when he got home late in the evening. She had created this image of herself as the perfect mother with perfect kids, and the possibility of Christine being ill had shattered that image. She needed to develop some new friends, and she needed to find some new activities that would give her and the kids time away from each other, and give her the opportunity to reclaim those parts of herself that were not "Mommy."

If, like Sheila, your self-concept is narrowly focused on just one or two roles, it's time to broaden your base by increasing the sources of self-esteem in your life. This doesn't mean getting involved in a hundred activities, half of which mean nothing to you. It means finding a few other things you want to focus part of your energy and your resources on, such as developing a new skill (for example, pottery), or a new relationship (for example, as a visitor to nursing home residents), or a connection with an organization that serves some cause (for example, becoming involved with the Humane Society). The key is to find new roles that connect to your basic values and needs, that provide opportunities to meet other people and form new relationships, and that bolster your positive sense of self. Then when something is wrong in one role in your life, you have these other roles to turn to for gratification, for a network of friends who will support you, and maintain a balanced sense of self.

Consider Finding New Friends

I mentioned above that one benefit to adding new roles to your life is that you add friends who can support you in times of trouble and give you a different perspective or advice regarding your troubles. Even if you don't need to add new roles to your life, you may need to add new friends if your current friends feed your overthinking rather than help you get past it. Perhaps you have become everyone's favorite shoulder to cry on, the friend whom everyone turns to for support and to unload their troubles. Problem is, when you need to unload on them, they can't handle it. They want you to be the strong one, the one who can always cope. If you are distressed and troubled, this threatens their need for you to be the strong one and they simply won't let this happen. So they dismiss your concerns: "You always get through things fine." Or they turn the tables and begin to air their worries: "You think that's bad. I was a total mess yesterday. Let me tell you about it."

Perhaps your friends try to be helpful, but they just can't because they are so overburdened with their own troubles. They try to listen but quickly become overwhelmed by your distress, or are preoccupied with their own. Although it's often true that "misery loves company," friends being miserable together can turn into an overthinking party that is destructive for everyone involved.

If most of your friends don't provide you with the kind of support that relieves your overthinking but instead adds to it, it may be time to consider finding new friends. That doesn't mean you have to dump the old ones. But having some friends who can support you the way you need when you are upset, help you move from overthinking into problem solving, and provide a role model for good coping with stress, can be invaluable as you reshape your life into one that is relatively free from overthinking.

Create a New Image of Yourself

We most often overthink those aspects of our self-concept that are a bit shaky. After all, if you have confidence in yourself, you don't have much reason to worry, and rather than overthink past mistakes, you can see them as opportunities for growth, and you believe you can prevent them from happening in the future. On the other hand, people who are completely hopeless about themselves and their world may not overthink very much either—they are so dead sure they are complete failures and life is utterly worthless that they don't have much to overthink about.

But when you are not entirely sure about yourself in some domain, such as your job performance, your relationship with your partner, or your leadership skills, then there is plenty to overthink. You fret about things that have happened in the past, kicking yourself for mistakes, questioning your own motives and the motives of other people. You're anxious about the future, wondering if you can rise to new challenges effectively. Often when we are overthinking our weak spots, we have this image of ourselves as bumbling or feeble or embarrassed or devastated, which creeps or floods into our consciousness as we begin to worry. This image feeds our anxiety, leading us either to avoid situations where we might fail or to become overwhelmed the second we begin to falter.

Such negative imagery is notorious for screwing up the performances of musicians, such as Sonia, an eighteen-year-old Russian-born pianist with deep brown eyes and wavy brown hair which she wears in a tight bun when she performs. Sonia had dreamed of being a concert pianist ever since she was a small child growing up in Moscow. She had tremendous talent and was trained by the best teachers in Russia during her child-hood. When Sonia was sixteen, her family moved to the United States so that Sonia could train in New York and her career could be launched. By age eighteen, Sonia was playing major concert halls throughout North America.

However, Sonia was developing a reputation for being unpredictable. Some of her performances were flawless, and Sonia seemed to be tremendously mature and composed. At other performances, she would suddenly stumble during a piece she had played hundreds of times before. Then, rather than regroup and resume her performance, she would either drag through the rest of the performance, making errors on most of the pieces, or would rush off the stage in tears, not to return that night.

Sonia's anxiety before every performance was becoming so great that her mother literally had to push her out on the stage. Before each performance, Sonia had become flooded with an image of herself sitting at the piano, the concert hall full of people staring intently at her, when she suddenly goes blank and cannot remember how to play a piece. Her body is filled with terror and her mind is completely empty. But she can see the faces of the people in the audience, looking disgusted, angry, and pitying. She can usually push this image out of her mind at the beginning of a concert by focusing intently on the music. But if she has any difficulty on a piece, the image suddenly reappears, clouding her thoughts and freezing her hands.

Finally, when Sonia's agent began to get nervous about being able to book new concerts for her, he pleaded with Sonia to see a therapist in New York who specialized in helping musicians overcome performance anxieties. This therapist made two major interventions with Sonia early in therapy. First, he got her mother to lay off. He sensed that Sonia's mother had been applying great pressure on Sonia to perform and to succeed since Sonia was a child, and this was feeding Sonia's performance problems. Second, he helped Sonia overcome her negative imagery. He explored with Sonia the minute details of her image of herself making a mistake on stage and freezing. This was excruciatingly difficult for Sonia, but she persisted.

As they explored this image, the therapist helped Sonia use relaxation exercises to counteract the anxiety that the image aroused in her. Then he worked with Sonia to develop a new, more positive image of herself at the keyboard. This wasn't an image in which everything always went perfectly. Sonia already had that idyllic image and would bounce between it and her negative, complete failure image. Instead, the therapist helped her develop an image of herself stumbling on a piece, but then regaining her concentration and resuming the piece successfully. They discussed how Sonia could use brief relaxation exercises, even at the moment during a real concert when she made an error in playing, to reduce her anxiety and arousal and give herself the mind space to call up her positive, coping self-image and regain her concentration on her music. Over the next few months, Sonia's performances became more consistent. She did make mistakes, but she seldom left the stage in tears. And no one needed to push her onto the stage any longer.

Like Sonia, we can replace those negative images of ourselves that drive much of our overthinking with more positive images. Sometimes it's as straightforward as what the therapist did with Sonia—using relaxation exercises to reduce our anxiety about the negative image and developing an image of ourselves coping with adversity and failure that we practice and use to replace the negative image. At other times, some of the other strategies discussed in chapters 4 and 5 are necessary before we can begin to replace our negative images. For example, we may need to forgive ourselves for mistakes we've made in the past before we can let go of a negative image of ourselves. For example, Crystal formerly drank too much, and at times was physically abusive to her children while she was drunk, hitting them hard when they misbehaved or annoyed her. Thanks to counseling, Crystal has been abstinent for six months. But she couldn't let go of the negative image of herself as a bad mother until she forgave herself for hitting her children when she was drunk. It wasn't until she forgave herself, and then developed an image of herself as a mother who was trying hard to overcome her weaknesses, that she really began to rebuild her relationship with her children.

Similarly, you may need to broaden your base of self-esteem, building new relationships and interests before you can change an image of yourself as wholly dependent on one role or relationship in your life. If when you look at yourself you see only somebody's wife, desperate to keep a marriage going because it's all you have, you need to broaden your base so that your self-concept includes other personal goals and sources of self-esteem. If when you look at yourself you see only a career that must succeed, you need to broaden your base to include more relationships that provide support and perspective on your life.

Once you've broken free of your overthinking, have moved to higher ground and solved some immediate problems, and are now ready to reshape your life to avoid falling into the pit again, take a good, hard look at your self-image. Work on what is negative, finding ways to correct faults and overcome weaknesses, to forgive past mistakes, to diversify your sources of self-esteem, and to re-create positive images of yourself that prevent new bouts of overthinking.

A Quick Reference

The strategies we've discussed in this chapter are designed to help you reshape your life for the long term. They will take longer to implement than the strategies in chapters 4 and 5, and it may take more time for you to see their fruits. But they can lead to permanent growth toward a more satisfying life and more personal control.

Strategy	Description	Example
Don't go there.	Choose not to get involved in situations that arouse overthinking.	Jan knew that spending too much time with her mother was sure to result in weeks of overthinking, so she kept her visits short.
Let go of unhealthy goals.	Let go of goals that are impossible or that cause you to act self-destructively.	Briana decided that rather than try to lose 50 pounds by starving herself, she would lose 20 with a diet prescribed by her doctor.

Be gentle with yourself.	Create opportunities to experience positive emotions and to affirm your personal strengths.	Sandy set aside 30 minutes a day for meditation, even though her family protested that she wasn't available to them at that time.
Find your story.	Try to find a satisfying story to understand your troubles.	Tillie read a dozen books on different religions' views of the afterlife to understand how she felt about her mother's death.
Broaden your base.	Develop multiple sources of self-esteem and support.	Fern realized her job as an attorney was her entire life, so she began volunteering at a local shelter for battered women.
Consider finding new friends.	Make sure you have friends who can help lift you out of overthinking instead of prolonging it.	All of Lilia's friends were graduate students like her, and they spent all their time complaining together, so she found nonstudent friends through her church who provided a different perspective on life.
Create a new image of yourself.	Replace negative images with positive ones, or diversity your image of yourself.	Rita replaced her image of herself as unable to lead people with an image of herself as a competent leader by learning new skills and practicing the new image.

Part III

Triggers for Overthinking

Although everyone has their own special topics for overthinking, some themes are common—intimate relationships, jobs and careers, children, parents and relatives, health problems, and losses or traumas. In Part III, I discuss how the strategies described in Part II of the book can be used to gain control over ruminations about these issues.

7

Married to My Worries:
Overthinking Intimate Relationships

One of the most common topics of overthinking for the people in our studies has been their intimate relationships—with spouses, partners, boyfriends or girlfriends. It makes sense that these relationships are so often the focus of concern. Our intimate relationships are a core part of our self-definition. We see ourselves at least partially through their eyes, and they are a reflection on us. So it is understandable that we worry about what they think of us, how the relationship is going, why they behave the way they do, how to keep them happy, and what other people think of our partners.

Reflecting on our intimate relationships is a good idea when it leads us to recognize problems and take corrective action, or when we are simply basking in the glow of relationships that are going well. But over-thinking can sabotage our relationships at every turn—when we try to select a partner, when we're dating, when we're first forming a committed relationship, when we begin having children. And the historical trends that have led to more overthinking in recent generations can make overthinking particularly dangerous in the context of intimate relationships.

From the outset, it is difficult to choose good life partners if we are not sure who we are or what we fundamentally believe. Although there is some truth to the adage "opposites attract," in most long-term relationships the couple shares core beliefs and interests. This provides them with a basis for making important decisions, such as how to spend their money or how to raise their children. It also provides them with an understanding and respect for each other's positions and interests that is an important source of trust, camaraderie, and shared activities.

But when we live in a vacuum of values, we can be too easily swayed by the opinions of others (and the media) as to what makes a good mate. If our sense of privilege has gotten the better of us—I deserve to have lots of money, a "showcase" partner, and to do what I want to do—then we resort to evaluating potential partners on superficial criteria, such as social status, income, attractiveness, or possibly how much this person annoys our parents. Eventually, we drift away from this person and begin to wonder what is wrong with the relationship. We may overthink endlessly whether this person hits the mark, or whether, if we stay in the relationship, we will ever get what we want out of life.

Once we choose a partner, we may find that society's obsessions with self-aggrandizement and quick-fix solutions to deep emotional problems make it hard to stay involved with that partner. If the relationship becomes rocky, we pop antidepressants, drink, or move quickly toward considering separation or divorce. If we feel stuck in a marriage, or the sex doesn't seem completely satisfying, infidelity seems a quick solution to our longings for emotional and physical satisfaction. When we have had multiple breakups of intimate relationships, frequent affairs, or endless arguments with our current spouse, we overthink what is wrong that we can't sustain close relationships.

Even when we are not in conflict with our lovers and partners, our navel-gazing culture encourages us to constantly take the pulse of these relationships, checking their health, wondering about changes and irregularities, and worrying about atrophy. Magazines provide us with endless quizzes to diagnose the health of our relationships, and we never quite get an A on the quiz. We are given impossible standards for everything, from the quantity and quality of our sexual encounters to the depth of our spiritual bonding. When we don't have a strong set of values to help us understand and appreciate our relationships, we are especially susceptible to these outside pressures and to the overthinking they can foster.

Can't Let It Go

Women are even more likely than men to fall into overthinking relationships. As we will explore in later chapters, women are prone to overthink all kinds of relationships, including relationships with parents and other family members, and relationships with children. Women's relationships with their spouses and partners are particularly likely to be the focus of their worries because women often suffer from two kinds of dependency on their partners—financial and psychological.

Although as a group women are much more financially independent of their partners now than a few decades ago, many women still depend on their partner's income to support themselves and their children. This kind of dependency can motivate a woman to put up with a lot in a relationship—from emotional distance to actual physical or sexual abuse from the partner. Feeling stuck, and wanting to protect herself and her children, the woman may become hypervigilant for signs that her partner may be dissatisfied with her or just generally getting upset. She can't afford for him to leave and wants to avoid his abuse. So she measures her every word and behavior in hopes of pleasing him, or at least calming him down. In between interactions with him, her thoughts may race about how to appease him, or perhaps how to leave him. But if she lacks education, job skills, and the support of others, and especially if she fears what he will do if she tries to leave, she may remain in the relationship, cowering when he is present and overthinking when he is absent.

Even when a woman is not financially dependent on her partner, she may be psychologically dependent. She may need his approval or a marriage to remain intact to feel good about herself. She may not know how to define herself apart from her relationship with her partner. Such neediness can lead a woman to monitor every aspect of her relationship: Why was he so cross this morning? Was it something I did? Is he happy in this marriage? What can I do to make him happier? Of course, we need to take stock of our relationships occasionally. But frantic watchfulness and chronic overthinking bouts about the relationship can do more harm than good. For one thing, it can drive away a partner. Psychologists Thomas Joiner of Florida State University and James Coyne of the

University of Pennsylvania have described the negative cycles of interaction that can happen when one partner is constantly soliciting reassur-
ance from the other.[1] The oversolicitous partner begs for guarantees
that the other partner loves her and understands her. The receiving
partner tries to reassure, but these reassurances are never quite enough,
so he may become frustrated and annoyed. This just feeds the anxiety of
the oversolicitous partner, so she questions him further about whether
he really loves her. He begins to wonder about this, but may feel guilty,
and thus promises his love. She sees his annoyance and perhaps his
guilty feelings, worries all the more, and tells him she doesn't think he
really loves her. He gets even more annoyed, and may either withdraw
or blow up at her. This interaction gives her a great deal to overthink.

Even if psychological dependence doesn't lead to these destructive
interactions with a partner, it can lead a woman to make bad decisions
about the relationship. In her overthinking bouts, she may see only the
problems in the relationship and not the assets, and may become hopeless about improving the relationship. This may lead her to leave a relationship that can be saved and is worth saving. Her overthinking bouts
may also involve a lot of self-blame and self-derision. She may become
convinced that she is not worth loving, or not able to have a good relationship. This can lead to all sorts of self-destructive activity, such as
binge eating or binge drinking, suicidal thoughts, or remaining in a bad
relationship because she thinks it's the only one she'll ever have.

Sherri, whom we meet in the story below, is vulnerable to overthinking in part because she is psychologically dependent on her relationship
with her husband, Bill. She has few sources of self-esteem outside this
relationship. She feels the need to maintain the relationship, even
though it is in trouble, for some pretty superficial reasons. As a result,
she doesn't really know what she wants from Bill, except for him to be
more sensitive and loving. Sherri is an avid reader of advice books and
columns about marriage, and to try to please Bill more has contorted
herself in all kinds of ways recommended by the advice-givers. Her desperation simply drives Bill further away, however, and his emotional distance gives her more to overthink.

Sherri's Overthinking Pit

The big day was approaching and Sherri still didn't know what she was going to get Bill. Their tenth wedding anniversary meant a lot to Sherri; in particular, it meant they had defied her parents' expectations that her marriage wouldn't last more than a few years. They had come close to separating any number of times. Sherri shuddered a bit as she caught the look of fear on her roundish face in the mirror. She shook her head to break the grip of the memories that flooded her mind, memories of Bill's fling with a younger woman a few years ago, and memories of the many knock-down, drag-out fights they had had over the years. She pulled her jet black hair back into a scrunchy and went to put on her uniform for work. "Damn," she thought, "the pants to this uniform are really tight." At 5'2", with the stocky frame she had inherited from her mother, Sherri had been battling her weight for her entire thirty-two years. She always wanted to look better—skinny so she could wear those skimpy outfits Bill seemed to like on other women, and athletic so she could keep up with him on the ski slopes when they went to Tahoe. Bill wasn't very tall himself, but he was in great shape and could move down the slopes at lightning speed. When he reached the bottom of the slopes, his black hair shone with perspiration as he strutted around the lodge talking animatedly about the condition of the snow that day.

As Sherri drove toward the hospital, she wondered if Bill would get her anything for their anniversary. He usually did the typical guy thing and forgot birthdays and anniversaries. This time she had done a lot to make sure he remembered. She consulted him on which restaurant they should go to the night of their anniversary. She wrote "Our 10th" on the calendar they kept on the refrigerator. She mentioned the anniversary to his mother when they talked on the phone, knowing she would remind Bill repeatedly. As she parked her car, and rode the elevator to the fifth floor to begin her night shift on the pediatric inpatient ward, Sherri was sure that this year would be different and they would have a romantic, fun anniversary.

That evening was quiet—the patients were sleeping better than usual, and there were no emergencies to deal with. After Sherri completed the usual round of taking vital signs and charting them, she had plenty of time to think. The memories that had visited her earlier in the day came back, particularly the image of Bill with that wispy little blonde who had nearly wrecked their marriage. Sherri still didn't understand why Bill had done it. She had begged him to tell her what was wrong, how she could change herself or their marriage so he would be happy. He couldn't seem to put his feelings into words, though. All he could say was, "It was just a fling. I let my hormones get the best of me." She couldn't take this answer, in part because it meant there was nothing she could do to prevent it from happening again. So she asked him, over and over, to tell her what was wrong and what she could do to ensure he never cheated again. Bill soon grew tired of Sherri's questions and pleadings, and eventually blew up. "For heaven's sake, Sherri, just let it go. I won't see her anymore. You're so damn needy—just get over it." She stopped asking him about the affair, but she had never gotten over it.

Ever since, she had been hypervigilant for signs he was cheating again. She had read a dozen books and hundreds of magazine articles about infidelity and about building good marriages. She had worked hard to follow the expert advice in those books and articles, buying sexy nightgowns and suggesting new sexual activities to Bill when they were being intimate, trying to be a better listener to him and show she cared about his work. Their marriage had seemed better in the last couple of years, although Sherri was still chronically nervous about it and spent a great deal of time analyzing things Bill had said or done. It didn't help that her sister, Audrey, seemed to be married to the perfect man, and her husband, Tom, was always buying her expensive little baubles and surprising her with romantic weekend getaways.

"Sherri. Sherri, wake up." Hilda, the nurse supervisor, jarred Sherri from her thoughts. "Your patient in 511 has pressed his nurse call light." Deeply embarrassed to have been caught a million miles away, Sherri got up to see what her young patient needed. The remainder of the night passed slowly, with just enough activity to keep Sherri from completely falling into her worries again, but not enough to fully occupy her mind, so the worries slipped in here and there.

She arrived back home just as Bill was leaving for his job as a biochemist for a major pharmaceutical company. Sherri knew that what Bill did for a living was important because she saw the miracles that modern drugs performed every day for her patients. She did have trouble, though, getting excited when he talked about the experiments that had gone right or wrong in a day. And he never seemed the least interested in her work as a nurse. They actually didn't talk much about anything of substance to each other. Sherri usually worked the night shift, while Bill typically worked ten hours a day, six days a week. When they did have a meal together, which wasn't that often, they typically dealt with business—who was going to go grocery shopping for Bill's mother, a ninety-three-year-old shut-in, whether they had enough money in their bank account to cover the mortgage this month, whether to hire someone to cut their grass or do it themselves.

As Bill was racing out the door, a bagel in hand, he paused long enough to say, "The BioTerm project is in trouble. The big brass thinks it's too expensive, wants to pull it. Jack wants me to go to Cleveland next week to try to talk some sense into them." Sherri's heart began to pound. "When next week?" she asked. "Probably leave on Thursday, and come back on Sunday so we can get good airfares. Gotta go, I'm late," Bill said, then jumped in his car and with a wave of his hand was gone.

Sherri grabbed hold of the doorjamb to steady herself. Next Friday was their anniversary. Bill would be gone for their anniversary. And he didn't seem to notice or care. Waves of anger, then panic, rushed over her.

> I should have known he'd find some way to ruin our anniversary. He doesn't care about me or our marriage. I can't stand this anymore, I've got to get out of this relationship. He's driving me crazy. I break my back to try to make him happy, and he just does what he wants with no thought of me. I quit. I just quit.
>
> But where will I go? I don't make enough money to support myself, at least not how I want to live. I'd end up sharing an apartment in the cheap part of town with some other nurse, just to get by. He's done it to me again—he knows I have to depend on his salary to live well, so he thinks he can get away with anything.
>
> What if he's not really going to Cleveland on business? What if he's cheating again? Maybe the fact that our anniversary is coming up has convinced him he doesn't want to stay married. Oh God, what am I going to do?

Sherri tried to think of someone to call. Her mother would just say, "I told you so," and her sister with the perfect marriage would just gloat. Bill's mother was too frail to handle this. Sherri walked through the kitchen like a zombie and plopped down on the couch. She flipped on the TV to one of those talk shows where people reveal their problems and the audience gives them dubious advice. The guests on the show today were of course a couple whose marriage was in trouble. There was no love left between them, they were saying, just a lot of sex. Some members of the audience suggested this wasn't such a bad thing, but others told them to pray for help, see a marriage counselor, or sacrifice all for each other. As Sherri watched, she yelled at some of the audience members, "You idiots. You don't know anything," and told the couple on the stage to give it up and just get divorced. Watching the show just pumped up her own overthinking, and she was now roaming around the house slamming doors and listing all the ways Bill was a lousy husband. She knew she should try to get some sleep, because she had to pull another night shift later on. There was no shutting off her thoughts, however, and it felt good to slam the doors and rag on Bill in her mind.

Bill made the mistake of calling her around noon. He had realized that his Cleveland trip would overlap with their anniversary, and had called to apologize and suggest they celebrate their anniversary a few days early. Sherri was completely ripe by the time the phone rang, and when she heard Bill's voice, she lit into him. "You sonofabitch. You don't give a damn about our marriage or how I feel. This is just another example of you doing whatever you please with no thought of how it will affect me. Go to hell!" And she hung up.

Sherri felt so good after yelling at Bill, she was elated. Finally, she had told him the truth. She tried to lie down to get some rest, but her own words rang in her ears, accompanied by, "I can't believe I said that to him!" After a time, her triumphant feelings waned, and the worried thoughts returned:

> What is he going to say when he gets home? What can I say? I can't apologize—I won't! But how are we going to get past this? Do I want us to get over it? Oh God, I don't know. I think I still love him. I don't know if he loves me, though. How can I live with a man if I'm not sure he loves me? How can I know how he feels?

What if he doesn't come home at all? What if he just leaves me right now? He's never left me after any of our other fights. But they were different. I've never said anything so mean to him before.

I wish I had someone to talk to. I wish Audrey wasn't so damn perfect. I need to talk to someone but I couldn't stand hearing how wonderful Tom is. Maybe I should call in to one of these shows to get some advice—I could do it anonymously so no one would know who I am.

For the next hour, Sherri thought through what she would say if she called in to a talk show to get advice what to do with Bill. She imagined telling all the things he had done that were insensitive, but realized she wouldn't be given the time to list them all. She then thought about which of his actions were the most egregious; she would convince everyone who listened that the failure of their marriage was all his fault. But then she imagined the talk show host questioning whether it really was Bill's fault. They like to zing the people who call those shows. Maybe the host would suggest that Sherri hadn't handled things well, that she wasn't attractive enough to Bill, that he was justified in looking to other women for satisfaction. She felt the shame and embarrassment she would experience if such accusations were made. She began to overthink whether she really might be to blame, at least partially, for her marital problems:

I'm sure I could have done something differently. After all, we were in love when we got married, despite what my mother thought. What happened that Bill lost interest in me? Could it be because he went on to get more education and I didn't? Does he think I'm boring or stupid? He sure doesn't think my work is worth talking about. Is it my weight? He can eat anything and stay trim, but I can't even look at a cookie without gaining a pound. I think it was a mistake for me to start working nights. I like it because it's less hectic, but maybe that's just a sign that I'm not very motivated about my work. I am boring. I have no hobbies. I have no friends. No wonder he wants to leave me. I wouldn't want to be married to such a slug, either.

When it came time to go to work that evening, Sherri had gotten no sleep and was almost dizzy with fatigue. She knew it wouldn't be safe for her to take care of sick children that night, so she called in sick. By the time Bill finally arrived home around midnight, Sherri was a complete wreck, psychologically and physically. She heard him come through the door and roused herself out of bed, where she had been staring at the ceiling, thoughts flying, for an hour. She entered the kitchen to find him opening a beer, and said in a tentative voice, "Bill, I'm sorry. I shouldn't have said those things." Without looking at her, he said, "Forget it. I'm tired. I'm going to bed." He walked past her, planting a perfunctory kiss on her head, and went into the bedroom. Sherri just stood at the entrance to the kitchen, shaking her head, knowing he must really be mad to be so silent and taciturn. He didn't want to talk about it because he didn't think their marriage was worth talking about, she was sure.

The next several days were like living in an ice palace. Neither Bill nor Sherri brought up the anniversary, the trip to Cleveland, or what Sherri had said to Bill on the phone. They just passed each other in the house, like roommates who were just sharing the rent. Sherri found the plane tickets to Cleveland on Bill's dresser when she returned home from work on Wednesday morning, so she knew he was still going. Later that day, he called home when he knew she would be out and left a message on the answering machine, saying he would be leaving Thursday afternoon and returning late Sunday night, and that he'd take his car and park it at the airport.

By the time Bill left on Thursday, Sherri was a complete wreck. She had hardly slept since she'd blown up at Bill the previous week. She kept replaying what she'd said to him in her head, sometimes feeling the anger behind her words full force again, and sometimes kicking herself for having said such stupid things. Because she was so fatigued and preoccupied, Sherri had called in sick to work three different nights in a week, something she had rarely done. Her supervisor, Hilda, began to raise questions about what was wrong with her.

Liberating Sherri

Sherri's story may feel familiar to you—overthinking whether her husband loved her, whether he was seeing someone else, what she could do to make herself more attractive to him. Women who, like Sherri, bank everything on pleasing their mates and maintaining their relationship with them are especially vulnerable to frequent overthinking. Any little indication that he's not happy can send them into frantic worrying about "What does it mean? What is he feeling? What can I do to make it better?" Deep down inside, they may resent their own sense of dependence on their partners. Feeling unappreciated and unaffirmed for all they do just gives them more to overthink.

They may try to talk to him about how they feel, as Sherri has tried to talk with Bill over the years. But psychologists John Gottman and Robert Levenson at the University of California, Berkeley, have found that many men assume the same strategy in these "talks," as Bill did—they stonewall, refusing to discuss the matter, telling their women partners that there's nothing to talk about or to get over it.[2] This just fuels a woman's worries about the relationship, and often enrages her. So she comes back for more, insisting he share his thoughts with her, perhaps becoming accusatory and hostile in her tone. He's likely to respond either by fleeing the scene or becoming angry, perhaps even violent. Nothing productive emerges from these talks and couples who frequently fall into this pattern are more likely to break up, according to Gottman and Levenson's research.

The night Bill left for Cleveland, Sherri plunged into an abyss of negative thoughts and worry:

> I've gotta get some help. I can't go on like this. I can't think. I can't function. What can I do? I can't call my mother. I can't call my sister. Maybe I ought to call a marriage counselor. But I don't know any. I don't just want to pick one out of the phone book. Who could I ask? The pastor at that church we've gone to a few times, maybe. I can't ask anyone at work—I don't want them to know. Maybe my doctor, maybe she'll know someone. I don't know. This might not be the right thing to do. I've never talked about my troubles with a stranger. Do I want my doctor to know I have a bad marriage? Oh, I've got to do something, anything.

Sherri picked up the phone before she lost her courage and called her doctor's office. She told the nurse she had something personal she wanted to ask the doctor, and was told the doctor would get back to her sometime that day. After what seemed an eternity, the phone rang. "This is Dr. O'Hara. What can I do for you, Sherri?" Sherri stumbled around, and finally blurted, "My marriage is in trouble. Do you know a good counselor?" Dr. O'Hara recommended a licensed family therapist named Carol Vanfossen and told Sherri she could find the number in the phone book. When she hung up, Sherri felt a bit relieved, but soon her doubts began to flood in again:

> Do I really want to go through with this? What if I don't like this woman? What if she gives me bad advice? What if Bill gets mad that I've talked to someone else about our problems?

Sherri's anxiety mounted, then turned to a sense of helplessness and hopelessness. "Stop it!" she said out loud. "Stop it and just call her!" She found Carol Vanfossen's number in the phone book and dialed it with a trembling hand. To her surprise, Carol answered the phone herself. Sherri managed to stammer, "Dr. O'Hara gave me your name. I'd like to talk to you about my marriage." Carol told Sherri she preferred to see married couples together rather than only one member of the couple, but Sherri told her she was desperate and didn't think her husband would agree to counseling. They made an appointment for the next day.

Sherri walked into Carol's freshly painted office building on a small side street downtown, looking for signs as to what this encounter would be like. There was a pleasant waiting room, with lots of plants and the standard office furniture. When Carol's office door opened, Sherri was surprised to see a woman about her age, tall, quite casually dressed, the kind of woman you might expect to see running one of the funky art galleries on Main Street. Sherri had pictured Carol as older and in a conservative suit.

Carol listened quietly as Sherri described both the recent incidents between her and Bill, and her view of their marriage over the last several years. Carol asked some questions about Sherri's work, family, friends, and pastimes. Then she gently asked, "Sherri, why do you want to save this marriage?" Sherri was so surprised at the question, she didn't know what to say. "I don't know. I love him, I suppose. I couldn't face my mother and sister if my marriage failed. I don't want to be alone."

For the rest of the hour, Carol worked to convince Sherri of two things. First, Sherri had to decide whether she truly wanted to be married to Bill, and if so she had to have better reasons than avoiding her mother's and sister's disapproval. Second, Sherri had to take better care of herself, whether or not she wanted to save the marriage. Carol pointed out what Sherri already knew—that her life revolved too much around Bill and she had no friends or activities that were all her own and brought her pleasure. They made another appointment to meet in two weeks, after Carol returned from a vacation.

Sherri and Bill were quickly walking down the path to dissolution when their journey was interrupted. Their blowup over the anniversary dinner was just another fight along the way, but luckily for Sherri it pushed her over a line into a frantic search for someone to talk to. Lacking friends, and believing her mother and sister would not be helpful, she turned to a marriage counselor, Carol. Actually, the steps Sherri took in deciding to find a marriage counselor and contact her were examples of good strategies for overcoming overthinking, even if Sherri didn't realize that was what she was doing. In one of her panicked moments, she simply told her thoughts to "Stop it!" because they were overwhelming her and tearing her down. Then she began to brainstorm what she could do in response to the argument with Bill, letting the possibilities flow. When she decided she should find a marriage counselor, she again brainstormed ways she could locate a good one. Then, when uncertainty gripped her, she plunged forward, forcing herself to dial the phone and make an appointment with Carol, just to be doing something to try to rescue her marriage.

Sherri may have been hoping Carol would give her a list of things to do to improve her marriage, like in the many magazine articles she read. Instead, Carol told her she needed to decide if she wanted to save her marriage and to come up with good reasons why. This drew Sherri's thoughts away from the minutiae of her interactions with Bill to the larger, more important questions in her life—a form of "adjusting your focus."

Sherri thought a great deal about Carol's words over the next few days while Bill was in Cleveland. She found that if she tried to think through Carol's questions about saving her marriage when she was alone at home and very tired, she would end up just going through a litany of all the things Bill had done to hurt her or all her deficits that would make Bill want to leave her. On the other hand, if she got out and did something pleasant for a while, like having a latte at her favorite coffee shop, then she could also remember some of the fun times they had had together. She felt guilty about calling in sick to work so many times in the last couple of weeks, so she volunteered to work both weekend nights. But to keep from being preoccupied with her marriage while she was working, she subconsciously made a date with herself to do that thinking when she was off duty and could go to her coffee shop, or take a walk in the park. During her breaks at work, she typically picked up a women's magazine and read one of the articles about saving your marriage, or having better sex with your partner. When she did that during her shift on Friday night, she was overcome with anxiety and worried thoughts. She vowed not to look at another one of those magazines for a long time.

Bill arrived home from Cleveland Sunday night when Sherri was at work, and by the time she got home the next morning, he was already at work. She felt hurt he hadn't left a note to tell her he was home. She considered saying something to him about it that evening. But then she decided this was one little battle she didn't need to fight with him. Normally after one of their fights Sherri would spend half the day preparing a terrific dinner for Bill, in hopes of appeasing and pleasing him. Then, if he didn't seem to appreciate it, or even worse if he called at the last minute and said he was staying late at work, she was devastated and yelled at him for his insensitivity. This time, Sherri stepped back and said to herself, "What do I need for myself this evening?" She thought for a while and realized that first and foremost she needed to be rested, so she could think straight in her interactions with Bill, and so she could go to work later that evening. Second, she needed not to be desperate. This meant no elaborate cooking, no hoping that Bill would be contrite and apologetic, and no believing that all the issues in their marriage had to be resolved tonight. Instead, she would order Chinese food after Bill came home, and she would see where the conversation took them.

Thankfully, Bill did come home for dinner that night and was pleasantly surprised to see Sherri looking more relaxed and rested than he had seen her for some time. They sat down with their hot and sour soup and Szechuan chicken, and she began to ask him how his trip went. He was again surprised not to be greeted either with angry accusations or icy stares from her. After he briefly described the negotiations over the BioTerm project, he got quiet for a few moments, then said, "I'm sorry I missed our anniversary. We'll make it up, okay?"

Sherri felt a mix of shock that he had apologized and rising anger that he thought they could just reschedule their anniversary dinner and everything would be fine. Before she said anything, however, she took a couple of deep breaths, thought to herself, "Pick your battles, girl," and then said, "I'd like to have an anniversary dinner sometime, Bill. But I also think we need to talk about what's going wrong in our marriage."

Bill sputtered something about their marriage being fine and got up to busy himself with the dishes. He clearly didn't want to talk about anything serious. Sherri decided she wasn't going to push him too hard that night, especially since she had to go to work. So she just replied, "Well, I think we do have some things to talk about. Tonight probably isn't the right time. But we've got to make some time."

"Sure, sure," was all Bill could get out, as he studiously avoided looking straight at Sherri. She got ready to go to work as he finished the dishes. They exchanged a brief kiss as she went out the back door.

Their rescheduled anniversary dinner happened that Friday night at Chez Daniel, the elegant new restaurant in town. After appetizers, a glass of wine, and the most enjoyable chitchat they had shared in months, Sherri didn't want to risk changing the mood. But she knew she couldn't avoid what was troubling her for much longer, and that it was difficult to get Bill to sit still long enough to have a conversation. So she began, "Bill, I've been really worried about us. Worried enough that I saw a marriage counselor while you were gone."

He was stunned and said he didn't think it was right to talk to strangers about their relationship. He started to say again that there was nothing wrong with their marriage, but Sherri interrupted, "There is something wrong. We hardly see each other, and when we do we're often angry. I don't feel much like a couple anymore."

What followed was a remarkably honest conversation about their relationship and themselves as individuals. Sherri let Bill know that she felt he was becoming distant from her, caring more about his work than about being with her, and she worried he was seeing someone else again. She remained calm, and chose her words carefully so they didn't sound angry and accusatory. Bill swore he wasn't seeing anyone else and admitted that he had been spending more time at work. He kept his cool, following her lead rather than responding nastily or refusing to talk. He told her he felt she was becoming too clingy toward him, too dependent on him, and one reason he spent so much time at work was that he sometimes felt badgered by her at home. They talked a bit about when they were younger and first married. As they walked through the history of their relationship, they agreed that they had married in part to spite their parents, and because they were so physically attracted to each other. After a year or two, this wasn't enough to sustain their relationship, and Bill became consumed with his graduate work as Sherri finished nursing school. They had spent the last several years living parallel lives, occasionally coming together for a vacation, but mostly existing on different planes, Bill focusing on work and Sherri grabbing at straws to keep Bill interested in her.

"Do you know what Carol asked me?" Sherri asked Bill. "She asked me why I wanted to save our marriage. I've been thinking a lot about the answer to that. I think the answer is because I really do love you. We may have gotten married for screwy reasons, but I do love you. And I think we can find new ways of being together."

Bill looked silently at her for a few long seconds. Then he said, "I do, too."

Working to take care of herself had many benefits for Sherri. It helped her realize that contemplating her future with Bill when she was tired and distressed only made her feel worse, but doing that thinking *after* she had done something nice for herself made her feel positive and in control. As a result, Sherri learned to consciously put off thinking about her marriage until she could do something for herself first. Taking better care of herself also led to an increase in self-confidence and self-respect for Sherri, which enabled her to talk with Bill about their problems in a calm but persistent manner, rather than in the desperation that usually characterized her conversations with him. When she felt the pang of an insensitive remark from Bill, she was able to feel that pain but maintain her composure and keep the conversation centered on what was important, rather than needing to confront him about his insensitivity.

When they did talk, Sherri and Bill began to move toward an understanding of "their story," how they went from the starry-eyed couple of ten years ago to the mess they were in right now. They could have decided that their marriage was built on a shaky foundation from the start, and that it was time to end it. Instead, they appear to have decided that the marriage was worth saving, if they could change their patterns of interacting with each other.

When Sherri went to her next appointment with Carol a couple of weeks later, she had already made some important changes in her life. She had switched to a day shift so she and Bill would be home together each evening. And she had started taking sculpting courses at one of the art galleries downtown. She was lousy at it, but she had a great time and was meeting fun people in the classes.

With great animation, she told Carol of the changes in her life and the improvements in her relationship with Bill, emphasizing how much more sensitively he was behaving toward her. Carol listened with a smile, and congratulated Sherri for taking such positive actions for herself. She warned, however, "You seem very focused on changing Bill, and that's pretty dangerous. We can never really change another person. We can only change ourselves."

Sherri was a bit put off by what seemed to be a reprimand from Carol. But as she drove home from the appointment, she realized how true it was—she had been reveling in how Bill had changed, but had also felt a twinge of anxiety about whether these changes would be permanent. And that left her vulnerable and dependent on him in a whole new way. When she got home, she sat down and wrote out all the ways she was still feeling dependent on Bill, putting what Carol had said at the top of the page. Some of the other items on the list were, "I wait to see what Bill wants to do instead of taking initiative." "I do things according to Bill's moods, not my own," and "I think too much about getting Bill's approval or appreciation for what I do." Halfway down the page, she wrote out the question, "How do I want to be close with but not dependent on Bill?" It was harder to come up with items for this list, but she wrote, "I want to share common interests instead of always taking his lead." "I want to do things because I care about them, not just because it will please Bill." Over the next several days, Sherri added to this list as she focused on sharing with Bill, instead of needing him.

Sherri had found a whole new way of being dependent on Bill by focusing on the changes he was showing as the source of improvements in their relationship. Carol pushed Sherri to let go of the unhealthy goal of changing Bill and to grab hold of the goal of broadening her base of self-esteem and support so she wasn't so dependent on Bill.

Sherri was making important headway, but she had a long way to go. Taking the sculpting class gave her a new outlet and source of friends, but it would help if she could find more support in her family. Sherri's tendency to compare her marriage to that of her sister, Audrey, put a wall between them. Sherri could actually be wrong about how perfect Audrey's marriage was—in their family, admitting to marital problems sounded as if it were taboo, so Audrey might be having troubles she's hiding from Sherri. Even if her marriage was indeed perfect, Audrey might be willing and able to support Sherri as she went through the difficult process of redefining herself and her role in the relationship to Bill.

If they were to remain together, Sherri and Bill would also need to find activities and interests that they share, rather than Sherri just following Bill around as he does what interests him. Many couples need to build in release time from the everyday stresses and strains that can drown long-term relationships, so that they can reestablish their common higher ground of goals and convictions. Sherri and Bill tended to spend what little time they had together talking domestic business. One important prescription for them would be to schedule a dinner out together at least once a week, and to make a contract with each other that they could not talk about house business at these dinners.

When a partner has been unfaithful, the wounded partner may choose not to forgive or feel it is impossible to forgive. Some cheating partners are not contrite about their infidelity, and may even persist in it. In such cases, the wounded partner may be forced to leave the relationship, if she can. If the infidelity is in the past, and both partners want to rebuild the relationship, forgiveness is often a necessary precursor. It's just too hard to reestablish the kind of trust and psychological intimacy that is necessary for a good relationship if one partner is living with a constant sense of betrayal. Sherri was still actively living with Bill's infidelity, with a combination of anger and panic occasionally rising to the surface and infusing her interactions with him. She is unlikely to have a satisfying, mature relationship with him unless she can forgive his infidelity and move on to focusing on their future together.

Not all relationships should or can be saved. Overthinking your relationship does nothing but tear you down, push you toward isolation, and increase the likelihood that you'll make unwise decisions about it. Breaking free of overthinking and moving to higher ground will give you the clarity and strength to evaluate your relationship more realistically, communicate more clearly, and make sensible choices about change.

8

Family Matters: Overthinking
Our Parents and Siblings

Our parents and siblings can evoke strong emotions in us. They are part of our self-definition, and we have a long history with them. They know our weaknesses and we know theirs. As we age, we are constantly renegotiating our relationships with them, often taking on new roles that are very difficult. Even simple negotiations, like who is going to take Mother to her doctor's appointment, can dredge up long-standing conflicts between family members and lead to major blowups. These conflicts are a frequent source of overthinking.

Some of us don't see our families very often, and we ruminate about it: Should I make more of an effort to see my elderly parents? Am I depriving my children of knowing their grandparents, aunts, uncles, and cousins? How will I feel when my family members begin dying away? Such thoughts can lead us to make positive choices in our lives—to spend a little more money and time visiting family and calling them, for example. But these thoughts can also spiral into ruminations: Why doesn't my family visit me more often instead of always expecting me to visit them? My siblings are so tight with each other—I'll never be a real member of the family. Does anyone in my family really care about me and my life?

One of the major themes of our modern entitlement obsession is that our families are to be held responsible for every wrong we can dredge up from our childhood, and that every style of parenting short of "perfect" (however that is defined by the expert of the day) constitutes emotional abuse. Indeed, some of us did grow up with abusive parents, and freeing ourselves from the effects of that abuse can be difficult. But most of us had parents who did an adequate, or better, job of raising us. There are always things that we wish they had done differently—we wish they had been more open with their expressions of love, less protective, allowed us more freedom. Entitlement values encourage us to see even minor "mistakes" by our parents as the source of significant troubles we have as adults. This can lead to rumination as we search through our childhood trying to dredge up some good reason for our weaknesses as adults. When our parents truly were inadequate or abusive, we can remain stuck in bitterly overthinking the wrongs they inflicted and replay images of angry confrontations with them.

A critical part of growing into a mature, fulfilled adult is to acknowledge our past and the foibles of our families, and to decide what aspects of our heritage we wish to reject and what aspects we wish to embrace. Simply denying your past—for example, denying that your mother's alcoholism affected you in any way—can allow that past to affect you in ways you don't even recognize. Remaining fixated on the past imprisons you and prevents you from overcoming it by making new choices in your life.

We often don't think that much about our childhood or our relationship to our parents or siblings until some crisis forces us into these thoughts. Such was the case with Faye, a forty-six-year-old elementary school teacher. She lived in the same town where she had been raised by her parents, Art and Nora, and had enjoyed a benign relationship with them for many years—taking her family over to her parents' home for occasional Sunday dinners, helping her parents as they reached their eighties and spent increasing amounts of time in physicians' offices. A health crisis with her father, however, stirred up decades-old resentments Faye had against her parents and her older brother, Jim.

Charting New Territory—Faye and Her Family

Faye knew her father was getting more forgetful. He would leave papers or objects in another room, then have no idea how they got there. Art had always been an irritable and critical man, so he usually accused his wife, Nora, of having moved them just to annoy him. Nora would quietly say, "Art, I wouldn't do that," and Art would stalk away grumbling something like, "Stupid woman."

One day recently, as Faye was tidying her classroom after school, she got a panicked call on her cell phone from her mother. "Your father went to the grocery store two hours ago and he still hasn't come back. I'm so worried—maybe he had an accident and he's hurt!" Her parents only had one car, so Faye drove her car over to the grocery store to see if she could find her father. She spotted his old blue sedan in the parking lot, and drove up to see her father sitting in the driver's seat, staring glassy-eyed out the windshield. She got out and tapped on his window. "Dad, Dad, are you all right?" Art looked startled, as though he didn't recognize Faye at first. Then a glimmer of recognition came across his face, and he started crying. Faye had never seen her father cry before, and it frightened her. "Dad, open your door. It's locked. Open your door, Dad." After what seemed an eternity, Art opened his door and Faye reached in to feel his forehead and take his pulse. He was warm, but he didn't seem to have a fever or an irregular pulse.

"Dad, what happened?" Faye asked.

"I don't know. How did I get here? Why are you here? Where are we?" replied Art. He seemed completely dazed. Then his angry personality took over. "Why did you bring me here? What are you doing to me?"

Faye took a deep breath and said, "Dad, I didn't bring you here, you drove here. We're at the grocery store—see, there's the sign. You're in your own car. Mom was worried. You've been gone for hours."

Art was really angry now, and sputtered, "Your mother is a stupid old woman. I have not been gone for hours. I just left the house, and I was just sitting here trying to remember all the things she told me to get at the store. Leave me alone. I'm going home now. I don't care what your mother needs at the store." He got back in his car, slammed the door, and started the engine. Faye tried to stop him, worried that he was not safe to drive, but to no avail. So she jumped in her own car and followed him home.

When they arrived at her parents' house, Art got out of his car and stormed inside, walking past Nora, who stood gaping at him, and into the bathroom. He slammed the door shut and Nora could hear him begin the shower. Faye came in shaking her head, and Nora immediately peppered her with questions about what happened. When Faye described her father's confusion, and that he had just been sitting in the car staring ahead blankly, tears began running down Nora's cheeks. Faye sensed this wasn't the first time something like this had happened.

"Mother, tell me right now what's going on. Has something like this happened before?"

"Yes. Several times. Your father saw the doctor last week. He said he thinks Art has Alzheimer's. Oh, Faye, what are we going to do? Art won't admit there's anything wrong. But it's getting worse quickly. Last night he was standing in the backyard, and didn't know where he was—in the backyard of the home he's lived in for thirty years!"

Faye was stunned. Neither of her parents had mentioned a word of this to her, even though she talked with them every few days on the phone and saw them at least once a week. As Nora kept talking, Faye realized that her mother had been hiding these incidents from Faye because she "didn't want her to worry" and because her father insisted there was nothing wrong and Nora should just keep quiet. This was totally typical of her mother. She had been making excuses for Art's nastiness and covering up the emotional wounds of his angry outbursts for their entire married life. Since she never wanted to "bother" her children, she always tried to take care of things herself.

This time was different, however. Faye knew enough about Alzheimer's to worry that her father could put himself and her mother in serious danger by getting lost or blacking out while he was driving. She also knew that her father was probably blaming her mother for all his lapses of memory and consciousness, heaping tension and stress on her.

"Did the doctor have any advice as to what to do?" Faye asked.

Nora got a somewhat wild-eyed look and said, "He said we might have to put Art in a nursing home fairly soon if the Alzheimer's progresses quickly. But I won't do that. I can take care of him. I won't put him in a home."

Faye looked at her eighty-three-year-old mother, thin, short, with barely the strength to pick up a five-pound sack of flour. There was no way she could stop Art, who was six inches taller and sixty pounds heavier, from doing anything he wanted to. And Nora rarely if ever drove a car these days because she got nervous and confused when she was behind the wheel. Still, the look of absolute determination on her mother's face made Faye back off. They talked for a while longer, then Faye left, saying she would come by every day to check on them.

As she drove home, Faye's ruminations were a mixture of worry and anger:

> How are we going to cope? My mother won't ask for help. I'm going to have to be there constantly to see what's going on. But I can't quit my job in the middle of the school year. I've got an obligation to the children. But I've got an obligation to my parents as well. What am I going to do? My father is such an ass. He has no right blaming my mother when things go wrong. Why does she put up with him?

Quite naturally, Faye entertained thoughts that maybe her father would die relatively quickly. She was flooded with guilt at these thoughts, however, and shut them out quickly. In their place came images of her father when she was a child, yelling at her, spanking her when she misbehaved, grounding her when she didn't do well on her report card. Her heart began to beat hard and she gripped the steering wheel so tightly her knuckles were white.

It is not unusual for a family crisis, like learning that a parent has Alzheimer's disease, to dredge up old memories from the past and put current conflicts into sharp relief. In our studies involving caregivers to dying family members, the caregivers often talked about buried issues between them and their siblings or parents coming to the surface amid the tension of the current crisis.[1] Some caregivers felt that the crisis had forced them to deal with these issues and overcome them for the first time in their lives. Others felt that these issues just added to their stress and that their relationships with other family members only got worse as a result of the crisis. Not surprisingly, the caregivers whose issues got resolved felt better emotionally than those whose issues only smoldered.

When she arrived home, Faye called her brother, Jim, who lived about two hours away. Jim was a successful lawyer, always busy and acting important, never finding time to visit their parents. Still, Faye needed to connect with her brother and let him know what was going on.

She finally got him on the phone after waiting on hold for nearly fifteen minutes. "Faye, I've only got a minute. I hope this is important." Faye told Jim directly the news she had learned that afternoon. He was quiet for a moment, then said, "That's too bad. This is going to be hard on Mom. Let me know if I can do anything."

Faye wanted to scream at him for his insensitivity, but instead said, "The doctor thinks we'll have to put Dad in a nursing home soon, but Mother refuses to consider it. I don't think she can handle him on her own."

Jim replied, "Can't you help them? You only work part of the day, right?" Faye knew that Jim thought that because the school day ended at 3 P.M. she only worked part-time.

Faye held back the angry words she wanted to scream at Jim, and instead said, "I can help them somewhat, but I can't be there all the time. In addition to my work, I have my own family to take care of."

"I know you'll work something out. You could always handle Dad better than I could. Gotta go." And before Faye could respond, Jim had hung up.

Faye was up nearly all night ruminating about her conversation with Jim and her interaction with her parents that day. Many of her thoughts were angry ones, but many were also focused on how she could juggle caring for her parents, her job, and her family all at the same time.

Like many women, Faye recognized her mother's tendency to sacrifice herself excessively for others, and Faye resented it, but still repeated it in her own life. When she thought of insisting that her father be put in a nursing home, she imagined her mother crying and begging her not to, and her father accusing her of betraying him. When she thought of asking her husband and children to take more responsibility around the house to free up some of her time, she felt guilty for burdening them so she could take care of her parents. So, like many women whose concerns focus mostly on pleasing others, Faye twisted herself into knots thinking of ways she could do it all, for everyone in her life.

For the next few months, Faye tried to do it all—work full-time, get meals for her family and take care of their house, and spend as much time with her parents as possible. Her mother greatly appreciated her presence, but her father accused her of "spying" on him and serving him rotten food. Art's wandering became more frequent, and his verbal abu-siveness became more harsh. Sometimes he would just start yelling and cursing at the top of his lungs, when no one else was in the room with him. This juggling act was exhausting Faye.

As Faye's stress level mounted, her overthinking bouts became more frequent. The themes were consistent: anger at Art for the emotional abuse he heaped on the family both now and in the past, frustration with her mother for not standing up to Art, resentment of her brother's self-importance and lack of helping, and a great deal of guilt for all these feel-ings toward her family. Faye was caught in that trap that many women find themselves in, continuing to sacrifice herself to keep her family happy, resenting the sacrifices she was making, but unable to break the pattern because the expectations of others had become her expectations for her-self. Faye just kept waiting around for someone in her family to change—her father to become more reasonable, her mother to take a stand and put Art in the nursing home, her brother to become sensitive and helpful.

One night Art went to bed leaving a lit cigarette balanced on the side of an ashtray in the family room. Nora didn't notice it and followed Art to bed. The cigarette fell off the ashtray onto a doily that covered the coffee table. The fire that ensued set off the smoke alarms in the house. Nora was awakened, realized the smoke alarm was going off, and tried to wake Art. He was completely confused, and pushed her away so that she fell off the bed. Smoke was beginning to waft into their bedroom, and when Nora tried to get up, searing pain shot through her leg. She called out to Art, but he appeared unconscious. Nora began to pull herself across the room toward the door. Happily, firemen burst into the room just then, scooped up Nora and Art in their arms, and took them outside to safety.

Faye met her parents at the hospital, where Nora was treated for a broken hip and smoke inhalation. Art was sitting in the room with her, but might as well have been on another planet. He just stared straight ahead and hardly seemed to notice when Faye entered the room. When she tried to talk with him, Art seemed to have little memory of the fire, or pushing her mother out of the bed. He just wanted to go home. For-tunately, the hospital wanted to keep him overnight for observation so Faye didn't have to decide what to do with him until at least the next day.

As she left the hospital in the wee hours of the morning, Faye's thoughts were running wildly:

> He nearly killed her this time. Something's got to be done. I don't care what she says. But he's just an old man with Alzheimer's. I shouldn't be blaming him. He can't help himself. What am I going to do? Maybe they should move in with us. But that's not fair to my family!

Knowing she would not fall asleep again, Faye drove over to her parents' home. She let herself in and began to inspect the house. Faye was concerned about the possibility of looters, so she decided to take her mother's jewelry and their lock box with their financial documents to her own house, then arrange for the house to be secured the next day. She opened the lock box to retrieve her parents' insurance documents and find out what had to be done to get the insurance company to pay for the damage. Her stomach grew tighter and her throat drier as she paged through each document in the box. Faye was no accountant, but she could tell that her parents' financial affairs were a real mess. There were old bonds and certificates of deposit that should have been cashed in months, even years, ago. Her father's will, which had been drawn up many years before, had several paragraphs crossed out in pen, with illegible paragraphs scrawled in the margins. He had obviously decided to change the will, but there was no way of telling what his new intentions were.

When she called her parents' insurance agent the next day, to her horror Faye found out that her parents' insurance premiums were overdue by two months. The agent said she had called Art several times, but he had hung up on her, thinking she was a telephone salesperson. Unbelievably, the final cancellation notice was due to be mailed from the insurance company that day. Faye raced down to the agent's office and paid the overdue premiums, then talked with the agent about the papers that needed to be filed for a claim on the house. This was the last straw for Faye:

> This can't go on. He's only going to get worse. Mother clearly can't handle this on her own. And I can't sacrifice my family or my job.

Then, of course, the guilty thoughts started flooding in. Faye also recognized the voice of her father, railing accusations against her for betraying him, and for not being strong enough. But this time, she fought back:

> Shut up, guilt. I'm not going to let guilt run my life any longer. And shut up, Dad. You're a sad, angry old man, but you've been that way my whole life. You're not going to change, even when you're dying. I'm sick of it. You're not going to control my life any longer.

With these declarations, Faye decided to stop listening to her father's voice and stop letting guilty ruminations force her to put up with her parents' impossible situation. She made one more decision in that moment—to stop waiting around for Jim to become sensitive, and to force him to take his share of the responsibility for her parents.

Faye called Jim's office, and this time refused to be put on hold. Jim was clearly annoyed when he got on the phone, but she cut him off, saying, "Last night, Mom and Dad were nearly killed in a fire that Dad accidently caused. Dad pushed Mom as she was trying to wake him, and she fell and broke her hip. I've discovered that their insurance premiums haven't been paid for months, and the rest of their finances are a disaster. I want you to come home, today, and help me clean up this mess."

Jim began to protest that there was no way he could leave his law practice on such short notice, but Faye would have none of it.

"You have neglected this family for years, leaving it to me to do everything for Mom and Dad. No more. You can straighten out their finances and papers much better than I can. I want you to come home, and I won't take no for an answer."

Jim, stunned at Faye's newly found assertiveness, stammered that he would be there by dinnertime.

Lowering her expectations for Jim moved Faye from overthinking his insensitivity to taking control of the situation and demanding what she needed from him. Next she had to confront her parents directly. As Faye considered how to talk with her parents, old angry thoughts about her father kept creeping in. Instead of thinking about how to tell them they had to go into some sort of care facility, she kept thinking of angry things she'd like to say to her father about his abusiveness over the years.

But then she realized this was getting her nowhere. Her father was never going to change. And yelling at him would accomplish nothing in his confused state of mind, except to hurt her mother. Faye told herself:

> I have a right to be angry, even to hate him. But I've got to accept who he is and move on. Otherwise, he's just going to keep winning battles he doesn't even realize he's fighting anymore.

Faye didn't exactly forgive her father, but she decided to accept who he was, accept her feelings about him, and then move on. This freed her from the grip of her angry thoughts and gave her the space to think about what she should do next.

Before going to her mother's room at the hospital, Faye stopped at the office of the social worker she had been introduced to the night before. They talked at length about different care facilities in town that would take her mother while she recuperated from her hip fracture, and her father permanently. The social worker told Faye about a facility that would take both her parents—they could live in an apartment-like space but have twenty-four-hour nursing care available on site and eat their meals with other residents in the facility's dining room. It was expensive, but it sounded like something Faye could be comfortable sending her parents to.

Presenting this to her parents was not easy, but Faye was steeled by the thought that she was doing what was best for her parents, as well as good for her and her family. Nora cried softly for a while, but faced with the fact that she couldn't return to her own, fire-damaged home, conceded that this might work out okay. Art didn't respond much at all. Faye didn't know if it was because of the smoke inhalation, the trauma of the fire, the Alzheimer's, or some realization of what he had done to Nora, but Art seemed to be even more confused and out of it than ever.

After she left her parents, Faye began second-guessing herself:

> Is this really the best thing to do for them? Why can't they move in with my family? We could convert part of the downstairs into an apartment for them. I don't want them to die in some institution. It would be cheaper for us to have them move in with us, even if I have to quit my job, than try to pay for this facility for them.

This time it wasn't Faye's father's voice that was creeping into her thoughts, but her mother's voice—the one that had convinced her all her life not to inconvenience anyone, to just manage everything on her own, to do anything to keep her father happy.

Faye didn't recognize this herself, but her husband, John, did. "Faye, you're trying to do it all again. Maybe your parents would like it better to live with us—although I'm not sure that's true of your father—but you love your job and it wouldn't be good for you to give it up. And quite frankly, I don't want to live with your parents, especially your dad."

Faye's first feeling about what John said was guilt, because she realized she had been ready to impose her parents on him and the kids. But then she realized she had created an impossible situation for herself again. If she put her parents into the care facility, she would feel guilty for that. If she demanded that they move in with her family despite John's objections, she would feel guilty for that. Her mother was always getting herself into catch-22's like this and Faye had learned this bad habit from her.

So Faye said to herself: Mother, I can't do it this time. I can't do it your way. The care facility is a better option for you and Dad, and for my family.

Ironically, Faye's mother probably would not have accepted living with Faye and her family, because it would be "bothering them," and so would have insisted that she and Art move into the care facility. But Faye's construction of her mother's voice in her head, telling her to sacrifice herself to make others happy, had nearly convinced her that this was what her parents would want. It often happens that the voices in our thoughts are more harsh and unreasonable than the true voices of the people they represent. This is part of what makes them such powerful material for overthinking. Fortunately for Faye, however, her conversation with John helped her to hear her mother's voice in her own guilty thoughts, and to reject it.

Life Span Overthinking

As our relationships with our families evolve over our life span, the focus of our ruminations about them changes. When we are teenagers, we may obsess about how embarrassing they are, how we can get away from them, or perhaps about problems our parents or siblings are having. When we are older, like Faye, we may overthink how to juggle our commitments to our family of origin with our commitments to our partners and children and to our careers. As our parents age, we may begin to worry about their health and about how we will feel when they pass away. Throughout our lives, we tend to rehash old wrongs committed by parents or siblings, to wish they would change in some way, and to worry if we are living up to parents' expectations.

The best remedies for concerns about your family will depend on the specific issues you have. At least four of the strategies described earlier in this book are especially useful in overcoming family-oriented overthinking. The first is accepting your feelings about your family. Anger and frustration are common in relationships with parents and siblings, because these people know how to push our buttons better than anyone else in our lives. But then we feel terribly guilty about being angry or frustrated because we believe, implicitly or explicitly, that we should love our parents and siblings. Accepting that our family drives us crazy, and that this is a perfectly understandable reaction, is often a necessary step before we can regain control of our thoughts and feelings.

A second key to coping with your family is forgiveness. This doesn't mean you have to believe that the sins committed against you by your family members were acceptable. If the harm one of them has inflicted on you is tremendous—in particular if you were abused by a family member—the best you may be able to do is to let go of your desire for revenge and move on. But letting go is necessary if you are to reclaim your life.

Third, you may need to lower your expectations for your family, especially the expectation that they are going to change in the ways you want them to. For example, if you continue to expect that your mother is going to revert from being stoic and constrained to being openly loving to you, you will only be disappointed every time she doesn't greet you effusively and may wonder if she really loves you. You can't change her basic temperament, but you can change how much you overthink it by accepting that she was born this way, or was raised to behave this way. Often when we change our own behaviors toward our parents or siblings, it breaks long-standing patterns of family dynamics that have served to maintain each individual's behaviors in the family. In other words, if you change how you react to your mother—perhaps becoming less anxious for signs of affection from her—she may relax and change her own behavior.

Finally, we all have issues with our families that are guaranteed to create conflict if they are raised openly. It may be your father's political views. It may be your brother's attitudes toward women. It may be your sister's decision to work full-time instead of staying at home with her kids (or vice versa). Often the best strategy for avoiding conflicts, and then avoiding overthinking these conflicts, is "don't go there." Confronting your father or brother or sister is unlikely to convince them that you know best. On many issues, we have to accept that our family members see the world very differently from us. Staying away from these issues is often the best medicine against overthinking, particularly when they are issues that do not affect us directly, and that they have a right to differ with us on.

Faye's ability to use strategies such as these to overcome overthinking her problems with her parents and brother allowed her to consider the options for her parents with a clearer head. Not everyone faced with Faye's situation would make the same decisions she did. But from Faye's story we can all learn the importance of conquering ruminations about family.

9

The Parent Trap:
Overthinking and Our Children

Children provide us with both great joys and deep frustrations. These conflicting emotions can be great fodder for overthinking. We have so much invested in our children—often far too much of our self-definition and self-worth. When our children are having trouble, we can view it as a reflection on ourselves—our skills as parents, our value as human beings. Unfortunately, we can't always control or change our children's behavior or attitudes, so it's inevitable that they will disappoint our expectations for them at least occasionally. This combination of lack of control, plus allowing our children's behavior to influence our own self-worth, creates ideal conditions for overthinking.

Several characteristics of our modern culture make child-oriented ruminations particularly likely. The complexity of modern life makes it difficult to know how to parent well. How much should we protect our children from the nasty side of popular culture? How can we protect them from the dangers that come from access to the Internet, television, guns, and the bad influences of other children? Are there dangers in overprotection? How can we possibly prepare our children for the world they will inhabit as adults, given how quickly the world is changing?

Today we have media experts giving us confusing, contradictory, and constantly changing advice on parenting. No matter what parents do there is some expert in the media telling them that what they are doing is wrong. One expert says that children *must* be cared for by their mothers as infants to optimize their development, and the next expert says that good day care is often better for a child than a mother reluctantly quitting her job. One expert says that parents *must* see to it that their children have a balanced diet for proper brain development, and the next expert says children are resilient and can grow up strong eating only pizza and hot dogs. The popular media also deliver a barrage of confusing—and often unhealthy—messages to our children about who they must be: it's okay to hit other people who annoy you; you have to have more toys than the other kids to be cool. If our children are operating in a vacuum of values, they suck up these media messages easily. If you are operating in a vacuum of values, it is more difficult for you to give your children guidance or to know how to parent them best.

So we overthink: Am I being too lenient or too strict? Do I really listen to my child? Have I made the right choices for my child? We fear our children will blame us much the same way we blame our parents for how we turned out. One friend of mine frequently says, "Every day I do something that I know my son is going to be talking about with his therapist in ten years."

Another aspect of modern society that is extremely damaging to parenting is our quick-fix obsession. If your child is having trouble in school, switch schools. If your child has behavioral problems, find a diagnosis and some medication to deal with it. If you worry that your child might get involved in drugs, sign him up for so many extracurricular activities that he doesn't have time for drugs. If your child seems unhappy or hostile, buy her something cool and expensive. If you want to know what is on your child's mind, ask her in the car on the way to her violin lesson. The long, slow, sometimes laborious work of knowing the child on a deep level, communicating with him or her, and teaching him or her important values is just too difficult for us to fit into our busy lives. So we settle for quick fixes, then ruminate endlessly when our children don't turn out the way we want them to.

Since women typically have primary responsibility for their children, and sometimes sole responsibility in single motherhood, children are a common topic of overthinking. Even if her husband or partner shares responsibility for child care, a woman will be held more accountable for her children's behavior and well-being than a man will be. So when their children are having difficulties, many women fret about what they are doing wrong. This can lead to positive changes in your behavior, but it can also deteriorate into chronic guilty ruminations about your failures as a mother.

Women are also very emotionally connected to their children, which can be a source of great empathy and richness in their relationship. But it can also be a source of great pain and worry as they reexperience the pains and sorrows of growing up as their children develop.

Often, rather than overthinking problems their children are having, women find themselves overthinking conflicts with their husbands or partners over child care. In our large community study, we asked women with children how much their husbands or partners (if they had one) shared in the daily activities of child care. Those women who said that there was no sharing—that they did all or nearly all of the child care—were more prone to ruminating.[1] It wasn't so much that the grind and burdens of child care—feeding, bathing, and dressing the children, transporting them around town, disciplining them if need be—led these women to overthink. It was the lack of equity with the husband or partner in the division of child care labor that was related to their overthinking. If you have a conflict with your spouse or partner about fundamental values of child rearing, such as what religion to raise your children in or appropriate means of disciplining them, it can really draw you into over-thinking.

Although women now have more freedom to choose whether or not to work outside the home, whatever choice they make is criticized by some portion of society. This provides ample fuel for guilty overthinking and self-doubt. If they work outside the home, women can feel guilty for not always being there when their children want or need them. If they don't work outside the home, they can feel demeaned by others who don't value their contributions as a full-time mother. In our community study, we found that women who were full-time homemakers and mothers reported overthinking just as much as women who worked outside the home and had children. So neither group escaped the pull of overthinking. The more these women were dissatisfied and uncomfortable with the amount of time they were spending with their children *or* on their jobs, the more they engaged in overthinking.

In this chapter, we will explore the story of Marcia, who has remained caught for years in cycles of overthinking her son's behavioral problems and her family's functioning. As is so often the case, this overthinking has not provided Marcia with insights into her family's problems. Instead, it has blinded her to the power she has to create positive changes in her son's behavior and her family's patterns of interaction.

Overthinking Mothering

Marcia and her husband, Peter, had agreed that children need to have a stay-at-home mom, and she happily quit her job as a schoolteacher when their first child, Adrienne, was born twelve years ago. Adrienne was the fulfillment of Marcia's fantasies about what it would be like to have a child. Like Marcia, she was fair-haired, with a roundish face and long skinny fingers. As a baby, Adrienne's temperament was just about perfect—she slept and ate well, was full of curiosity and loving affection for everyone around her, and reached important milestones, like walking, extremely early. Adrienne continued to be just about perfect in elementary school. Her marks for every subject were always "excellent" and she never seemed to get in trouble. Marcia began taking Adrienne to violin lessons when she was six, and by the time she was nine, Adrienne was playing solo recitals. Her violin teacher even suggested Adrienne should be sent to a school for musically gifted children. She was the kind of child about whom other parents often said, "Marcia, you are so lucky."

Marcia wasn't so lucky with Timothy, her second child. As so often happens, Timothy had the opposite temperament to Adrienne's. He was a fussy baby, and now, at seven years of age, he still didn't sleep through the night on his own. Timothy liked to play with other children, but other children often complained that Timothy always wanted to do things his way, and that he got mad too easily. In kindergarten, and now in first grade, Timothy frequently got into trouble for being disruptive in class, and wasn't advancing as expected in his reading or arithmetic skills. Marcia tried to get Timothy interested in music, but he had no patience for it. He loved sports, but was so awkward and uncoordinated that he couldn't play any sport particularly well. Between his lack of athletic talent and his temper, he was usually the last chosen for sports teams, which sometimes led to explosive outbursts at the other children.

The contrast between Adrienne and Timothy was frequently pointed out to Marcia by teachers, by Peter, and by Marcia's mother. "Adrienne is so special, so perfect—I wonder what happened with Timothy?" What was Marcia supposed to say in response? That yes, Timothy was a disappointment, a dud? Despite his shortcomings, Marcia loved Timothy greatly, and believed that one day he would "blossom." But comments from others typically sent Marcia spinning into overthinking:

> They seem to be asking for some explanation. I don't know why Timothy is so different from Adrienne. They act like it's my fault. Especially Peter and my mother. I've tried to give him everything I gave Adrienne—why has he turned out so different from Adrienne? I'm so tired of going into the school for parent-teacher conferences. The teachers always spell out what Timothy is doing wrong, as if I've never heard it before. Then they stare at me, expecting me to say something or do something. Maybe it is my fault. Maybe I need to be more disciplined with him at home. Peter always thinks so. He says if I just lay down the law with Timothy, he'll shape up.

Marcia tried to be more strict with Timothy, but that usually resulted in shouting matches between them. If Peter walked in on one of these, he'd explode at Timothy and send him to his room. Then there would be silence between Peter and Marcia for the rest of the evening, with Peter fuming that Marcia couldn't handle Timothy, and Marcia fuming that Peter had interfered, but also wondering why she couldn't handle Timothy. She'd be up for a couple of hours that night, overthinking the incident in bed, feeling helpless and guilty.

Many women let this unhealthy pattern of interactions, and overthinking these interactions, go on for years, as did Marcia. At times of high conflict with their children, their spouses, the children's teachers, and others, they are so overwhelmed with the immediate situation that they have trouble stepping back to evaluate what needs to be done. When things are calm, they are so relieved and thankful that they want to believe things are now better. As a result, they never deal with the larger issues driving their high-conflict times. They overthink what's wrong, but this only sends them into tailspins of anger at others, concern about their children, and guilt at their own parenting.

They may grab at straws, trying to fix "the problem." One of Timothy's teachers told Marcia that Timothy clearly had attention deficit hyperactivity disorder, and this explained his behavior and lack of achievement. Marcia was relieved that there might be a label and a cure for Timothy's problems, and took him to his pediatrician, requesting that Timothy be put on Ritalin. The pediatrician insisted that Timothy be evaluated by a psychologist who specialized in assessing and treating ADHD before she would agree to prescribe Ritalin. Marcia was annoyed that she had to have Timothy evaluated before he could be put on medication, but went along. The psychologist, Dr. Glass, took a detailed history of Timothy's development and behavior, asked a lot of questions about the family, and administered some cognitive tests to Timothy.

When Marcia and Peter went to Dr. Glass's office to hear her recommendations for Timothy, they fully expected to be told he needed to go on Ritalin or some similar drug. Instead, Dr. Glass said, "Timothy may have ADHD, but it's not clear to me. He does need help controlling his behavior, and catching up in his reading and arithmetic skills. I also think the two of you need to make some changes in your ways of responding to Timothy, and learn new ways to encourage and discipline him." Marcia sat stunned, but Peter erupted, "How can you blame us for this? We have one perfectly good child—we're good parents. There's something wrong with Timothy. Why can't you see that? There is nothing wrong with this family!" He shoved his chair back and stormed out of the office.

Although Marcia agreed with Peter's angry words to Dr. Glass, she was also terribly embarrassed at his behavior and began apologizing. Like many women who hold themselves responsible for everyone's happiness and well-being, she couldn't accept her own anger at Dr. Glass and instead worried what Dr. Glass thought of her based on Peter's behavior. Dr. Glass calmly smiled, as if this were not a new experience to her, and said, "Marcia, you are not responsible for Peter's behavior. And Timothy's behavior is not your fault. But you can change Timothy's behavior by changing your own behavior toward him, I'm sure of that. It may not be all he needs, but it will help him a great deal. I'd like you to do one thing for me. Sit down at some quiet time when the children and Peter are gone, and write down what your expectations are for Timothy— your hopes and dreams for him. Then, next to each thing on your list, write down where you think this expectation comes from. If you're willing, I'd like to see you, and Peter, again in a week."

When Marcia caught up with Peter in the parking lot, he barked, "What took you so long?" Marcia mumbled something then got in the car and buckled her seat belt. All the way home, Peter continued to rant and rave about Dr. Glass and give Marcia orders: "How dare she suggest we need to change! She must be incompetent. If that pediatrician won't give you drugs for Timothy without her recommendation, then you need to find a new pediatrician."

That evening when the kids had gone to bed and Peter was downstairs watching television, Marcia sat down with some paper and a pen. She thought that writing out her expectations for Timothy would somehow prove Dr. Glass wrong. And she hoped it would make her feel better. She had been silently overthinking what Dr. Glass had said and Peter's reaction to it all day:

> How could she say that we needed to change our behavior? Does she think we cause Timothy's school problems somehow? Everyone is always holding me responsible for Timothy. Peter was such a jerk, I was so embarrassed. And then he talks to me like I'm a child, or one of his employees, telling me what I have to do about Timothy. He never listens, he just gives orders.

Marcia shook herself all over to try to clear her head, then poised to write down her list of expectations for Timothy. Within a few minutes, she had written:

1. Do well in school.
2. Don't get into trouble.
3. Do well at some extracurricular activity.
4. Get along with the other children.

When she read over the list, it seemed perfectly reasonable. Then she thought about the other half of Dr. Glass's assignment for her—to consider where these expectations came from. On the surface, this seemed absurd. These were the kinds of expectations every parent had for their children, goals most children had no trouble achieving. After all, Adrienne had . . .

Then Marcia caught herself. She realized that as she was writing each of these items down, she was imagining Timothy bringing home A's from school, just like Adrienne, and playing the violin, just like Adrienne, and being popular, just like Adrienne. She was using Adrienne as the standard for what Timothy should be able to do.

When parents carry out the exercise that Dr. Glass gave to Marcia, they often find that their expectations for their children are based on inappropriate standards. Sometimes these standards are other children, and sometimes they are standards imposed on them by other people. Marcia was holding Timothy to Adrienne's image because that's what Peter, her mother, the teachers, and many others were doing. She needed to stop comparing Timothy to Adrienne. She also needed to stop listening to the voices of Peter, her mother, and the teachers, demanding that Timothy be like Adrienne. Initially, this realization triggered guilty overthinking in Marcia:

> How could I do this to Timothy? He must feel so terrible to always be compared to Adrienne. How could I let other people do this to him?

Fortunately, it occurred to Marcia that this overthinking was not doing any good, that it was not helping her or Timothy. So she used the "thought police" technique—she squeezed her eyes shut and told herself to stop this self-pity because it wasn't helping Timothy. She wanted to think this through so that her insight might help her to understand Timothy better.

Then she asked herself a different question, adjusting her focus: "What do I hope for Timothy, based on who he is?" Marcia loved Timothy enough to want him to be happy for himself, doing things that he wanted to do, and doing his best, not Adrienne's best. But the more she thought, the more she realized she didn't know what Timothy wanted to do, or what he was capable of. She, like everyone else, had been so fixated on why Timothy wasn't like Adrienne that she wasn't really sure who Timothy was.

Tremendous guilt swept over Marcia. How could she not know her own child? How could she be so unloving that she had denied his individuality all these years? Usually, once Marcia had thoughts like these she would go to bed and beat herself up mentally for hours. But again, she squeezed her eyes tight and told herself she wasn't going to indulge in these thoughts about herself. She was going to raise her sights and keep focused on what was important: understanding what Timothy wanted and needed for his life. Her love for Timothy was going to win out over her self-loathing.

So Marcia asked herself another adjustment-focusing question: "How can I find out what Timothy wants, and what his capabilities are?" On the back of her piece of paper she began to brainstorm:

1. Find out more about Dr. Glass's evaluations of Timothy—what does she think he's good at, and what can be done to help him do better at reading and math?
2. Spend more time with Timothy—but don't push him so much. Listen to him and watch him more.
3. Talk to Timothy about what he likes (instead of always talking to him about what he's doing wrong).

Marcia headed for bed feeling more upbeat and hopeful about Timothy than she had for a long time. She stopped by his bedroom and smiled when she saw him sprawled across his bed sideways, half covered in his blankets. She actually looked forward to spending time with him, because the pressure to "fix" him was off.

Marcia was still angry with herself and felt guilty for having wasted so much time doing what she thought others wanted her to do with Timothy—yelling at him, disciplining him, trying to make him act like Adrienne. But she knew that she had to let go of these self-directed thoughts, forgive herself, and spend her energy learning what Timothy needed.

Self-forgiveness can be critical to good parenting. When your actions toward your child are driven by guilt, they can be self-indulgent and harmful. Instead of doing what your son or daughter needs from you, you do what makes you feel good and lowers your guilt about your past parenting mistakes. Along with self-forgiveness must come repentance. It's no good to forgive yourself for behaving badly toward your children if you keep on behaving that way. For example, if you frequently lose your temper at your children, and tell yourself it's because your parents were violent toward you, or it's because you are frustrated at work, but you continue to lose your temper, that's not forgiveness—it's rationalization.

For the next several days, when Marcia picked Timothy up at school, rather than asking him if he'd been a good boy and kept out of trouble, she asked him what was his favorite thing that happened at school that day. Timothy seemed surprised at the question at first, and had difficulty answering it. Over the week, however, Marcia noticed that Timothy often mentioned some incident that occurred during a sports game: "Jimmy Peterson hit a home run that won the game for our team!" She was surprised that he continued to like sports so much, given how unathletic he was. But as she listened closer, she noticed that he often wasn't talking about a fantastic play he had made during a game, but a play made by one of the other children. He also often rattled off statistics for ballplayers on professional teams. Marcia had no idea Timothy knew so much about professional sports. No one else in the family had any interest in such things, so they were seldom a topic of conversation. In the meantime, Timothy had amassed a great knowledge of the records of professional baseball, football, soccer, and hockey players. He had kept this knowledge to himself, because no one was ever interested in his interests.

Marcia's revelations about Timothy are typical of the kinds of insights parents can have when they adjust their focus away from controlling their children to understanding them. You can spend so much time and energy winning arguments with your children, or pushing them to do "what's right," that you won't hear them tell you what their concerns are, or what they really want and why. Particularly when you invest your self-worth in your children's success, you can be completely blind to who they are as people. You become consumed with how your children's behavior reflects on you as a parent. If your child is talented, popular, well-behaved, then you feel good about yourself. If your child is lacking in any way, then you feel guilty and ashamed.

Children pick up on these expectations and respond. They may knock themselves out doing activities they don't really enjoy, trying to accomplish goals they can't or don't care about accomplishing, worrying about disappointing Mom or Dad. Other children, perhaps including Timothy, rebel, rejecting Mom and Dad's expectations of them, sometimes to the point of being self-destructive.

Understanding how much Timothy loved sports gave Marcia an idea: Why not use his love of sports to help him with some of the behaviors he needed to change? It occurred to her that he must be doing quite a bit of reading to learn all his sports trivia. Maybe they could build his reading skills through books about sports. And all the sports statistics he had memorized involved math—could these sports examples help him understand more about math? Marcia called Timothy's teacher the next day to discuss these ideas with her.

Marcia kept the appointment with Dr. Glass that she had made the week before. She didn't tell Peter. She knew he wouldn't go, and she didn't want him to prevent her from going. Marcia admitted to Dr. Glass that she had realized she was holding Timothy to an "Adrienne standard," and this was not healthy for him. Dr. Glass responded, "It takes some parents forever to realize something like that. You did it in a day." Marcia quizzed Dr. Glass on the details of her tests of Timothy's cognitive abilities to get a better sense of what Dr. Glass thought Timothy's academic strengths and weaknesses were. Marcia also told Dr. Glass of her ideas to encourage Timothy to practice reading and math using sports stories and examples. She was feeling really good about this appointment and all the support she was getting from Dr. Glass, when the psychologist sprang this on her: "You know, Marcia, you're going to have to deal with Peter's attitude toward Timothy and his style of interacting with him eventually."

Like many women, Marcia didn't want to confront her husband's behavior toward their children—she wanted to be able to fix the family problems all by herself. Some women face much bigger family problems than Marcia, with husbands or partners who are physically or sexually abusive toward their children. This certainly was not true of Peter, but his explosive outbursts at Timothy were wrecking Timothy's self-esteem, causing him to retreat into himself, giving him reason to rebel, and providing a terrible model for how to handle frustration. Marcia was

afraid to become the target of Peter's anger by criticizing him or confronting him. Besides overthinking the problem, she typically tried to
engineer situations to avoid it.

Dr. Glass sensed Marcia's reluctance to deal with Peter. She asked if
Peter had ever been violent toward her or the children, or if Marcia
feared he could become violent, and Marcia said no. Dr. Glass asked
Marcia to describe a recent situation in which Peter had gotten upset
with Timothy, and how Marcia had responded to that situation. Marcia
described a blowup that had occurred about a week ago, how Peter had
yelled at Timothy, asking him what was wrong with him. Timothy had
gone silent and retreated to his room. Marcia admitted that she had stood
there saying nothing, although she was furious at Peter for being so harsh
with Timothy. Then she and Peter had given each other the silent treatment the rest of the evening.

Dr. Glass then asked Marcia if they could replay this scene, with Dr.
Glass acting the role of Peter, and Marcia trying to respond differently
to him. Marcia knew this was what they called role-playing, and she
didn't want to do it. She had no idea how to act differently with Peter.
But she went along. She knew she was supposed to be more forceful with
Peter and stick up for Timothy. So the first time through role-playing,
when Dr. Glass began to say the things Peter had said, Marcia interrupted her and said, "Stop yelling at him! He's just a little boy! Leave
him alone! You're so mean to him!"

Dr. Glass helped Marcia understand how hard it would be for Peter
to hear what she was saying and respond to it sympathetically. He would
feel angry, defensive at being accused, and they'd likely end up in a
shouting match. She suggested that Marcia might be able to have a
greater and more positive effect on Peter if she waited to talk with him
after he had calmed down. Then she described the difference between
an aggressive response, like the one Marcia had used role-playing, and
an assertive response, in which Marcia told Peter how his behavior made
her feel, calmly and without accusations.

They tried role-playing again. Marcia said she would wait for a few
minutes after Timothy had stormed out of the room, then say something like, "Peter, when you yell at Timothy like that, he feels bad and
doesn't understand, and I feel bad. I think we need to find a different way

of communicating with him." Dr. Glass said she was impressed at how quickly Marcia had picked up on the ideas behind assertive responses, and they talked about worries Marcia might have in acting assertively with Peter.

Over the next couple of days, a great deal of Marcia's overthinking concerned the idea of being assertive with Peter. He hadn't always been so domineering. When they were first married, they shared a lot of interests in music and theater, and had lively discussions in which Marcia was perfectly comfortable expressing her point of view. As Peter gained more status and responsibility in his job as an account executive for a large plastics manufacturer, he worked longer hours and their conversations became more infrequent. Peter became the manager of a large division of the company and slowly began to act like a manager at home as well, giving orders and issuing opinions he expected Marcia to accept without question. After Adrienne was born and Marcia quit her job, her scope of activities had narrowed to the baby and their home. Although Marcia was somewhat involved in the school that Adrienne and Timothy went to, the vast majority of her time was spent transporting the children to some activity or doing housework. Peter tried to sound interested in Marcia's stories about the children, but seldom had much of a reaction unless Marcia reported that Timothy had gotten into trouble again, when he became frustrated and angry. All in all, the couple rarely talked to each other about topics other than household business, Adrienne's latest award or accomplishment, or Timothy's latest transgression.

As Marcia's thoughts circled round and round, she didn't come to understand this larger picture of her relationship to Peter. The overthinking focused her attention narrowly on recent arguments with Peter, on her feelings of anger at him, and her sense of guilt and incompetence:

> He treats me like one of his employees. He thinks he can just give me orders and it's my job to carry them out. Why have I put up with this for all these years? Because I'm stuck, that's why. I can't confront him because I can't risk losing him. The kids need their father. But he's such a lousy father! Timothy would certainly be

better off without him. Or would he? A boy needs his dad—that's what everyone says. Why am I so weak in dealing with Peter? I just let him walk all over me. I don't think I can change our marriage. I feel so stuck.

Marcia's thoughts were surging like this one afternoon when Timothy tapped her on the shoulder, and said, "Mom! Mom! Look here, I finished this homework page my teacher gave me. I added up all the baseball players on these different teams. Can you tell me if I got the right answer?"

Marcia was overcome with pride in Timothy—this was the first time he had voluntarily done homework. As she looked over the page, she saw that he had gotten the right answer. He had done math homework on his own, and he had gotten the right answer! Marcia was filled with determination. She was going to stand up to Peter and try to change his interactions with Timothy, for Timothy's sake, no matter how unsure she was. After all, as Dr. Glass had said, Peter had no history of violence, so the worst that would probably happen was that he'd get angry and shout at her. But she'd lived through that many times already and she could get through it again if it happened.

Many couples drift away from each other, as Marcia and Peter had, as their lives become filled with separate activities and different interests. Peter had become consumed with work and with his image of himself as "in control" and a manager, and inappropriately brought that into his interactions with his family. Marcia's world had shrunk to include only her children and her home. This is a dangerous position in which, unfortunately, many women find themselves. When all your self-esteem and social support are tied up in your family, it leaves you extremely vulnerable. If anything goes wrong in the family, as was true in Marcia's family, your whole world caves in.

Our children can be our best motivation for changing our own behavior. We may be complacent about the rut we have fallen into in the relationship with our partner or we may just decide to give up the relationship if repairing it seems like too much work. But our love for our children and our desire to protect their well-being can be a powerful motivator to take stock of our relationship and make needed changes.

That evening after the children had gone to bed, Marcia went into the family room to find Peter reading the newspaper. This struck Marcia as a good time to try to talk about his interactions with Timothy.

"Peter," she said, "can we talk? It's about Timothy."

"What has he done now?" was Peter's reply.

"He did something wonderful. He finished his math homework, on his own, and he got the answer right. He was so proud of himself, and I'm proud of him, too."

"It's about time he buckled down on that math homework," Peter said sarcastically.

"Peter," Marcia began tentatively, "it makes me upset when you are so critical of Timothy, and I know it upsets him, too. I think he might do a lot better if you could be more encouraging toward him."

"I'm not critical of Timothy," Peter said defensively. "I'm just trying to get him to fly straight. He'll never pull good grades if he doesn't work harder and behave himself more."

"I think you are critical of Timothy. Most of your interactions with him are negative—you're yelling at him for something. Peter, I've discovered that Timothy has lots of interests we didn't even know about, in sports figures and trivia. When I talk to him about these subjects, he just lights up. How could we not have known he cares about such things? We've both been more focused on what's wrong with him than on what's right with him. And we're both guilty of comparing him to Adrienne all the time." Marcia paused and waited for Peter to erupt.

"He likes sports trivia? But how could he? I don't care about sports, you don't, Adrienne doesn't. Where did he get that from?"

Marcia replied, "Who knows where he got it from—it doesn't matter. And it doesn't matter that none of the rest of us care about sports. What matters is that it makes him happy. And when he reads about sports or does math problems about sports, he does a really good job, better than I thought he could." Marcia watched Peter's face, expecting annoyance and dismissal. Instead, she saw his eyes soften and his body relax.

"So you think we compare him to Adrienne too much, huh?" he began. "I suppose that could be true. She is a hard act to follow."

Marcia was so surprised at Peter's admission that she nearly didn't know what to say. It occurred to her to accuse Peter of being the biggest perpetrator of the "Adrienne gold standard," but she remembered what Dr. Glass said about accusations driving people away. So instead, Marcia took responsibility for her own negative behavior toward Timothy and described how different their interactions had been since she'd begun to listen to him and learn about his interests. Taking cues from Marcia, Peter acknowledged that his relationship with Timothy had deteriorated and that he rarely spent any time just being with him, doing what Timothy wanted to do. He suggested that he could take Timothy to a minor league baseball game the next Saturday.

Building a New Family

There was a slow but steady transformation in the family over the next couple of months as Peter and Marcia both tried to connect positively with Timothy. He didn't cease to get into trouble at school, but the frequency of phone calls and notes from Timothy's teacher reporting a fight with another child or Timothy's refusal to do an assignment in class definitely decreased over this time. After consulting with Dr. Glass, Marcia found a tutor to work with Timothy on his reading and math skills. The young man knew almost as much as Timothy did about sports statistics. Marcia was clear that she had to lean on others—particularly Dr. Glass—for advice and support in helping Timothy and changing their family patterns.

The frequency of Marcia's bouts of overthinking also decreased, although they didn't cease completely. One particularly vicious bout occurred after Peter and Timothy had lapsed into one of their yelling matches. Peter had been much less critical of Timothy in recent weeks, but when Timothy was sent home from school for punching another boy in the stomach, Peter lost it and began yelling. Timothy responded by accusing his father of being unwilling to listen to his side of the story, and running to his room.

Marcia's heart broke as this argument raged on, and in the quiet after the storm, her thoughts raced:

> How could I have thought that things were different? Peter will never change. I don't think I can stand this anymore. But I can't

handle Timothy on my own. How could he punch another child? Have I been too lenient on him? What is wrong with him? Does he have bad genes for temper, that he clearly got from Peter? It all seems so hopeless! I just don't know what to do. I can't stand this any longer!

Marcia's tears flowed with her thoughts, and Peter was surprised when he walked into their bedroom and saw the state she was in. He knew instantly she was upset about the argument he'd had with Timothy.

"I'm sorry, I guess I really blew it tonight," he began. "I've been so proud of how much progress Timothy was making, then to hear he had hit another kid, I just lost it. I'll go talk to him and apologize to him. But Marcia, do you think we need some help, maybe from that Dr. Glass we talked to a few months ago?"

Marcia still hadn't told Peter she'd consulted Dr. Glass several times already, and to hear him admit they needed help and offer to apologize to Timothy instantly began to mend her heart. She sputtered some sort of agreement with Peter and hugged him tightly. He went off to talk with Timothy.

As Marcia sat up on the bed wiping her wet eyes, she thought, "We're going to get help. This family is going to be okay." When she looked in the mirror and saw her red swollen face, she said to herself, "I'm pathetic. I can't live on this roller coaster all the time. I'm too wrapped up in this family. I've got to get a life outside this family for some emotional balance."

Broadening your base of self-esteem and social support by having multiple activities and interests is not only critical to your well-being, it can be beneficial to your children's well-being as well. When a mother is focused singularly on her children, they can feel smothered. They may fail to grow into the independence they need to be mature adults. But when a mother has roles outside her family that are also important to her, children can learn to respect her interests and autonomy from them. Having multiple roles also gives a woman a base to fall back on in times of trouble in her family. The friends she develops through volunteer activities or work can provide crucial advice and support when her family faces difficulties. Having work or volunteer activities that exercise your talents can also give you the strength and self-confidence you need to cope with family problems.

Marcia needed to engage in at least one more strategy to avoid falling into future traps of overthinking in the long term. She needed to develop a new image of herself, discarding her self-image as the person solely responsible for her family's welfare and Timothy's behavior, and moving toward a self-image as one member of the family, concerned about the other members' welfare, but not the only one responsible for the family's well-being. She also needed to create new images of the family and each of its members. Marcia has a tendency to see the family as either all good—everyone is happy and everything is going well—or all bad—the family is a mess and it's hopeless to change it. She also seems to view Peter and the children this way—either Peter is a great dad or a terrible dad, and either Timothy is making great progress or he's defective. This kind of either-or viewpoint promotes overthinking because you can easily be overwhelmed by catastrophic negative thoughts if something goes wrong, but when things are going well, you don't want to risk "rocking the boat" by trying to make important changes.

Instead, Marcia needs to cultivate more complex views of her family and its members that integrate both their strengths and their weaknesses. Peter can be a jerk, but he definitely loves his children and is willing to change his interactions with them. Timothy has a number of behaviors that need changing, but he is a loving boy with great potential. Having a more complex view of her family would provide Marcia with the kind of distance she needs to see any individual blowup in the family in the larger picture of the family's functioning, and to prevent her from falling into helpless, hopeless overthinking. It also gives her the motivation and direction to keep building on the strengths in her family and working to overcome the weaknesses.

Marcia and her family had a long way to go. But by breaking free of her overthinking, adjusting her focus on Timothy, and attempting to make changes in her family despite her doubts, Marcia had already had a powerful positive effect on her family in a matter of a few months. Marcia had gotten some useful advice from Dr. Glass. But mostly she discovered that once she put aside her overthinking, she could be creative in helping Timothy overcome his behavioral and academic problems. She also had the courage to confront Peter for his style of interacting with Timothy and to help him transform those interactions.

You will never be completely free of concerns about your children—it's a natural part of parenting to worry about their well-being. These concerns need not grow into debilitating overthinking, however. Using the strategies described in this book, you can learn to address your concerns as parents by mobilizing your deep knowledge of your children, and making life's tough decisions based on a secure relationship with your children.

10

Always on the Job:
Overthinking Work and Careers

Work is a frequent focus of our overthinking. We spend a great deal of time at our jobs—some of us are at our workplace much more than eight hours per day, and our jobs consume the vast majority of our waking hours. A conflict with a coworker, a snide remark by your boss, or simple boredom or frustration with the tasks of the day become giant in your mind if what you do all day is work. Our work holds many meanings for us, which also makes it powerful fuel for overthinking. What we do for a living is an important facet of our self-concept. If you are stuck in a job you think is beneath your skills and capabilities, you may feel frustrated and demeaned. If your job does not satisfy important goals in your life or leads you to compromise your values, you may feel ashamed. On a more concrete level, events at work can threaten our livelihoods and the welfare of our families. A pay reduction or layoff can put your mortgage into jeopardy, prevent you from paying your children's college tuition, or force you to drastically reduce your quality of living.

The work world has changed dramatically in the last couple of decades in ways that make it even richer territory for overthinking than it previously was. Employees used to be able to count on a high degree of stability and security in their jobs as long as they performed competently. These days, constant corporate mergers, the volatile stock market, the focus on the quarterly bottom line, and the rapid pace of technological change have led to tremendous instabilities in the workplace. People who worked faithfully in the same job for thirty years are losing their jobs just a few years short of retirement. A good education can be obsolete in five years because the technology of a profession has changed so rapidly. The dramatic rise and fall of thousands of dot-com companies around the turn of the millennium was a great illustration of how people at the top of the hierarchy can be at the bottom in a matter of weeks.

The historical changes in our social psyche that generally contribute to more overthinking come into play with great force in the workplace. Our global sense of entitlement leads us to expect to have a fulfilling job with great pay and rapid advancement. Especially if we go to the right college and get the right grades, we shouldn't have to work as hard as our parents did to make a living and build our career. The outrageous success of young entrepreneurs—college dropouts who create Fortune 500 companies in their parents' garage—gives us a standard for "real success" that is about as attainable as becoming a pro basketball player. Yet somehow we think that if we can just get the right break, meet the right people, our instant success story will be realized. This makes it very hard to be satisfied with real life. We never seem to be making enough money. We never get the recognition we deserve.

So, operating from our belief in quick fixes, we switch jobs in hopes that the next one will be more satisfying. Sometimes we get lucky and the next job is our dream job. More often, however, the concerns that fed our overthinking will follow us because we never really dealt with the root cause of our distress—deficits in our competencies or interpersonal skills, a mismatch between our true interests and our profession, the absence of a clear direction or purpose in our career. Thus we feel pressured to move from one place to another, never happy in our job, increasingly overthinking what is wrong with us and our world.

If you live with a vacuum of values, it's particularly hard to recognize your work-related deficits or to determine what type of job would be most satisfying for you. How can you find a job that meets your life goals if you don't know what those goals are? If we have work-related goals, they may simply be to make more money and achieve more status. But these things rarely satisfy our deepest needs to have a meaningful life. Janice, a college professor, maintained a singular focus on getting tenure at a highly competitive and prestigious university, to the detriment of her marriage and personal life, for seven long and arduous years. When she finally achieved this goal, she found herself deeply depressed: What do I do now? This just doesn't feel as good as I thought it would. And I've wrecked the rest of my life, just to be stuck here in this job that I'm not even sure I like.

Or we may be striving for work-related goals that are not our own but are imposed on us by our parents, our spouse, or other important people in our lives. Consider, for example, Randi, a tall, muscular eighteen-year-old blond woman who is graced with tremendous athletic skills. All her life Randi has loved tennis and became very good, winning several regional titles and one national title. Randi desperately wanted to pursue a professional career in tennis and had been offered tennis scholarships to several large colleges. Her parents, who were religious fundamentalists, wanted Randi to attend a small college run by their church and study to become a missionary, as they had in their own youth. They never explicitly told Randi she couldn't accept one of her tennis scholarships or go to a secular college. They made it clear, however, that they believed the Lord had a plan for Randi that involved missionary work and not tennis.

Randi followed her parents' dream instead of her own and attended her church's college. She tried to satisfy her tennis longings by playing for the college's team, but the other students were not in her league and she was frequently frustrated. She dutifully completed a degree in elementary teaching so she could become a teacher in a missionary school. Her life was filled, however, with thoughts about the dream she had abandoned, and with guilt for not appreciating the path she had taken.

· · ·

Finally, work gives women their own special issues to overthink. Much of the gender discrimination and harassment in the workplace is now covert instead of overt. Instead of your boss refusing to promote you because you are a woman, he is more likely not to notice your contributions as much as he notices those of your male colleagues. And although he may not ask you directly for sex in exchange for a promotion, he may come on to you, denying the obvious power difference between you and him. The more covert and subtle forms of discrimination and harassment that characterize today's workplace can be hard to decipher. Was your boss taking credit for your work because he doesn't value you as a woman, or because he is a jerk who does this to all his employees? Was he really inappropriate in inviting you to his house to discuss your department's budget over dinner, or was he treating you like a member of the "in crowd," the way he treats some of your male colleagues? This is great stuff for overthinking.

Women overthink the workplace because it is fundamentally an interpersonal setting and women are so interpersonally oriented. There are the inevitable conflicts and disagreements to ruminate about. You may have to work closely with someone you don't respect or trust, or simply don't like, and this can lead to preoccupations with why that person behaves so badly or to paranoia about what he or she might do. Then there are the evaluations. We are being evaluated every day by everyone in our lives, but at work the evaluations are made explicit. They are supposed to be objective and helpful, but they are almost always highly subjective, and usually quite threatening. Moreover, women take them personally. Psychologist Tomi-Ann Roberts of Colorado College and I did a study in which we compared women's and men's responses to performance evaluations.[1] The task they were being evaluated on wasn't an important one in real life—it involved solving abstract geometric puzzles. After they completed the task, the evaluator randomly gave them a report that was either positive in tone ("You did better than most people") or negative in tone ("You didn't do as well as most people"). You may be able to guess what the men did with the evaluations—they accepted the positive ones as highly valid, but blew off the negative ones as invalid. This left the men feeling good about themselves and their performance no matter what the evaluator said. The women took both the positive and negative evaluations to heart. In particular, their self-esteem went down after the negative evaluation and they became sad. All this over a stranger's evaluation of their performance on some silly puzzles! You can imagine how much more potent a boss's evaluation of your performance on the job can be for a woman.

The consequences of overthinking work can be severe. Most jobs involve problem solving and overthinking interferes with good problem solving by making you think more negatively about the problem and sapping your confidence in any solution you come up with. At the micro level, overthinking can impede your accomplishment of even the smallest work assignment. For example, Vera, a fifty-year-old clerk in a large accounting firm, was asked by her supervisor to rearrange the employee mailboxes after some employees had left and new employees had been hired. This seemed like a simple task at first, but as Vera stood looking at the boxes, considering ways of organizing them, she began to worry about the employees' reactions to possible arrangements. If she ordered the boxes by an employee's status in the company, she might offend someone who felt he or she had not been placed high enough in the hierarchy. If she simply ordered the boxes alphabetically, the higher-ranking employees might feel slighted in not having their rank acknowledged. Vera could imagine confrontations with specific employees she expected would react badly to a particular arrangement—these scenes played vividly in her mind, causing her anxiety level to soar. Vera stood immobilized for over an hour, just staring at the boxes and worrying. Her supervisor walked in and yelled, "Haven't you gotten this done yet? For heaven's sake, this is about as simple a job as they come!"

On the more macro level, it's easy to see how chronic overthinking about work can threaten your job security by impairing your performance. If Vera's supervisor catches her standing and staring instead of completing an assignment too many times, Vera may be out of a job. If you become immobilized in your job, or don't make good decisions, because overthinking is clouding your mind and draining your confidence, your career may be stalled. In a large survey study we did a few years ago, we found that chronic overthinkers reported their jobs were more insecure; that they hadn't accomplished as much in their career as they had wanted to; and that they were generally less satisfied with their jobs, compared to people who didn't tend to overthink.[2]

So what do you do if you find yourself frequently overthinking work? Abby's story provides some clues. She was a chronic overthinker for years and, as we shall see, her worklife suffered greatly from it. Abby eventually dug herself out of the overthinking pit, however, and was able to reverse some of the effects it had had on her career.

Abby's Career in Overthinking

You know the minute you see her that Abby has style and a sense of fashion. Her clothes are always a bit different, a bit funky, but somehow perfect. Her slender six-foot frame can make anything look good, and at forty-two, she's not afraid to wear the most revealing clothes for the right effect. This style serves her well in her job as a buyer for a large chain of clothing stores. She seems to know what new lines of clothing are likely to be the rage six months from now when they hit the selling floor. More than once her purchases, although they appeared outlandish at the time, made the company a mint when young women flocked to buy them the moment they arrived at the stores.

Abby's career as a clothing buyer has not always been smooth, however. Indeed, she had no idea she'd end up in this career when she graduated college with a degree in history and a minor in art. She didn't want to go to graduate school in history so she did what many history majors do after college—she got a job as a teller in a bank. All day long she stood at her little window, cashing checks and processing deposits, bored out of her mind. She wasn't making enough money to rent an apartment on her own so she was still living with her parents. Her dad, who was not the most supportive father in the world, reminded her regularly that he had spent over $70,000 on her college education—and what was she doing handling other people's money instead of making good money for herself? Abby tried to ignore him, but at night as she tried to go to sleep, overthinking would invade:

> Dad's right. All that money he spent, and I had to major in history. What did I think I was going to do with a degree in history? I didn't think, that's the answer. I just glided through college without really thinking about what I was doing. And here I am in this deadly job with no idea what I want to do. I can't stand this for much longer. What am I going to do?

After about six months in her bank job, Abby was so frustrated and depressed that when she wasn't working she just sat around the house all the time watching TV. Her father came home one afternoon to find her lying on the couch watching the soaps, and exploded with, "Why aren't you working? No daughter of mine is going to spend her days watching television. Get up and do something! If you have so much time on your hands, get a second job so you can contribute something to this family!" Abby didn't try to tell him this was her usual afternoon off from the bank. She just flew up the stairs to her room, slammed the door, and lay down on her bed to cry, then overthink:

> This is it! I can't live with this man! I'm going to move out whether I can afford it or not. And I'm going to quit that stupid bank job. I'll show him! I can find another job, one that pays better. And I'm not going to talk to him again until he apologizes.

Abby called her friend Gina to ask if she could stay at her apartment for a couple of nights, packed a bag, and left that evening. Her mother stood crying at the door, but her father hunkered down in the den with the TV blaring and ignored Abby's departure.

The next morning, Abby called the bank to say she wouldn't be coming in for her shift because she quit. This gave her a terrific feeling of relief and triumph, although it did cross her mind that it might be hard to get a good recommendation from her supervisor at the bank after quitting so abruptly. After Gina left for work, Abby looked through the want ads for a new job. So many of them required special skills, such as in computer repair or nursing. There were clerical jobs, but after her experience at the bank, Abby was convinced she wasn't cut out for those. She wouldn't even consider flipping burgers. After an hour or two of looking through these ads, Abby began to be concerned:

> What if I can't find a job? Oh my God, the worst thing in the world would be to go crawling back to my parents, unemployed. I'd never hear the end of it. I'm not qualified for anything, at least not anything I want to do. What do I want to do? I don't know, just make enough money to shut my father up. Surely this college degree is good for something—it sure cost enough. I've got to play that up. I should be able to land a decent job if people know where I graduated from.

Abby continued to look through the want ads and came across an ad for an assistant manager in a local clothing store. Thinking maybe she could get discounts on the clothes if she worked there, she called the number listed in the ad and made an appointment for an interview.

For the interview, Abby dressed in the terrific outfit she had bought with her graduation money. It wasn't exactly conservative—the neckline

plunged very low and the skirt was very tight—but she looked spectacu-
lar in it. When she arrived at the store offices for the interview, the
receptionist gave her a look that was mixed with doubt and envy. Abby
was kept waiting for nearly an hour, during which she engaged in angry
and ambivalent overthinking:

> This waiting stinks. They know they can do this because they
> hold all the cards. After I land this job, I'm going to complain to
> this person's supervisor! What if I don't land this job? This is the
> only one that looked remotely interesting. I can't go back to that
> bank job, or anything like it. I've got to be nice to this inter-
> viewer. And I've got to make sure she knows where I went to
> school. What if she doesn't care? How did I get into this mess?

Abby was startled from her thoughts when the clerk called her name
and led her back to another office. There sat a large fifty-ish woman
named Mrs. Weeks. Abby heard an audible "Hmmph" when she looked
at Abby's outfit. Worried thoughts flooded Abby's mind, preventing her
from speaking for a few moments.

Mrs. Weeks began the interview with, "How are you qualified for this
job?" Abby replied by noting the college she had graduated from, saying
that she had always been interested in the fashion industry. Looking
utterly unimpressed, Mrs. Weeks asked what Abby's major had been in
college, and what retail experience she had had. Abby's face fell, and she
admitted that her major had been history and she had absolutely no retail
experience. The interview dribbled on for a few minutes as Abby's heart
sank lower and lower, realizing she had probably made a fool of herself.
Eventually, Mrs. Weeks mercifully ended the interview, and as Abby got
up to leave, expecting she could never face even shopping in this store
again, Mrs. Weeks said, "You know, we are always in need of salespeople.
If you'd like to get some retail experience, you could work here as a salesperson on the floor." Abby was so grateful to be handed this bone by Mrs.
Weeks that she immediately said yes to the offer and left to fill out paperwork in Human Resources.

Abby started her new job a week later, and soon discovered that she
liked the work, especially helping customers choose clothes that high-
lighted their best features. She was frequently frustrated, though, that

the store didn't carry certain styles she thought many customers would find appealing—she didn't like having to encourage customers to buy clothes that she knew were not exactly what they were looking for or needed.

Abby, on the other hand, looked good all the time. She had a real fashion sense, and quickly caught on to the culture of the store so that she was choosing clothes that were at the same level of conservatism as the store managers', but always more stylish and original than what most employees of the store were wearing. Unfortunately, she was using too much of her new income to purchase clothes at the store, lured by the deep discount she got as an employee. This made it difficult for her to have her portion of the rent for the apartment she was now sharing with Gina.

A few weeks after she began working at the store, Abby was given the job of rearranging some of the clothing displays by her department manager. The main store manager saw her new displays and liked them a great deal. They were much more artistically appealing and eye-catching than previous displays had been. One day the buyer for the store, a short, wiry woman named Helene, was on the sales floor inspecting the layout of the merchandise when she overheard Abby telling another salesclerk that, yet again, she had been waiting on a middle-aged woman who was ready and willing to spend a lot of money on some new clothes, but the clothing lines the store carried just didn't meet her needs. Abby described the style she thought this woman and many women like her would go for. Helene was particularly interested in this conversation because she had just made the decision a couple of days before to buy a new line of clothing that fit Abby's description. She began a conversation with Abby and was terribly impressed with her ideas for what would sell to various types of customers. Right there on the sales floor, Helene asked Abby if she'd like to become her assistant. Stunned at the offer, Abby stammered an acceptance. Thus, Abby's career as a buyer was launched.

The next few months were a blur of accompanying Helene on buying trips to New York, learning the business of buying for a store, becoming familiar with all the lines currently carried by the store, and doing a great deal of grunt work for Helene. Helene was an enthusiastic teacher, and Abby realized she was getting a crash course in the fashion industry. She didn't always feel appreciated by Helene, however, for the long hours she put in or for her suggestions as to what Helene should buy for the store. She also thought she wasn't making enough money.

These frustrations were especially salient in the early part of each week. Through Gina, Abby had developed a new set of friends who liked to go out dancing on the weekends, staying at clubs until the wee hours of the morning and often drinking a lot. On Mondays, Abby was usually very tired and still a bit hungover. Somehow this made everything at work seem a bit bleaker. On her way to work, Abby would usually find herself in an overthinking bout:

> I dread going to work today. There'll be endless meetings with the department heads, and I'll have to sit there like a lump acting as Helene's secretary. Nobody cares what I say at those meetings. All they care about is having their fresh coffee and doughnuts. This job is going nowhere. I've gotta get out of there, do something different.

As she sat through the morning's meetings, Abby continued to ruminate about her frustrations with her job, and about her judgments of the department managers:

> Some of these people are so stupid! I could do their job so much better than they can. They don't have a clue what the customers want. All they are concerned about is when their salespeople take their lunch break. No wonder this store isn't making a good profit! I just can't stand this any longer.

Abby was so consumed by her thoughts that she didn't hear Helene ask her to go to her office to fetch a quarterly sales report she had forgotten to bring. When Helene raised her voice to get Abby's attention, Abby snapped out of her frustrated reveries, embarrassed both that Helene had caught her not paying attention and that she was being asked to be a gofer yet again.

On her way to the office, Abby's overthinking soared, leading her to make an impulsive decision:

> That's it, I'm getting out of here. I won't be treated like this any longer. I'm going to quit this afternoon!

At lunchtime, Abby made a call to a buyer she knew at the rival store in town, who had once told Abby if she ever wanted to switch allegiances, to give her a call. Abby didn't know this woman, named Bridget, well, but she figured that anyone would be better to work for than Helene. They made an appointment to talk that evening, and Abby hung up the phone feeling triumphant and emboldened. She went immediately to Helene's office and told her she was quitting. Helene was stunned, and asked why Abby would want to quit. Abby's mind ran over the angry ruminations she had been having all day, but she knew she couldn't voice them all to Helene. She stumbled around, saying something about wanting a position with more independence, and wanting more money. When Helene asked what she was going to do for another job, Abby fudged and said that Bridget had already hired her as her assistant. Helene smirked, and said, "Oh, you'll *love* working for Bridget. I hear she's just a peach of a boss." And then Helene tried to persuade Abby to stay, pointing out she had a bright future in this store and she was on a good trajectory to a more senior position with the company. Abby stuck to her guns, and as she left the office, Helene said, "I think you're really going to regret this decision, Abby."

On the way home, Helene's words rang in Abby's head, especially the snide remark about Bridget being a "peach of a boss":

> What did she mean? Was she just being nasty because she lost the battle? What if she's right? How could I have quit that job before I know for sure that Bridget will hire me? Oh man, what have I done? I can't go crawling back to Helene. I'm so stupid. I'm so tired! I felt so good at noontime but now I feel so bad.

Abby met Bridget that evening at a small restaurant, looking much less chipper and confident than she had sounded on the phone earlier that day. Fortunately, Bridget did offer her a job as an assistant, at a starting pay that was somewhat below what Abby had been making with Helene. Abby was so grateful for the job, however, that she didn't even mention the pay issue.

Within a week of working for Bridget, Abby knew where Helene's snide comment had come from. Bridget was a nasty woman, forever critical of everyone and everything around her. Abby learned that Bridget had been through three assistants in the last year, and Abby was not surprised people didn't last long in this position. Bridget expected Abby to work sixty to seventy hours per week, and be on call the remainder of the time. Buying trips were planned at the last moment, and Bridget was always dissatisfied with something—the flight arrangements, the hotel Abby booked them into, Abby's inability to get them reservations at the best restaurants in New York on a day's notice.

On the way home from a buying trip, wedged into a seat in coach while Bridget sat in first class, Abby fell into overthinking:

> This is impossible! Why did I leave Helene? I would have been better off staying there! What can I do? I can't do anything! I'm stuck! I can't do anything right! What my dad said was true—I'll never have a career or make a good living! I can't stand this! I just can't stand this another week!

By the time they reached the airport, Abby was so angry at Bridget that she couldn't speak to her. She just trudged alongside her, sulking. Abby expected Bridget to get a cab home from the airport, but instead Bridget expected Abby to drive her home to her apartment, which was on the opposite side of town from Abby's. Abby continued to fume as she drove, ignoring Bridget's banter about how incompetent or unattractive certain department managers at their store were. When Bridget began to criticize Helene as a "has been" and "frumpy girl who doesn't understand fashion," Abby exploded. "How dare you say such things about Helene! She was a great boss and taught me everything I know. She certainly was a better boss than you! You are such a bitch!"

Bridget became very quiet, and Abby did too, realizing she had probably made a huge mistake, though she was still fuming to the point she could hardly drive straight. She pulled up in front of Bridget's apartment building, and as Bridget got out of the car, she quietly said to Abby, "Don't bother coming to work tomorrow. You're fired. I'll have your personal things sent to you." Then she slammed the door.

Abby's head dropped to the steering wheel as she nearly began to cry. But she held it together enough to get home, where, once she was in her pajamas and in bed, she began to panic:

I'm sunk. There are only two large clothing stores in this town and I've burned my bridges at both of them. I'm going to be a bank teller all my life. I probably couldn't even get a job in a bank now, with the lousy references I've got. I can't pay the rent. I can't even feed myself. My parents are going to expect me to move home with them, but I can't bear that. I'd rather die.

Abby was up most of the night overthinking conversations she had had with Bridget, with Helene, with her parents, berating herself for being so stubborn and prideful, but then berating others for not appreciating her or giving her a chance. She eventually drifted off to sleep, awash in despair at being unemployed again, with no apparent good options.

When she awoke later in the morning, hopelessness had fully set in. She couldn't get out of bed and she didn't care about eating. Gina came home that afternoon to find Abby in her pajamas, sitting on the couch staring at the television. She asked if Abby was ill, to which Abby replied, "No, just stupid." Gina pried a bit further and learned that Abby had been fired. Although Gina immediately worried about Abby's ability to cover her part of the rent, she was sympathetic and supportive as Abby told her what had happened. Gina made a couple of suggestions for what Abby might do to find a new job, such as contact the local job counseling agency, or look into positions at some of the smaller clothing stores in town. Filled with the irritability that comes with angry and self-loathing ruminations, Abby snapped, "You don't understand. I'm not ready to do anything yet. I've got to think this over."

Abby continued to think things over for several days, becoming more depressed and unmotivated with each overthinking bout. At the end of a week seeing Abby just sit around the apartment looking glum, Gina let her have it: "You've got to get off your ass and do something! You'll never find another job sitting around here! I'm not going to float your portion of the rent for much longer. Either get a job or move out." Deep in her heart, Abby knew Gina was right, but what she felt at the moment was betrayed and abandoned. She slunk back into her room and crawled into bed. Gina felt terrible for her outburst and went to Abby's room to talk with her. Abby just pulled the covers over her head and refused to talk.

Fortunately for Abby, Gina wouldn't give up that easily. She went into the kitchen and found the phone number for the job counseling service, then called and made an appointment for Abby for the next day. When she told Abby this later that evening, Abby was furious at her heavy-handedness. Gina didn't budge, though, and said, "You go to this appointment, or you move out. Period."

Somehow Abby got herself dressed and to the appointment, and even thought along the way that it would be nice to talk about her job woes with a sympathetic listener. The counselor she was assigned, a woman named Marilyn, was not exactly warm and fuzzy, however. She saw through Abby's complaints about her bosses immediately and asked Abby pointed questions about what she wanted to do with her life. Abby's only answer was, "I want to make good money," to which Marilyn replied, "That's not a career plan, my dear. You have some work to do."

Reconstructing Abby

Abby's tendency to fall into angry bouts of overthinking nearly wrecked her career. They led her to take a number of impulsive actions that felt good at the moment but had potentially disastrous outcomes, such as quitting jobs abruptly. It was only after Abby began to recognize her pattern of negative thinking and impulsive action that she began to have some control over the direction of her career.

Over their first few counseling sessions, Marilyn pointed out that Abby had fallen into every job she'd had and had lost or quit every job because she acted on angry impulses. More conversation and Abby's answers on a psychological test convinced Marilyn that the fashion industry was a good place for Abby. There was, of course, the problem of the burned bridges with the two main department stores in town. Abby wasn't going to get a good job in the clothing industry anywhere without good references. She simply had to go back to Helene and acknowledge she had made a mistake in quitting abruptly. Abby protested this idea, but Marilyn was persuasive. They rehearsed together what Abby would say to Helene, and different ways Helene would respond. Marilyn helped Abby think of responses to any negative reactions Helene might have and with ways of coping with her anxiety about approaching Helene.

Abby called Helene to ask for an appointment, and a surprised Helene agreed to meet with her. Abby began the conversation just as she had

rehearsed with Marilyn, taking responsibility for her actions and apologizing for her rudeness in quitting abruptly. Abby's only goal in the conversation was to repair the damage she had done in her relationship with Helene
so she could ask her for a recommendation later on. She was flabbergasted
when Helene offered her the old job back. "I've had another assistant since
you left, but she's not much more than a secretary for me. You've got real
potential and talent, Abby. I'd rather have you working for me."

Abby thought at first she might be hallucinating this conversation.
Even so, she said yes to Helene's offer, and left for home feeling dazed
and giddy. On the way home, she made two important decisions. First,
she was going to take some night classes at the community college in
marketing and design so she would be more qualified for promotion
within the store. Second, she was going to continue working with Marilyn, even if she had to hire her for private counseling sessions. Abby had
finally realized that she had a bad habit of getting herself worked up
about frustrations on the job, and then acting impulsively in an attempt
to quell her frustrations.

Those frustrations cropped up within a couple of weeks of starting to
work with Helene again. Abby found herself rant-and-rave overthinking
after Helene disagreed with Abby's suggestion that the store begin to
feature a new line of clothes by a young designer she had read about:

> She only thinks of me as her servant. She said she valued my
> ideas, but it doesn't show—she just does what she thinks is best
> and ignores me, except for sending me to run errands!

This time, however, when Abby heard herself indulging in these
rant-and-rave overthinkings, instead of acting impulsively she took
them to Marilyn, who asked her what evidence she had that Helene
didn't respect her opinions. Earlier in the week, when Abby had been
upset with Helene, it seemed there were mountains of evidence that
Helene wasn't treating her right. Now, with her mind clearer and facing
Marilyn's steady gaze, those mountains seemed very small. In fact, Abby
could recount many instances in which Helene had agreed with something she had suggested, and had even complimented her on an idea in
front of other employees.

Marilyn explained to Abby that when she was upset, she could only see things through the lens of that upset, and couldn't see things that contradicted her mood. That's how Abby's angry ruminations took on a life of their own, to the point where she was completely convinced she was being wronged and deserved to retaliate against those who were abusing her. Marilyn asked when Abby was most prone to falling into these angry thoughts, and discovered it was often early in the week when Abby was worn out from her weekend activities. "Alcohol is a depressant, Abby, and when your brain is still under the influence of its depressant effects, all you can think about is depressing things." Abby made a deal with Marilyn that she would cut back on her weekend partying, particularly her consumption of alcohol and all-night outings, and would consider finding some new friends whose lives didn't revolve around weekend escapades.

Many of us find it is extremely helpful, and sometimes absolutely necessary, to work with a professional counselor to overcome self-defeating patterns of thought and behavior. Marilyn taught Abby that when her ruminations were driven by her mood at the moment, they seldom gave a complete and valid picture of what was happening in her life. Instead, when she was angry, all she could see were reasons to be angry, and when she was sad and upset with herself, all she could see were the things she had done wrong. Abby learned to question the picture painted by her overthinking and ask what was missing. What were different ways of looking at the same situation? This inevitably took the wind out of her overthinking, calmed her down, and helped her to think more clearly.

Abby found new friends through the classes she took at the community college. She found herself gravitating toward a couple of women who, like herself, were young, single, and getting serious about improving their career choices and paths. Abby also discovered that she loved these classes, in a way that she had never loved her college classes in history. She could relate much of what the instructors said to her experiences working in the department stores—sometimes she thought the instructors were wrong in the theories or practices they advocated, but much of what they said helped Abby understand how Helene and the store managers made decisions about what to buy or what to display most prominently. Increasingly, Abby peppered Helene with questions about the fashion industry and the store's marketing policy. Her suggestions to Helene grew more informed and impressive each month, and Helene began giving Abby new and more interesting responsibilities.

Greater satisfaction with her job didn't completely prevent Abby from overthinking, of course. One Friday, when she was exhausted and fed up with a million little things that had gone wrong that week, an overthinking bout began:

> This job doesn't pay enough. I have no flexibility in my schedule. And then there was that blowout last week with Julia over her display. It was ridiculous, horrendous! I don't know how she could have thought I'd approve it. I don't think I'll ever get promoted out of this position. I'll be stuck here dealing with the everyday drudgery, and Julia will probably be promoted above me. My job is miserable, and it's making me miserable.

Abby desperately wanted just to leave the store and go get a drink with her old friends to blow off some steam. She reached into the drawer of her desk to get her purse, and saw a card on which she had written: WHAT WOULD MARILYN SUGGEST I DO? That stopped her in her tracks, because she knew the answer was not "get a drink with the old friends."

It can be tough to give up the self-righteous feelings pumped up by angry overthinking—the sense of entitlement, that you have been victimized and deserve retribution, that other people should rescue you from your predicament. As in Abby's case, although these thoughts can feel really good for a while, they can lead you to make really bad choices, such as lashing out at others in ways that permanently damage relationships, failing to recognize and overcome your own faults and deficits. In the work world, this can translate into lost opportunities for career growth, constant frustration on the job, and even unemployment.

Abby decided to sit down at her computer and write out the thoughts in her head without censoring them. She had filled two pages before she stopped and went to get a soda from the machine in the employees' lounge. When she returned to her office and read through what she had written, Abby asked herself what Marilyn had so often asked her: "What's the other side of the coin?" Meaning what is another way of looking at this situation, or what would the other person say about this. Her searing criticisms of others lost much of their heat when she forced herself to answer these questions.

Abby was startled to hear another voice as she read through her thoughts—the hypercritical voice of her father, asking her why she wasn't making more money. She had kept the notes she had made during previous bouts of overthinking, and as she read through those she again heard her father's voice ringing through what she'd written. Never before had Abby realized just how much she had taken on her father's tendency to be critical as well as his obsession with making money. "I don't want to be this way," she thought. "I don't want to be so critical of others, and especially not of myself. I don't want to care only about money." From then on, when Abby heard herself snarling at what someone else had done, or raging at herself for not being perfect or not earning enough, she quietly whispered to herself, "Stop it, Dad."

Writing out her thoughts on her computer also helped Abby take a different perspective on them. Realizing that her father's voice permeated her negative thoughts was a turning point for her, helping her to reject criticism and concern with money as her father's obsessions and not her own. Listening to her father's voice not only made Abby feel bad, it led her to pursue two unhealthy goals. The first was the narrow goal of making more money. This is not an unimportant goal, of course, but focusing only on making more money distracts you from other important job-related goals, such as finding an outlet for your special talents. The other goal Abby seemed to be pursuing, thanks to the influence of her father's critical voice, was the goal of always being appreciated and taken care of by her boss. Her dad had not appreciated her, so Abby turned to people like Helene for acknowledgment that she was a good and worthy person. When Helene didn't fully appreciate her, Abby felt betrayed and her father's criticisms of her ran rampant in her head. Fortunately, Abby developed the ability to recognize when it was her father's negative voice she was listening to, and to discard these thoughts by whispering to herself, "Stop it, Dad."

One Tuesday, just before a meeting in which Abby was going to assist Helene in presenting the proposed summer fashion buys to the store manager, she spilled coffee on her new suit jacket. As she stood in front of the mirror attempting to dab away the stain, Abby's overthinking took off:

> You idiot, you can't do anything right. You were a klutz as a kid and you're still a klutz. Just a silly little klutz, pretending to be some big, important department store buyer.

Abby looked at herself in the mirror and saw that nervous little girl that her father often called "Stumblebum." She felt small and embarrassed and wanted to flee. Her commitment to Helene kept her from bolting, and as she thought more about Helene, her image in the mirror seemed to slowly change. She stood up a bit taller, and instead of seeing only the stain on her jacket, she saw that the outfit she had put together was stunning on her. She saw a healthy-looking, mature young woman who could stand up for her ideas. She saw an energetic person who was on the rise in her career. "This is who I am," Abby thought, "not that little girl my father saw." She stopped trying to get rid of the stain on her jacket and simply took it off. The skirt and silk blouse she was wearing looked fine by themselves, but she decided to make a quick pass through her favorite section of the store and pick another jacket off the racks. She quickly snipped the tags off the jacket, told the clerk to put it on her account, and headed for the store's boardroom for the meeting.

Abby gained even greater freedom from the image of herself that had been shaped by her father's criticisms by actively choosing to focus on the new image she was creating of herself as competent, mature, and working toward goals that she cared about. Previously, when she had tried to counteract the negative image of herself as a silly, klutzy girl, she had temporarily taken on the self-image as a woman wronged by others, full of hubris and entitled to retribution. This new image she was creating didn't rely on hurting others to prop up her own self-esteem. Instead, she was working hard to gain the skills, knowledge, and maturity to achieve goals she had set for herself. She could cope with the little frustrations of the day because she had raised her eyes to focus on what was important to her—demonstrating her competence and learning her job—rather than on focusing on issues such as who was or was not being nice to her that day. Whenever she felt a pique of anger or frustration, rather than fanning it with her thoughts, she would now feel her pain and move on either to overcome what had made her frustrated or forget it and refocus on the key job for her at the moment.

Early in her work with Marilyn, Abby admitted that her overthinking bouts often came on Mondays or Tuesdays when she was tired from all-night weekend parties and still feeling the depressant effects of the alcohol she had consumed. This malaise made it much more likely that little irritations at work would seem huge, and that she could perceive only the dissatisfying aspects of the job. Until Marilyn explained this to her, however, Abby thought she was seeing the job for what it was—boring, ungratifying, full of incompetent people who drove her crazy. Misunderstanding the sources of our negative feelings is a big ingredient to bad decisions. Abby quit her job on one of these days, convinced that it was dead-end, hopeless, and the only solution was to escape from it, when the real source of her upset was a hangover. This is a classic example of the need to "Keep It Simple" when you are searching for the causes of your negative feelings. There indeed may be some deep dark reasons why you are feeling lousy—for Abby it turned out that her relationship with her father drove many of her self-critical ruminations—but it's hard to discern the true meanings of your feelings through the haze of fatigue and the side effects of chemicals such as alcohol.

· · ·

The reconstruction of Abby's image of herself as a professional and the skills she developed for overcoming her overthinking tendencies didn't come overnight. It took months of working with Marilyn and slowly building her strength to fight off her father's voice and the impulsive habits she had developed early in her career. Some people's careers flounder for years as a result of uncontrolled overthinking and the unwise decisions they make in the midst of overthinking. They never fully evaluate what they want to do for a career, and instead indulge in quick fixes for their emotions—switching jobs unnecessarily, living only for the weekends. On the job they are unhappy and less productive than they could be. Off the job, they avoid thinking about it, but harbor a deep, gnawing dread of returning on Monday morning.

It is possible, as Abby showed, to conquer work-related overthinking and its deleterious effects on your career. Using strategies such as Abby used, and others described in chapters 4, 5, and 6 of this book, you can break free of career-damaging thought patterns and design a new course for your career that can improve your well-being and increase your chances of achieving significant career goals.

11

Toxic Thoughts:
Overthinking Health Problems

Many of you reading this book will be young and healthy enough that you haven't yet had to cope with serious health problems. But such problems are inevitable at some time in your life. Health problems can be potent material for overthinking, for many reasons: Our lives may be threatened by a disease. Even if our illness is not life-threatening, it might lead to disability, disfigurement, pain, lost work, or intrusive medical procedures. We may not have enough money to pay for our medical care. Understanding what is wrong with us can be tough. Physicians often don't communicate well with patients, or we might get conflicting opinions from different physicians. We have to make decisions about our own health care that we may not feel competent or comfortable making. We may wonder if our physicians are making the right decisions on our behalf. The health care system often seems to be full of rude, overworked people who don't give a damn about our dignity and well-being. Finally, unlike many problems in our lives, illness is often not something we can "fix" entirely by our own actions. We may be able to reduce the impact of the illness on our lives, but we may not be able to overcome it entirely, even with the help of the best medicine. Thus, we must cope with the illness and its meanings and consequences day in and day out for weeks, months, even years.

Overthinking Life and Death

All of these issues were the focus of Michelle's overthinking during the many months she battled breast cancer. Over her thirty-three years of life, Michelle had always kept her fear of developing breast cancer firmly tucked in the back of her mind. Her mother and two of her aunts—tall, boxy midwestern women with the Nordic features of their ancestors—had all suffered from breast cancer. Both her aunts had died from the disease, but her mother was still alive and now healthy four years after first being diagnosed. Michelle shared her mother's straight blond hair and blue eyes, but avoided the high-fat diet she had grown up with and jogged daily, so that she was lean and in great physical shape. She wasn't going to give the genes for breast cancer that she might have inherited any assistance if she could help it.

But in a routine gynecological exam shortly after her thirty-third birthday, it happened. The doctor felt a lump. Terror raced through Michelle's mind, her body suddenly felt a hundred pounds heavier, and her overthinking began:

> I always knew this was possible. But I never believed it would happen. I'm so young. This is really bad. I don't think I can take this. My mother is going to have a stroke when I tell her. How can she handle this? My dad—my dad will be even worse. Why didn't I feel this lump? Did I just not want to feel it? Could the doctor be wrong? I'm going to lose control. I'm going to lose control right now and break down.

Meanwhile, Michelle's doctor was telling her not to panic, and that she would order a mammogram to be done immediately. Michelle barely heard her, because her own thoughts were racing through her mind.

Michelle had a lot to overthink. She was facing an illness that had killed two of her aunts, had struck her mother, and for which she had a strong genetic predisposition. Even a woman who had no family history of breast cancer would have many fears to overthink after being diagnosed, but a diagnosis of breast cancer in a young woman with a strong family history like Michelle's is especially volatile fuel for anxious ruminations.

Michelle knew she had to listen to the doctor, however, so she literally shook her head vigorously for a couple of seconds to break away from overthinking. Her doctor was a bit startled, but Michelle explained that she was trying to clear her head so she could listen.

As she drove home, Michelle couldn't help but play through everything the doctor said:

> She said the lump was small and that was good. But my God, I have a strong family history of breast cancer and I'm only thirty-three! She was just trying to cheer me up. What was she really thinking? How can I find out what the odds are that it's cancer? Do I want to know? Oh, how am I going to tell my parents?

Not paying enough attention to her driving, Michelle ran off the road. Fortunately, she was able to keep control of the car, but this drew her attention away from her overthinking for a few moments, which gave her the chance to say to herself:

> I'm not going to let this kill me by causing a traffic accident! Stop it, Michelle. You don't know anything yet except that there's a lump. It's okay to be anxious about this, but don't let yourself freak out completely. I'm simply not going to tell my parents yet, until I know something more.

Michelle's overthinking preoccupied her to the point that it put her life in danger. Recent research suggests that overthinking can keep a woman from taking care of herself in other critical ways. In a study of women who detected lumps in their breasts, Sonja Lyubomirsky of the University of California, Riverside, found that those women who were especially prone to overthinking waited one month longer to tell their physicians about the lump than women who did not tend to overthink.[1] This makes sense when you think about the effects of rumination on thinking and problem solving. It makes you more pessimistic, which could make a woman feel more helpless and hopeless that anything could be done about a lump in her breast. Overthinking makes it harder to generate positive steps you might take to deal with a problem you discover.

And overthinking makes you more unsure and uncertain about taking any action to solve your problems.

Michelle resumed paying attention to the road and resolved once she got home that she was going to hold on to hope that nothing was wrong. That evening, after her seven-year-old son, Tory, had gone to bed, Michelle told her husband, Jason, about the lump. She let the tears flow, and Jason wrapped her in his arms, stroked her long hair, and let her cry.

Within a few days, Michelle had the mammogram, and it confirmed that there was a suspicious mass in Michelle's left breast. The doctor did a fine-needle biopsy the same day, and it showed highly abnormal cells. Michelle sat shivering in her hospital gown as her doctor told her the results of the biopsy. Sirens were going off in her head so loudly she could hardly hear the doctor's words. There was something about surgery. In a week. On the eighteenth. Did Michelle want to rule out a mastectomy? She thought she had said she wasn't sure. More sirens:

> God, why didn't I have Jason come with me? He offered. I said I could handle it. I can't hear. I can't think. Surgery. I've got to get my head together so I can ask questions.

Michelle cut her doctor off in the middle of a sentence, saying, "I have to catch my breath and get my mind back. I can't listen to you right now. Can you give me a couple of minutes?" The doctor looked a bit annoyed, but complied with Michelle's request and left the room. Michelle knew she was about to burst into tears. She didn't want to be sobbing when the doctor returned, so she began to do deep-breathing exercises. She inhaled deeply through her nostrils, quietly saying "in" as the air entered and feeling its coolness. Then she exhaled slowly, quietly saying "out" and feeling her body relax. Within a minute she was feeling calmer. Then she said to herself:

> I can break down and bawl my eyes out at home in privacy. I've only got a few minutes with the doctor when she comes back and I need to understand this. I need to ask questions. What do I want to know before I leave here? What would I tell my friend to ask if she were in the same situation?

Michelle pulled a pad of paper and a pen from her purse and made a list of the questions she wanted to ask. Exactly what kind of surgery was the doctor recommending? Was surgery absolutely necessary? What were the alternatives? Would she still need chemo and radiation? What were the risks of the surgery? What were the risks of waiting and not doing surgery now?

When the doctor returned, Michelle asked all her questions, and listened as carefully as possible to the answers. She wasn't entirely convinced by her doctor's arguments that surgery was the best option. So she asked to be referred for a second opinion. This annoyed her doctor greatly, and Michelle felt a surge of guilt and embarrassment. But then she stepped back mentally and chided herself for feeling guilty for taking care of herself. She stuck to her guns, and her doctor gave her a referral to a breast cancer specialist at the university hospital.

Michelle's overthinking almost kept her from asking the questions she needed to ask, and particularly from demanding a second opinion. Sensing her own doctor's annoyance at having to arrange for a second opinion, Michelle began to have guilty thoughts about inconveniencing her doctor. Such guilt is unfortunately common for women—we can't stand the thought of bothering someone else, especially an important doctor, with our doubts and worries. So we often just don't mention them. But then we overthink these worries, often blowing them up bigger and bigger with each overthinking bout, and we kick ourselves for not asking all the questions we have about our own health.

The three weeks between that visit and her appointment with the specialist were torture. Was she being foolish for delaying action on this lump by insisting on a second opinion? What if the cancer was growing aggressively? How far could it develop in three weeks? Michelle shared these thoughts with Jason. He told her he was proud that she had insisted on a second opinion. This quelled her thoughts about the wait a bit. But in the meantime, there was plenty more to worry about. Michelle's fiercest overthinking happened at night. She'd fall asleep in exhaustion, but awaken around 2 A.M. and begin overthinking:

What's going to happen to Tory if I die? Jason's a good father, but Tory needs me. Jason's too harsh with him at times. Jason needs me, too. We do so well together. We don't deserve to have this happen to us. Tory's too young to lose his mother. Jason doesn't deserve to be saddled with single parenthood. Will he have enough money to raise Jason without my salary? I don't want to tell my colleagues at work about this. I don't want to have to answer questions and have them look at me strangely. People treat cancer patients differently. It's not fair, but they do. Even if I live through this, they'll treat me differently for the rest of my life. I can't tell anyone about this. My parents. How am I going to handle my parents? They've been through so much already. It's not fair that they have to go through this, too. I shouldn't be thinking this way. Who says life is fair? Do I have enough faith? What will happen to me if I die? Do I believe strongly enough in God?

For several nights, her overthinking bouts kept Michelle awake for hours. Then she would be completely strung out all day at her job as a writer for a women's magazine. Her fatigue fed a growing depression over her health concerns.

One day as she was staring at her computer screen, morbidly ruminating about whether Jason would still find her attractive after breast surgery, she yelled "Stop!" loud enough that the woman in the cubicle next to hers was startled. Michelle took a few deep breaths, and then said to herself, "This is tearing me up. I don't want to live in misery. I'm not going to let this take over my life." She got up from her desk, marched down the hall and into the elevator, and left the building to take a brisk walk around the block. When she got to a small park near her office, she sat down on a bench and began to pray to God for help in coping with her worries. She literally cupped her hands together and symbolically held out her fears for God to take. A woman pushing a stroller past Michelle's bench looked at her oddly, but Michelle felt a wave of relief sweep over her.

When you are faced with a serious illness, it is natural that many of your ruminations will be about the possibility of death. Michelle is a religious woman, and her faith in God comforted her through her harrowing experience, but her religious beliefs were also tested by this experience. Some people when told they may die immediately accept this as part of God's will. Many religious people, though, have the kinds of questions Michelle had about the meaning of this experience and about the strength of their faith. Michelle asked why God put this great burden of breast cancer on her and her family. How could she ever know if she had enough faith? Was it even okay that she was asking such questions—did this mean she didn't have enough faith?

Eventually, Michelle found some resolution for her questions. But my colleagues and I have found in our studies of people facing serious illnesses, or the serious illnesses of loved ones, that these questions about faith and meaning can present some of the most troubling types of overthinking.[2] People who have a strong tendency to overthink can have an especially hard time with questions of meaning and faith. There can be great guilt over the sense that you are questioning or doubting God or your own religious doctrines. Most of us don't think much about death until it stares us in the face, and so we can be surprised by the flimsiness of our beliefs about what happens after death, or what the meaning of hardship in our lives is. The pat answers that we may have mouthed previously—death is just part of life, or hardship makes you grow—can seem shallow and empty when it's our death or our hardship we're talking about. Because overthinking makes you so much more uncertain about any answer you might arrive at, it is doubly hard to find some meaning or claim your faith in times of great stress. Just when you think you've come to a resolution of the difficult religious or existential questions a crisis poses, your overthinking mind pipes up to say, "Yeah, but . . ."

Michelle was also confronted by other forms of overthinking that are common for women. She worried about what was going to happen to all the people in her life that she cares for—her son, Tory, her husband, Jason, her parents. She overthought about the impact of the news of her cancer on her parents, especially her mother. She agonized over what would happen to Tory if she died. She wondered if Jason would find her attractive after her surgery. Women take care of others, and even in our darkest moments of fear and pain, our thoughts are often consumed with worries about the people we love.

Michelle got off the park bench and called her office from her cell phone to say she was taking the rest of the day off as a personal day. It was about time for Tory to be out of school, so she scurried back to the parking garage, jumped in her navy blue Volvo, and went to pick him up before he got on the bus he usually took home. Michelle and Tory first

stopped by their favorite ice-cream store for a treat, then went to a park
near their house for a little soccer practice. Tory's skinny little body
zipped this way and that as he dribbled the ball around Michelle's
attempts to intercept him. Keeping up with Tory took all Michelle's concentration and energy, and the exercise felt great. By the end of the
afternoon, Michelle felt more relief, physically and mentally, than she
had felt since her doctor discovered the lump.

For the next several days until her appointment, Michelle worked to
keep life as normal and upbeat as possible. She went back to work and
plunged into researching a new article for her magazine. When she felt
herself slipping into overthinking, she'd listen to what she was saying to
herself, write it out on her computer, then put it aside for a while. When
she came back to it, she'd ask herself which of her concerns were things
she should ask about when she met with the second doctor, which ones
were things she could do something about, and which ones were wild-
eyed worries that were the result of her anxiety. Michelle tried looking
on the Internet for information about breast cancer, but found that most
of it was either too vague or too technical. She often felt more confused
and more scared after reading something on the Net, because she didn't
know what really applied to her specific case.

When her appointment with the breast specialist finally arrived,
Michelle was armed with a long list of questions. She created a mental
image of herself as strong and competent and in control. She asked Jason
to go with her to the appointment to provide a second pair of ears to
listen to what the doctor said, as well as emotional support. The two of
them were seated in a sterile, white examining room and after a while
the door opened. A tall, balding man with a confident stride and a broad
smile strode into the room, introducing himself as Dr. Phillips.

"I've gone over all your test results and your history. I have to concur
with your gynecologist that a surgical biopsy, followed by removal of any
cancerous tissue, is warranted in your case."

Although Michelle had felt prepared for this judgment, she still felt
stunned. She took a deep breath and said, "I have some questions." For
the next half hour, she peppered Dr. Phillips with her questions about
alternatives, what to expect after the surgery, risks, and so on. Jason
piped in with a question or two of his own. When Dr. Phillips left the
exam room, Michelle looked at Jason and said quietly, "I guess I have to

do this." Then her tears flowed. Jason held her tightly as she sobbed. After a few minutes, Michelle felt spent, and began to take deep breaths. She eventually went over to the sink in the room and splashed cold water in her face as Jason gently rubbed her back. When she felt more composed, she turned to Jason and said, "I want to go for a walk. Can we go out to the river?"

They headed for a park where they could walk along the river for miles. As they walked, Michelle spilled all the most anxious and nasty ruminations she had had about her illness and the surgery—her fear of dying, her fear Jason would no longer find her attractive, her concerns about Tory, her worries about telling her parents. Jason listened, and although he didn't dismiss any of her concerns, he gently pointed out things the doctor had said that contradicted specific concerns Michelle raised. When she said, "I'm going to look horrible after this surgery," Jason responded, "Phillips said a mastectomy was not likely to be necessary and the incision he'd make would be quite small. You're so beautiful that one little scar is not going to change how you look at all." Jason helped her think through ways of handling some of her concerns. They decided they'd drive over to her parents this weekend and tell them together, then stay for several hours to help her parents get past the initial shock. They walked and talked for a couple of hours, ending up at the park café to eat sloppy chili dogs.

The weekend arrived, and Michelle and Jason drove to her parents, while Tory stayed at a friend's house. Michelle's parents knew something must be up to warrant this unusual type of visit. Michelle said the words she had rehearsed for the last couple of days, "They think I have breast cancer; I'm having surgery next week," feeling almost surreal as the words left her mouth. Instead of breaking into sobs, Michelle's mother took a deep breath and said, "Honey, I got through this, and you will, too. We'll do it together." Tears streamed down Michelle's face as her mother and father both reached out to hold her. The afternoon was bathed in love and support. Michelle shared what the doctor had told her to expect. Her mother shared how she had coped with her surgery and the many fears she'd had over the years. Jason and Michelle's dad sat together in the garden, occasionally talking directly about Michelle or her mother, but mostly chatting about other things, sharing the kind of indirect support that men often give each other.

Michelle was very lucky to have such a supportive husband. Jason listened to her and comforted her. He quelled her worries that he wouldn't find her attractive after the surgery. Michelle was also blessed with parents, particularly her mother, who understood what she was going through and were dedicated to helping her get through her cancer experience in a positive way.

The incredible relief Michelle felt after telling her parents gave her the courage to tell her boss and coworkers about her surgery. She was forced to anyway, because she'd be absent from work for some time. But having let go of this news once with her parents gave her some psychological distance from it, so she felt she could tell her coworkers without bursting into tears.

The reactions were mixed. Most of her female coworkers were completely supportive, offering to take care of Tory when needed, to cover for her at work, and generally just be there in any way she wanted. Telling more people about her surgery made it somehow feel more manageable to Michelle, compared to how it felt when the thoughts and images were just swirling around in her head. Michelle was uplifted by the genuine concern and support offered by the women. Some of the men in her office were also outgoing in their offers of help, though a few of them just stood in silence, unable to say anything when Michelle told them.

One coworker, Rhonda, plunged Michelle back into overthinking. Michelle hadn't told Rhonda about her surgery directly because Rhonda wasn't a close friend or someone who needed to know. Rhonda heard about it around the office, and came to Michelle's cubicle to talk with her. She launched into a story of how her sister-in-law had had breast cancer surgery, and it had gone badly. Rhonda didn't know if the surgeon was incompetent, or what, but it took months for her sister-in-law to feel better. Then she lived in constant fear of the cancer coming back. Rhonda didn't want to scare Michelle, of course, but she thought Michelle should be realistic about the possibilities.

For the next few hours, Michelle tried to work but Rhonda's depressing story kept creeping into her thoughts, and images of herself disfigured, in pain, depressed, anxious, began forming. Fortunately, Michelle was scheduled to have lunch with her friend Heather, and when she shared Rhonda's story, Heather simply said, "That bitch. Rhonda had no business telling you that story. Heaven knows if it's even true. You've got the best doctors and it will do you no good to expect the worst at this point. You've got to have twice as much character and resilience as anyone related to Rhonda. You will get through this."

After lunch, Michelle wrote down Heather's encouraging words on a card and put it in her desk. Then she decided she'd write a story about her experiences for her magazine. If telling the story of her journey through breast cancer treatment might help other women, then she would feel better. She felt better writing it all down. As she sat at her computer and typed, tears streamed down her face. Still, Michelle felt a tremendous release of tension as she spilled the details of her experiences and thoughts into words.

Michelle discovered something that many of us find true when we reveal our concerns to others. Somehow, after telling our thoughts, they seem more concrete and manageable than when they were floating around filling up all the spaces in our head. Sometimes other people provide answers to our questions or help us dismiss specific worries. But often just the airing of our ruminations shrinks them, puts them in a box, and gives us the sense that we control these thoughts instead of their controlling us.

Of course, telling others about our concerns also creates the opportunity for those people to feed the concerns, just as Rhonda fed Michelle's most morbid imaginations about her surgery. Then we have to cope not only with our original worries, but with broodings about our reactions to the jerky behavior of others when we are down. Sharing these nasty experiences with friends you can rely on for support and clarity, as Michelle did with her friend Heather, can be critical to containing the negative effects of these interactions.

The day came for Michelle's surgery, and as she was being admitted to the hospital, she felt dizzy with anxiety. Jason held her hand, doing as much of the paperwork as he could, then read the consent forms to Michelle and showed her where she had to sign. As they wheeled Michelle into the operating room on the gurney, Jason walked beside her, whispering, "You're going to be fine. I'll be right here when you're done. You're going to be fine."

The experience of the operation was bizarre. Michelle was only under partial anesthesia, so she could hear the surgeon talking to her and

to the other people in the room, the music playing, the clinking of surgical tools. Time seemed to pass very slowly, and she was sure she was
drifting in and out of consciousness. Finally, she heard Dr. Phillips's
strong voice calling her to awareness, "Michelle, Michelle can you hear
me? The lump is definitely cancerous. But the good news is that it hasn't
spread far, and it's not in your lymph nodes. We caught it early."
Michelle shut her eyes and thanked God, then mumbled something like
"good" to Dr. Phillips.

In the recovery room, as the anesthesia began to wear off, questions
began to flood Michelle's mind. "What does this mean that I had a cancerous lump at thirty-three? Does it mean I will probably get cancer
again?" "Did Dr. Phillips say he got it all?" "Will I have to do chemo?"
"What if he didn't get it all? How can he know?" When Dr. Phillips
came by to check on her, her questions to him flowed. Yes, she should
have chemo to ensure that all of the cancer was eradicated. Yes, this does
indicate she is at high risk for future breast cancer, so they will have to
follow her closely. But that did not mean she was doomed to die of cancer. Michelle was thankful that Jason and her mother were standing
there when Dr. Phillips was answering her questions, because the anesthesia had not worn off completely and she wasn't sure she was going to
remember all his answers.

Coping with the Long Haul

In the next few months, as Michelle dealt with the side effects of the
chemo and radiation, she tried to develop a way of coping with the anxiety of knowing she was at high risk for breast cancer. Overthinking bouts
still overcame her at times:

> Why do I have to live with this cloud over my head all the time? I
> hate it. I want life to get back to the way it was before we discov-
> ered the lump. I hate feeling like a walking time bomb. How will
> I know it if I get another lump? I didn't feel the first one until the
> doctor discovered it. What if they don't detect the next one until
> it's too late?

One day, in the midst of one of these bouts, Tory came up to Michelle and said, "Mommy, you look sad. What are you thinking about? I don't want you to be sad." Michelle looked at Tory and, holding back the tears, responded, "Honey, I'm just worrying about something. And you're right, I don't want to be sad, either. Let's go play outside." After an hour of pitching softballs to Tory, Michelle went back into the house, and silently prayed, "God, I will do my best to cope well with this. Please help me."

Then Michelle resolved to do whatever she could to regain a sense of control over her health and get back to as normal a life as possible. She went to her bedroom and found the brochures her gynecologist had given her on breast self-examination and read them through. She decided to ask the gynecologist in her next office visit to show her again exactly how to do a proper self-exam. She made a list of questions to ask the gynecologist during that visit.

Michelle also made a list of the things she does during her day that give her pleasure, including finishing writing an article, playing with Tory, and cooking a nice dinner for Jason and Tory. She decided she would finish her article about her breast cancer experiences, first interviewing a few more cancer specialists and other women who had gone through surgery. Writing the article would get her memories and images of her own surgery down on paper rather than letting them only circle around in her mind. In the article, she would include ideas for how to cope with breast cancer that she had gleaned from her own experience, her mother's experience, and the experiences of the other women she interviewed. She hoped these ideas would help other women, and making a list of the ideas would give her something to refer to when she found herself sliding back into anxiety, sadness, and overthinking.

Michelle decided she would start leaving work an hour earlier so she'd have more time at home with Tory before dinner. She resolved to get some exercise with him at least a couple of afternoons a week, by playing ball in a park or going swimming. She'd get her family back on the healthy diet she used to prepare for them before her surgery. She'd add an extra vegetable to every dinner to increase their intake of cancer-fighting foods.

Michelle didn't cut herself off from her feelings and worries completely. When a wave of anxiety or overthinking came upon her, she told herself, "This is natural. I have a right to feel this way." Then, after a few minutes of letting the thoughts and feelings flow, she said to herself, "I don't want these feelings to overwhelm me. What am I worried about? What can I learn from this?" She'd try to listen to her thoughts, perhaps writing them down. If there was something she could do to deal with one of her concerns—information she needed to get, or a conversation she needed to have with her physician or her husband, for example—she would write it down and resolve to do it.

For the existential questions that came to her mind—"Why did this have to happen to me?" "What is the meaning of this for my life?"—she developed a set of answers that helped her cope: "Only God knows why I'm experiencing this; I just want to learn to live positively with this; I've grown greatly as a person through this experience." Over the next few years, Michelle wrote several more articles on breast cancer for her magazine, and did some public speaking to educate and support women with cancer. These helped her fulfill her new goal of turning her cancer experience into a vehicle for helping others.

Short-term strategies helped Michelle gain some control over her thoughts so that she could sort out her ruminations. Michelle didn't quash her overthinking altogether. She knew it was a natural response to the crisis she was facing. But she didn't let it rule her, either. Once she broke its grip on her mind for a while, she was better able to determine what concerns she needed to pay attention to and do something about, and which she wanted to dismiss.

Michelle also used a number of longer-term strategies to move out of overthinking and into problem solving, or at least into effective management of her cancer experience. She needed a lot of information to make good decisions about her medical care. Her doctors were obviously the best sources of this information. After using short-term strategies to break loose of her screaming ruminations, Michelle made lists of questions. Indeed, a question she often asked herself to stop her overthinking was: "What do I need to know from my doctor to understand this?" Michelle then persistently asked her questions until she felt she understood her situation and her options. Sometimes she brought along Jason or her mother to help her listen to the answers and decipher them. But the critical strategy for Michelle was to write down these questions and refer to her lists in her meetings with the doctors, rather than relying on being able to remember and articulate all her questions in the chaos and terror of the office visits.

Michelle also tried to get information from the Internet about her condition. She didn't find this helpful because of the conflicting viewpoints she found and the material that was available was often too technical. But many people do find the Internet to be a good source of information about medical illnesses. The key to successful use of the Internet is to investigate the reliability of the sources, use only those that are reputable organizations or individuals, and look for a consensus among these reputable sources as to what is most highly recommended.

Part of Michelle's list making also involved listing the themes of her overthinking, leaving the list for a while, then going back to evaluate it. She asked herself which concerns she could do something about, which ones she needed more information to address, and which ones represented her uncontrolled fears. Writing down her concerns gave Michelle some distance from them, and the evaluation of their validity helped her sort out the ones she wanted to ignore and the ones she could take some control over.

Besides writing magazine articles about her own experiences and the experiences of other women with cancer, Michelle did public speaking to break the stigma of cancer and to educate women about the importance of breast self-exams and regular gynecological checkups. Some people accused Michelle of being Pollyanna-ish when she talked about what she had learned and how she had grown in her fight against cancer. This rocked Michelle at first, but then she realized that her optimism and focus on the positive was what she needed to do, and she couldn't let others steal that from her. Research by psychologists such as Shelley Taylor of the University of California, Los Angeles, confirms that Michelle's optimism will do her a lot of good, not only by making her feel better, but possibly by making her better able to fight her cancer.[3] Taylor, and a number of other psychologists, have done dozens of studies showing that hope and optimism are potent medicine against a number of diseases, including cancers. For example, optimists show better immune system functioning than pessimists, and since cancer is a disease of the immune system, optimists' bodies may do a better job of fighting their cancer. Optimists also fare better than pessimists after heart bypass surgery, and in fighting HIV, the virus that causes AIDS. In short, people who remain optimistic even in the face of a life-threatening ill-ness recover faster and even live longer than people who become fatalis-tic and pessimistic.

Michelle's optimism wasn't a pie-in-the-sky, everything's-going-to-be-fine kind of denial that some people use to face illness and hardship. Michelle knew she was in trouble and that her family history of breast cancer, and her young age, didn't make for a rosy prognosis. But she chose to remain hopeful and keep up her fighting spirit. She also chose to take control of her medical care and her life as much as possible, rather than succumbing to feelings of helplessness and being diseased and damaged.

Our health is something many of us take for granted when we are young. If we are confronted by a major illness, we are often stunned that it could happen to us. Even if illness doesn't strike until we are older, it still often hits us as a surprise, because we still think of our-selves as twenty or thirty or forty. Questions abound: Why did this hap-pen to me? What did I do wrong? Is the diagnosis correct? How will I ever know? How can I decide between alternative treatments? So it is completely natural for a serious illness to cause us to overthink. If we have chronic pain or discomfort, it can be even harder not to be self-preoccupied.

Even when overthinking is a natural response to a crisis, however, it can be toxic. It can diminish our ability to make good decisions about our medical care. It can drag our moods down so that we are dealing with severe depression or anxiety, as well as our medical illness. It may even impair our body's ability to heal itself.

Thus it is essential to break free of overthinking and move to higher ground where you can manage your illness and the medical world as effectively as possible. Michelle's journey provides several ideas for how to do this. But every woman must develop her own strategies for grab-bing hold of her overthinking, learning what she can from it, and defeat-ing the toxic ruminations that are pulling her down.

12

Can't Get Over It:
Overthinking Loss and Trauma

Intellectually, we know it's inevitable that we'll someday experience the death of someone close to us, a parent, a sibling, a partner, a close friend, perhaps even a child. But most of us don't think about it much, particularly if we've never experienced an important loss before. We think even less about the possibility of being the victim of a major trauma, such as a sexual assault, losing our home in a fire, or being paralyzed in a car accident.

Imagining ourselves losing someone we love or experiencing a trauma hurts, and that's one good reason we avoid such thoughts. We also tend to deny that such terrible things can happen to us. Researchers Shelley Taylor of the University of California, Los Angeles, and Jonathon Brown of the University of Washington summarized hundreds of research studies showing that most people tend to believe that bad things are less likely to happen to them than to other people: they are less likely to get a serious illness, to have a bad marriage, to fail in their career, or even to lose money in gambling than other people.[1] When a tragedy does befall us, particularly if it comes completely out of the blue, it violates our fundamental belief that we are in control. We can feel powerless, helpless, immobilized. Even worse, tragedies can call into question our self-image as a good person, because they challenge our belief in what psychologist Mel Lerner called a "just world"—in which good things happen to good people and bad things happen to bad people.[2] If we are the victim of a trauma, what does this mean about us—that we are bad? That there is no justice in the world? That we got what we deserved?

No wonder the loss of a loved one or being the victim of a traumatic event can spark virulent ruminations about the meaning of life, about our religious or philosophical beliefs, and about how we are living our lives. To some extent, such rumination is perfectly natural and can be healthy. It can lead to a clarification of your values and beliefs. It can cause you to reprioritize your life. It can deepen your appreciation of each new day.

But loss and trauma can also trigger overthinking that can last for months, even years. Some people never find the answers to the profound questions raised by their tragedy. Others remain stuck with a sense of helplessness and victimization that robs them of the ability to rebuild their lives. Still others turn to alcohol or drugs to numb their feelings and drown out their overthinking.

We are probably more likely to fall into overthinking when we are confronted with a loss or trauma than were people in previous generations. Decades ago when people experienced a loss or personal trauma, they often had two powerful sources of comfort and support that helped them cope. First, they had a network of family members and friends, a local community of loved ones, who were there for them in any way they needed—financially, practically, emotionally. Many of these family members and friends had experienced their own losses and traumas, and thus could empathize and comfort in a way that comes only from experience. Second, our ancestors frequently held beliefs, often religious in nature, that helped them understand and accept their experiences. Death, disability, and loss were part of a natural order that they understood and found ways to live with.

Today, often we have neither of these resources when we face loss or trauma. We tend to live far away from our families of origin and may have only a superficial social network of acquaintances where we live. These acquaintances may provide some support in our times of loss and trauma, but they do not really know us or know what we need without our even having to ask. Everyone is busy, so as soon as the funeral is over, or you are discharged from the hospital, or the proper condolences have been expressed, family and friends go back to work and to their busy lives and expect you to do the same. I found in my bereavement studies that many people were overcome with angry overthinking, not about the fact they had lost someone they loved greatly, but about the insensitive reactions of others to their loss.[3] Marjorie, a fifty-year-old homemaker whose mother died after battling lung cancer for a year, told me:

> When I first told people that my mother had cancer, they were very concerned, and said, "Can I do anything? Let us help out in any way we can." But those people never called. They never asked again how they could help. If I ran into them in the grocery store, it was obvious that most of them had completely forgotten my mother was dying. If they did remember, they'd ask me how I was doing, but that was it. Once she died, lots of people came to the funeral. But it was like that was the end of it. No one mentioned it again, everyone assumed the whole ordeal was over for me once she actually died.

These days, many of us also do not have a religious or spiritual connection that is more than skin deep. We may whisper the occasional prayer for help, but we do not actively cultivate a relationship to a higher being or a set of deep spiritual values that can provide answers to the fundamental questions of meaning that loss and trauma raise. Thus, we are left to overthink and question. We overthink about our anger against those who have abandoned us or traumatized us. We fixate on our isolation and emptiness. We worry about our inability to "bounce back." We question why this happened to us.

Coming to terms with a loss or a personal tragedy takes time. We must reorder our lives. And we must answer the many questions in our heart. But as a society, we have little time or patience for processes such as grief or coming to terms with a trauma. If a person is not "over it" in some prescribed amount of time (usually a few weeks), we tell them, implicitly or explicitly, just to get on with it, or go get some help. When they go for help, increasingly it comes in the form of a pill—a little medication will do the trick quickly and efficiently. The spiritual, philosophical, and psychological journey they might need to make is too messy and inefficient for our pace of life. Even when we do make that journey, our vacuum of values leaves us with nothing but to overthink the big questions that loss and trauma raise.

It doesn't have to be so, however. In my research on bereavement, I found hundreds of people, young and old, who not only coped with their loss but turned the loss into a transforming growth experience.[4] Indeed, between 70 and 80 percent of bereaved people said they found something positive in their loss. These people were not talking about inheriting a large sum of money. Instead, they said they grew in character and maturity. They recognized strengths and skills in themselves they didn't realize they had. They gained new perspectives on life. They reprioritized their goals. They deepened their relationships with others.

These people who coped include Alicia, whose partner died of cancer. This petite thirty-one-year-old secretary nursed her partner for months as the cancer and the treatments he underwent for it incapacitated his body. But her perspective on her experience is anything but negative:

> I would never wish this experience on anyone. But somehow I feel lucky to have had it. I feel it was a gift to have gone through this, to learn so much about myself and about love. I have grown so much. I feel so much more alive now. I will never take life for granted again, and for that I am so grateful.

Similarly, research on people facing myriad personal traumas, including being the victim of an assault, being paralyzed in a freak accident, or losing everything in a natural disaster, shows that many people eventually emerge feeling that they are better people because of their traumatic experience and have a greater appreciation for life.[5]

In this chapter, I explore how people who suffer a huge loss or personal trauma move from the inevitable questions and natural ruminations that arise from such experiences into personal growth and the ability to feel joy again. The message is not for people to "get over it," but to go through it, to make the journey through the issues that their loss or trauma raise for them. This journey can be a difficult one. But I will describe how people have used strategies such as the ones discussed in this book to break free from toxic overthinking and make progress toward growth and understanding.

The Strength of Her Convictions:
Alicia's Story

When Alicia learned that her partner, David, had a brain tumor, she thought the world was coming to an end. She had met David two years before at a party and was instantly captivated by his sarcastic wit, his intense brown-eyed gaze, and his absolutely perfect body. At 6'1", David towered over Alicia, who, at 5'1" and 102 pounds, would have made a perfect Tinkerbell in a production of *Peter Pan*. David fell just as hard for Alicia, and within a couple of months they were living together in a small apartment in the North Beach area of San Francisco.

Their life together was blissful—passionate sex, weekend sailing on the bay, and a love of just talking to each other as they sipped wine and watched a candle slowly burn down. Their bliss was interrupted when David was in a serious car accident. The driver of a delivery truck had fallen asleep at the wheel and veered over into David's lane on Highway 101. David's car was rammed up against the guardrail, flipped over the rail, and landed on its roof. David was extracted from the car by firefighters and rushed to the hospital unconscious and with multiple broken bones. A CT scan was ordered to determine whether there was any damage to his brain. No injuries that could have been caused by the accident could be seen, but a large, ominous mass did show up deep within David's brain. The chief physician, Dr. Armstrong, ordered an MRI to further investigate the mass.

When Dr. Armstrong arrived at David's hospital room later that evening, his face was grim. Alicia was sitting at David's bedside, quietly talking about their plans for David's return home. A visible shiver went down Alicia's spine when she saw Dr. Armstrong's face. "I'm afraid," the graying physician said, "the radiologist and neurologist who have reviewed your CT and MRI data think you may have a tumor. They want to do a few more tests, but this may require exploratory surgery."

"I can't have a brain tumor," responded David in horror. "I was fine before the accident. Are you sure it's not some injury caused by the crash?"

"No, it's unlikely to be caused by the crash—it's too deep and there are no injuries closer to the surface of your brain where we would expect to see them if the accident had caused brain damage." Dr. Armstrong then queried David for several minutes about any symptoms or changes he might have noticed before the accident. There had been some headaches, but David had attributed them to all the pressure he was under at work. And there was that time, a few weeks before the accident, when David became dizzy at the top of some stairs and fell down them. But he hadn't slept much the night before and thought he had just been disoriented because of sleep deprivation.

Shortly after Dr. Armstrong left, the hospital staff told Alicia that visiting hours were over and she needed to leave. She protested, but David insisted she go home to get some sleep. As she walked down the hospital corridor, Alicia's fears began to overwhelm her:

> What if they're right? They can't be right. It's not fair. I can't lose David. He doesn't deserve to die. I can't stand this! I can't stand the thought of losing him!

As Alicia rode the elevator down to the parking garage, fear engulfed her body. She couldn't breathe and her heart was racing. "Oh my God, I'm going to have a heart attack right here in the hospital!" She began hyperventilating and grabbed hold of the railing in the elevator thinking she was going to faint. When the elevator door opened, a nurse entered and saw Alicia was in trouble. She brought her out of the elevator, sat her down in a chair, and took her pulse. Alicia's heart rate was high, but it was steady. The nurse asked her to take a couple of deep breaths. Somehow Alicia was able to tell her, "My partner . . . (gasp) . . . brain tumor . . . (gasp) . . . afraid (gasp) . . . he will die." The nurse understood that Alicia might be having a panic attack—a sudden burst of anxious feelings and physiological arousal that can make you feel you're suffocating, having a heart attack, and going to die. Alicia was taken to the emergency room, where tests showed that she wasn't having a heart attack or any other physical emergency. The psychiatrist on duty talked her down from the panic attack by helping her to get her breathing under control, then she was discharged with a prescription for anti-anxiety medication.

Alicia's questions and angry overthinking may be understandable, but they were nonetheless doing her harm. The panic attacks she experienced were probably the direct result of the physiological arousal that can be caused by uncontrolled overthinking. Alicia wouldn't have died from her panic attacks, but they were definitely frightening, and if they became frequent, could become debilitating.

Alicia took a taxi home because she was afraid to drive. She felt numb and empty as the cab careened up and down the hills of San Francisco. She hardly remembered paying the cab driver or walking up the stairs to the apartment she shared with David. As soon as she entered the apartment, though, the panicked thoughts came racing back, accompanied by a deep sense of anger and injustice at what she and David might be facing.

> How can he have a brain tumor! He's only in his thirties. These things aren't supposed to happen until you're older. We've only been together a year. It can't be over so fast. This isn't fair. I finally found someone I can love, and I'm going to lose him. Everyone I know has been in love a dozen times. This is my first time, the first time I've ever really loved someone, and he's going to be taken away from me. It's not fair.

These thoughts continued through the night, so by morning Alicia was so tired and full of anger that she was dizzy. She showered and dressed, but couldn't face eating any breakfast, even though she hadn't eaten since lunch the day before. In the backseat of the taxi on the way to the hospital, Alicia stared at the people walking down the street on their way to work on this day, which was unusually clear for San Francisco.

> They are just going about their daily lives. They're happy, munching on doughnuts, talking with other people. Why can't David and I go back to just living our lives? We had so much joy. We weren't doing anything wrong. Why can't things just be normal again?

Intermingled with these thoughts, Alicia heard the voice of the priest at her parents' church chastising her for thinking this way: "God doesn't guarantee us happiness. Everyone must experience pain in life. Turn to God and He will help you bear it." Far from diminishing her anger, these words only made Alicia angrier:

What good is faith if it doesn't give you a better life? Why can't God ensure that his followers be happy? I don't want to be put to any tests. I want to live a normal life just like all those non-believers.

Alicia is an ordinary woman who had ordinary expectations for her life. She was faced with extraordinary stress, however, when David became ill. Her anger and sense of injustice were completely understandable. Most of us, if we were cheated out of the most important thing in our life, would be angry and question why. The sense of being cheated is especially common among people who lose a loved one at an early age, before it is "supposed to" happen. The questions Alicia had about her religious beliefs are also understandable given what she was facing. We found in our bereavement study that although religious beliefs can help some people weather extraordinary loss and trauma, these beliefs can also be severely challenged by these traumas, so that some people actually lose their faith as a result.

When Alicia entered David's hospital room, he immediately noticed the wild-eyed look on her face. "What happened to you?" he asked. Alicia felt she'd been caught and didn't want to tell David what she'd been going through for the last twelve hours. "Nothing," she said, "I'm just tired, that's all."

They were interrupted by an aide coming to take David to yet another test. Alicia waited in the lobby for David to return and watched as a parade of people looking worried and desperate passed by in the hallway. Seeing older people who were sick only fueled Alicia's anger.

You're not supposed to get sick until you're that old. Then you expect it. It's not supposed to happen when you're young. You still have too much to give, too much to live through.

What stopped Alicia's angry ramblings was the sight of a young boy, about six years old, with thick jet-black hair, being pushed down the hallway in a wheelchair by his parents. The boy looked thin and pale and had a couple of intravenous tubes attached to his arm. The boy was smiling. He was telling his parents a joke, and they were laughing with him. As the boy smiled, his blue eyes danced and his face grew a bit pinker.

His parents' faces, however, showed a deep, tired sadness underneath the smiles they were sharing with their son. There was a great deal of emotional pain there, sadness and fear. Still, they laughed with their son, and the father came back with his own joke that caused the son to roll his eyes and shake his head in disbelief at his father's silliness.

"That's really unfair," thought Alicia. "Little children don't deserve to be sick or to die. And parents don't deserve to face losing a child." Alicia was flooded with guilt for having felt victimized by David's illness. "How can I believe nothing bad should happen to me when bad things happen to little children and their parents?" She was so confused, so overwhelmed. She didn't just want to stuff her feelings away and deny them. But she didn't want to be consumed with anger or guilt, either. She wanted to understand what was happening and choose how she was going to respond, rather than feeling so helpless.

Just then the nurse tapped Alicia on the shoulder and told her David was back in his room where she could join him. He had been sedated for the test and might sleep for an hour or so. Alicia quietly entered the hospital room and sat down by the window to watch David as he rested.

> He's so beautiful. He's so peaceful right now. What do I want for him and me? I want him to live, obviously. I also want him to know I love him and I will be with him no matter what. I want him to be as happy as he can be. I want him to get the best medical care. I want him to have the best chance possible.

When David stirred and looked over at Alicia, gone was the wild-eyed look he had seen on her face earlier and in its place was a look of deep, deep love, mixed with concern. "Hi, Al," he said in a gravelly voice. "Whatcha doing?" "Just loving you," she said with a sincere smile. They talked quietly for a while about what tests the doctor had ordered and how David was feeling. As the day passed, they ate a bit of lunch together, watched some TV, but mostly talked about different things— whether Alicia should call David's mother now or wait until they knew more, how Alicia should water the plants that David usually took care of, whether the Oakland A's would make it to the playoffs this year.

What helped Alicia break free of overthinking and move to higher ground? The first break was triggered by Alicia's chance encounter with the little boy in the wheelchair who was joking with his parents. The notion of "unfairness" took on a whole new meaning when Alicia saw this little boy and his parents struggling to smile and support each other in the midst of their pain. This shift in perspective interrupted Alicia's overthinking long enough that she could step back and realize she didn't want to remain mired in angry questions. Initially, she didn't know what she wanted her perspective to be on David's illness, but that came to her when she saw him a few moments later, sleeping peacefully. She chose to focus on loving and supporting David in every way possible, and knew that angry overthinking was not going to help her do this. This conscious choice on her part was the single most effective coping strategy Alicia employed through her ordeal.

Around 6:30 P.M., as David was trying to choke down some dinner, Dr. Armstrong came in. Again his face was grim, and David and Alicia immediately reached for each other's hands. Dr. Armstrong quickly got to the point. "It's clearly a tumor, and the surgeon wants to operate day after tomorrow. He'll try to get it all. It will depend on what kind of cells they are and how fast they're growing." David and Alicia were stunned and couldn't say much. They both had known it could be a tumor, but had also somehow believed it would all be proven to be a mistake—that the new tests would show there was nothing seriously wrong with David. The truth seemed unbelievable.

After Dr. Armstrong left, David was the first to speak. "Shit." Alicia was fighting back tears when David continued, "Well, I guess I have to do this." Alicia's anger burst forward again and she exploded. "No, you don't have to do this! You shouldn't have to do this! This is so crazy! This shouldn't be happening! It's not fair!"

David was surprised, to say the least, at Alicia's outburst. "Fair is not the point, darling. I have a tumor, and I have to deal with it." At first, Alicia was furious at David's rationality. Then she saw tears well up in his eyes. Her fury melted away, replaced by an overpowering desire to comfort and hold him. She leaned over and, careful not to disturb his IVs, put her arms around him. They both wept for a while, holding each other and sniffling. When they came apart, Alicia said, "We're going to deal with this together. I'll always be here for you, David. I love you so much."

To some extent, Alicia was dragged kicking and screaming into coping positively with her trauma by David's strength and calm. But she had her own inner strength, fueled by her deep love for David, that allowed her actively to choose how she wanted to think and behave during this crisis. Many people discover strengths in themselves they didn't know they had when faced with unimaginable stress. They become assertive when they would normally be passive; they keep going when everyone expects them to falter.

Later when Alicia went home the angry thoughts surfaced again, but this time she said to herself, "No, that's not where I want to go. I want to focus on David and what I need to do to support him. I won't understand all this and be able to deal with it by being angry. I may never understand this. But I want to be here with David and I can't do that if I'm preoccupied with angry thoughts." That night, Alicia made a list of people she needed to call—David's mother and employer, her employer to let her know she'd be away from work for a while, and some friends they were scheduled to go have dinner with next weekend. She also decided to call her mother, not because she had to, but because she instinctively wanted to. Alicia didn't have a great sleep that night, but she didn't stay awake all night with angry overthinking, either.

Some of the phone calls the next morning were hard. Alicia never really liked David's mother, and dreaded calling her. When Mrs. Jenner answered the phone in her shrill voice, Alicia bristled, remembering the million little criticisms Mrs. Jenner had made in an offhand way of David or Alicia since they had been together. "Oh, it's you," was Mrs. Jenner's reply when Alicia identified herself. "Where's David?" Alicia proceeded, as calmly and matter-of-factly as she could, to tell Mrs. Jenner what was happening. The older woman was nearly speechless, for the first time since Alicia had met her, and it was clear she had begun to cry softly near the end of the conversation. Alicia felt truly sorry for her and promised to pick her up at the airport the next day.

The next person on the list was David's employer, a guy named Bill, whom David always described as money hungry. Bill said he was sorry to hear David was sick, but Alicia felt he was just mouthing platitudes. Bill's real concern then surfaced—how long would David be away and how expensive was this surgery going to be (that is, how much might his insurance premiums for employees go up). Alicia, of course, didn't know the answer to either question and told Bill so.

The next call, to her employer, was better. Madeline was a decent woman who had built her small retail business after her husband had abandoned her and their two preschool children. Alicia didn't feel close to Madeline, but she trusted her, and Madeline lived up to that trust. "Of course, you take some time off. Let me know how things go. When he's out of the hospital, I'll bring over some food."

Alicia had expected the same kind of concern when she called their friends to cancel dinner. Instead, what she got was near silence. Their friend Danny, upon hearing that David had a brain tumor, simply said, "I'm sorry. Here—talk to Barb." Barb got on the phone, unaware of the bombshell Alicia was about to drop, and began chattering about what restaurant they should go to on Saturday. "Barb, we can't go. David's in the hospital. They think he has a brain tumor and they are going to operate tomorrow." Barb could only say, "What?" Alicia repeated the news again and Barb replied, "I don't understand. How can this be true? I thought he just had a car accident. You said he was not hurt that badly in the accident. Are you sure you trust the doctors?" Alicia definitely didn't need to be grilled on the accuracy of her facts, so she made an excuse to hang up on Barb as quickly as possible.

Alicia felt the need to talk with her mother then, and dialed the number. When her mother answered the phone, Alicia instantly let her news spill out and found herself overcome with tears. "Just take a few minutes, baby, and breathe. I'll still be here," was her mother's perfect reply. Alicia sobbed for a while as her mother stayed on the phone and occasionally said, "It's okay, baby, I'm here." When she felt able to talk again, she said, "Mom, how am I going to get through this? I don't know what to do." Her mother replied, "You'll get through this, Alicia, just like I got through your father's death. It's going to be hard, damn hard. But you are strong and your love for David is strong. Hold on to that love and listen to it. You'll know what to do."

Alicia told her mother about the insensitivity of David's boss and her friends. "Some people are jerks, Alicia. I learned that when your father was dying. People don't know how to respond. They have their own agendas. They don't want their orderly lives disturbed. So they say rotten things, unhelpful things, insensitive things. Find the good people,

Alicia, and let them help you and support you. Forget the others. They aren't worth thinking about."

Many people facing the illness or loss of a loved one reach out to others. Alicia was lucky to have a mother who understood what she was going through and could offer such important advice on how to cope. First, Alicia's mother gave her the room to sob and scream and let her emotions flow for a while, then helped calm her by encouraging Alicia to breathe. Her mother also advised Alicia to lower her expectations of others, and to forgive and forget the insensitivities of people who don't know how to respond supportively. This helped Alicia let go of angry overthinking about the reactions of David's boss and some of their friends to the news of David's illness. Finally, Alicia's mother gave her confidence in the instincts and understandings that grew out of her love for David, assuring her that she would know how to deal with whatever happened. Whenever Alicia was overwhelmed with sadness, fear, anger, or confusion, she came back to what her mother had said and recentered herself on her love for David.

Alicia began sobbing again when she got off the phone, but this time it was "relief crying," that letting go of sadness and fear that can make the body feel released and more relaxed. She took a long, warm shower, letting the water run down her back and the soapsuds pool at her feet. She dressed in one of the outfits David liked to see her in, and headed off for the hospital. The day was filled with more tests and their first meeting with the surgeon, Dr. Scanlon, a tall, lanky man with a very firm handshake. He was extremely confident and straightforward, telling them what he would do in the surgery and how David could expect to feel afterward. He also made it clear there was a chance the tumor was malignant, and he couldn't remove it all in the surgery. If that was the case, David would have to undergo chemotherapy in hopes of killing the remaining cancer cells.

When Alicia drove Mrs. Jenner to her hotel that evening, the two of them were silent much of the way. As they pulled up in front of the hotel, Mrs. Jenner turned and said, "You really love him, don't you? I know he loves you. I love him, so very much, as only a mother can. He's going to need our love. Love will pull him through." With that, Mrs. Jenner abruptly opened the door and went quickly into the hotel.

Alicia wasn't entirely sure what Mrs. Jenner meant. Two weeks before, if David's mother had said something as ambiguous to Alicia, it would have sent her into hours of overthinking Mrs. Jenner's meaning and intent. Now it seemed so irrelevant. Alicia was sure the woman was hurting deeply. Alicia was also sure that she wanted to stay focused on supporting David and taking care of herself so she could support him.

The day of the surgery was hell. It went on for eleven hours, with little word as to how it was progressing. Alicia paced and drank Diet Pepsi and jumped up every time someone in green surgery scrubs came through the door. Mrs. Jenner sat motionless and silent, staring at the TV screen in the corner of the waiting room. Finally, Dr. Scanlon came out looking fatigued. Alicia also thought she saw disappointment in his face. His news was not good—in fact, about as bad as it could have been. David's tumor was malignant. It was impinging on the brain stem, a part of the brain that controlled vital functions of the body. They had removed as much as they could, but it was a fast-growing kind of cancer. There would need to be chemotherapy. Nothing was guaranteed. They would do the best they could.

All Alicia could think was:

> Oh no. This can't be true. God please make it not true. Oh, please, please, please, make it not true.

They walked to the ICU, where they saw David lying in the bed, completely ashen, his head wrapped in a bandage, and tubes coming out of him in several places. Mrs. Jenner stopped just inside the door and reached out to take Alicia's hand. The two women stood looking at this man they loved, grateful he had survived the surgery. But both knew instinctively that he was going to die. Neither of them voiced this. But they understood that they shared this knowledge.

As the weeks unfolded, what the tumor and surgery had not done to David's body the chemotherapy did. He was constantly nauseous, couldn't eat, and lost many pounds. Just as he would feel a bit better, it would be time for another dose of chemo, and he would be sick as a dog again. The worst thing was that it didn't seem to be having much of an effect on the remaining cancer. The tests continued to indicate growth of the cancer cells. Finally, the oncologist said the chemo had done as much good as it was going to, and put an end to that misery.

When David's strength returned somewhat, Alicia began to think of what they could do to return life to some degree of normality. There were a million wonderful places in Northern California where Alicia and David had loved to spend time before he became ill—the wine country north of San Francisco, the pier in Santa Cruz, the elephant seal preserve a couple of hours to the south. She decided that, if David wanted to, they would take day trips to revisit their old favorites. These day trips were not filled with the carefree laughter and talk that had characterized their earlier visits to the same places, but they were soothing and uplifting nonetheless. Sometimes David and Alicia talked about his illness, their fears, and the future. Most of the time, they just enjoyed each other's company and the surroundings.

When David became unable to bear these trips physically, they narrowed their focus to the area around their apartment. They spent hours in their favorite coffeehouse, sipping, talking, and watching the local characters walk by. They drove down to the San Francisco piers and watched the ferries go back and forth to Alcatraz. They went out to one of the Italian restaurants in their neighborhood when David felt up to eating.

Alicia and David knew instinctively that putting a little bliss back into their lives with these short outings would help them cope both mentally and physically. Even brief periods of positive emotions can break cycles of overthinking, open your mind, and help you feel stronger to face what is ahead. In contrast, isolating yourself in times of great stress, remaining focused on the unfairness and hopelessness of it all, tears you down. It may even hasten the progression of disease.

Alicia felt the doctors were not doing enough. All they seemed to care about was trying the newest drug that might slow the progress of David's cancer. None of these drugs had accomplished that, however, and most had made him violently ill or weak. Alicia did some research on pain relief at the library and on the Web, and kept coming across references to hospice and palliative care. When she asked Dr. Armstrong about this, he said it wasn't time for hospice yet, that they wanted to try some experimental medications in hopes that they could slow David's cancer. Alicia knew, though, that doctors are often reluctant to bring in hospice because they can't admit that they can't save a patient. David wanted to contact hospice, hoping that he could get some relief from his pain. Alicia was unsure—were they giving up, should they continue to try the experimental medications and hold out hope, what if they didn't like the hospice people? This new crisis triggered fresh overthinking for Alicia:

> This is ultimately David's decision, but should I try to talk him out of it? What does it mean to be turning to hospice? Am I letting go of him by agreeing to let hospice come in? What if the new medicines could have some effect? Shouldn't we try everything?

For the first time since they found out about David's tumor, Alicia and David became tense with each other. David knew what he wanted, but he also knew that it was Alicia who would have to deal with the hospice people much of the time, and he didn't want to impose them on her if she didn't want them. Alicia became mired in indecision as her overthinking confused and upset her.

After a serious argument one morning, Alicia called her mother, crying and slightly hysterical. She voiced the back-and-forth overthinking that had tormented her for the last week and had kept her and David from agreeing to move forward on either the experimental medications or calling in hospice. "Alicia," her mother said firmly, "you'll never know for sure what is the best option. Remember what I said, listen to your love, and it will help you know what to do."

Alicia's mother's advice fits with our research showing that rumination feeds uncertainty, and makes it difficult to "just do something." But moving forward even in the face of uncertainty can be critical to overcoming disabling overthinking.[6]

Alicia was annoyed at her mother's philosophical answer—she wanted a concrete opinion as to which option she and David should choose. As she gave in to her overthinking again, Alicia's thoughts began to question whether she was coping "the right way" with David's illness. Should she be more stoic like Mrs. Jenner? Some of her friends seemed to think she was already too cheerful and together, that she should be more of a chronic wreck given the seriousness of David's condition.

Surely if she was coping better, she would not be so uncertain as to what the next step should be in David's care.

As these thoughts screamed in her head, Alicia began to feel dizzy. Her breathing became shallow, and she could feel her heart beating hard.

> Oh no, I can't have another panic attack! What did they tell me to do? Breathe. In deeply through my nose, out slowly. Count each breath. In deeply, out slowly. It's just stress, there is nothing wrong with my body. In deeply, out slowly.

When she could feel her anxiety subsiding, Alicia knew it was time to break away from her overthinking and clear her head. She grabbed her jacket and set off for a walk in the San Francisco fog. She headed toward the bay, seeking the solace of water. She tried to walk slowly and breathe in the cool, damp air. "I'm not going to deal with my worries for a whole half hour. I'm going to look in shop windows, enjoy the exercise, and see what's going on down by the water. I deserve it." The relief that Alicia felt come over her body was sweet and deep. She languished in her sense of calm and relaxation. When a worried thought came to her, she pushed it aside for the time being and concentrated on whatever she was passing by at the moment. Alicia had broken free of her overthinking with a quick, pleasant, energetic distraction.

When she returned to their apartment an hour or so later, Alicia realized she had come to a decision. She hadn't really thought about the choice she and David were facing while she was walking. But the space she opened up by pushing her overthinking away let her see and hear what she should do. She would tell David that if he wanted to call hospice, she was all for it.

Within a couple days of calling the hospice, David and Alicia were visited by a nurse and a social worker, whom they instantly liked. Both of these health professionals seemed so present with David and Alicia, unlike the hurried nurses and doctors they were accustomed to talking to. They explained what hospice offered: in-home care oriented toward the relief of pain, information on what David could expect to happen as his cancer advanced, advice on legal and financial issues that David and Alicia should consider while he was still able to make decisions, and respite care—relief for Alicia so she could leave David occasionally and get away by herself. It was extremely painful to hear them talk so directly about David's illness and the fact that he was likely to die within a couple of months. But it was also a tremendous relief to have them answer questions straightforwardly.

Although David agreed to try two new experimental drugs, his condition deteriorated rapidly over the next month. He became so weak he couldn't leave the apartment, and his pain was so severe that he had to be on constant pain medication, which made him dopey. Alicia was with him morning and night, keeping a monologue running much of the time. One day, after three weeks of this, the hospice nurse said to her, "Alicia, you've got to take care of yourself also. Taking a couple of hours for yourself doesn't mean you love David any less."

The hospice nurse was wise to push Alicia to take some time for herself, if for no other reason than it would help her remain supportive of David. Many caregivers become so exhausted physically and emotionally that they become ill themselves. Alicia resisted for another day or two, but when she began to feel panic attacks coming on every few hours, she knew she had to get away. When the hospice nurse came again, Alicia drove over the Golden Gate Bridge and parked where she could take a walk along the ocean.

As the sea spray wet her face, she let her tears flow. As her sobs intensified, her old anger came back. "Why is this happening? Why does David have to die? Why can't we have a life together?" She sat on the sand screaming these questions at the waves and at God. Eventually her screams and sobs subsided and she sat numbly looking over the waves. Conversations she had had with lots of people came floating into her head. Most were inane conversations with friends who couldn't understand what she was going through. Then she remembered something a hospice nurse had said one evening: "Alicia, David is so lucky to have you. I can see his body relax and his face brighten a bit, even through the pain medication, when he hears your voice."

Alicia began to replay all the things she and David had done together since he was diagnosed with the cancer, and all the ways she had tried to support him and show her love. She started to feel strong again, and purposeful. She was going through this because David needed her. She didn't know why he had to die—probably there was no "why." But she had been able to make him happy and to make his last months as good as possible. And she had known love that was more profound than she had ever dreamed possible. She felt she had learned a great deal about herself and about life in the last few months. She couldn't really articulate what she had learned yet, but she knew she was much wiser and had a much deeper appreciation of life than was true just a year ago. Alicia began to cry again, but this time softly, not out of anger and fear. Instead, she was actually crying with joy at what she had grown to know and what she had been able to do for David in the last few months.

David died two weeks later, peacefully lying in bed in their apartment. Alicia had known instinctively that he was going to die for months, and in his last few days she knew it was very near. She kept close to him, talking with him when he emerged for a few moments from his grogginess. The pride and strength and peace she had found on the beach stayed with her and grew in those last days.

In our studies of bereavement, and other researchers' studies of traumas in addition to loss, it seems that it doesn't really matter what type of meaning people find in their experience—what's important is that they find some meaning and some way of understanding what has happened to them that allows them to accept it. People who can't find any meaning or understanding tend to stay mired in overthinking about why they experienced such a trauma, why they can't "get over" the trauma, and why they can't seem to relate to other people any longer. Meaning can't be imposed by other people, however. In fact, some of the most bitter comments we've heard from bereaved people are about the attempts of others to tell them how they should feel about their loss: "You should feel happy that she's with God now." "It was all part of a master plan." "He lived a good life, you should be happy he passed away so peacefully." Instead, we need to be supported as we grieve a loss or trauma, and as we muck around trying to find our own idiosyncratic meaning for it.

When Alicia talked to an interviewer in my bereavement project about a month after David's death, she said:

> If you had asked me a couple of years ago whether I could have lived through David's death and come out okay, I would have said no. I didn't think I had that kind of strength. But I learned that I

do. I learned that love gives you superhuman strength. I don't feel invincible now. But I feel as though I can take what life brings me because I've put my expectations aside. I used to think, "I'm young, I've got my whole life ahead of me." Now I know that I could go any day, just as David died young. So I appreciate life so much more than I did, and so much more than I see most of my friends doing. When we realized David was dying we decided to live each day as fully as we could. I'm not going to stop that now. Life means so much more to me now than it did before. And I'm proud of myself. I'm proud of what I've grown into.

The Trauma of Abuse

Every loss or trauma presents unique challenges to the people living through it. There are some events that are extremely difficult to understand in any satisfying way. This seems to be particularly true of manmade traumas or disasters, such as a sexual assault, having someone you love murdered, or being the victim of a terrorist attack. These kinds of traumas are especially potent fuel for overthinking because they violate our basic trust in others and raise questions about the goodness of humanity.

For example, many women who have been sexually assaulted become trapped in chronic overthinking, not only about the details of their assault but about larger questions that the assault raises: Why did this happen to me? Did I do anything to make this happen? How could he have done that to me? When the perpetrator of the abuse is a family member or close friend, the woman has even more questions about how this could have happened, and concerns about how to prevent it from happening again. These are compelling questions and concerns, and they just can't be turned off at will. Remaining mired in this overthinking, however, will only pull the woman's mood and self-esteem down even more. Women who have been sexually assaulted are at high risk for depression, an anxiety disorder called post-traumatic stress disorder, and substance abuse. Overthinking can also keep a woman immobilized when she may need to take action to protect herself.

So how can a woman deal with such a situation? Many women can't deal with it alone—they are too overwhelmed by their memories and fears, and their safety concerns are too real. They may need to seek professional help. Even that is difficult when you are trapped in overthinking, however. Below I offer a list of suggestions how to apply the strategies in this book to break free of overthinking and begin to reclaim your life if you have been sexually abused. Some of these may make more sense than others, given the specifics of your situation. I hope the list will help you generate your own ideas.

• If you just can't let go of thoughts about your sexual assault experience (or experiences), try to keep in mind that overthinking is not giving you insight into these experiences, but clouding your mind about what you should do in response. Also, tell yourself you won't let your abuser win by letting your overthinking overcome your life. Try to step back from questions about why this happened for a while—realize answers to those questions may never come, but if they do, it will take some time for them to come.

• Abuse survivors often feel they will never be able to feel happy again, and as a result withdraw from their usual activities or isolate themselves from others. To regain your equilibrium, it's important to seek out soothing and comforting things to do, which might lift your mood a bit. If "seek your bliss" sounds completely impossible, try seeking a tiny ray of sunshine, perhaps by spending more time outdoors, reestablishing an old hobby, or leaning more on your best friends.

• Sometimes writing out the angry, fearful, and self-blaming overthinking concerns can help put some boundaries around them. Try letting your thoughts flow on paper, on a computer screen, or as you speak into a tape recorder, saying whatever comes to your mind as your overthinking comes up. If you are working with a therapist, you might want to share these recordings with her, so she can get a better idea of your most troubling thoughts.

• If your assault experience is in the past, accept that it's perfectly normal for you to feel the emotional pain of this experience for a long time to come. If you find yourself asking, "Why can't I get over this?" consider answering, "Because this was a huge, traumatic event that it is very hard to recover from." Realize that you don't have to be "over" your experience to begin reclaiming your life. Indeed, you may feel the emotional consequences of this experience for the rest of your life. But these emotions don't have to rule you or overcome you.

• If you are still in an abusive relationship, don't wait to be rescued from it, either by some white knight or because your partner suddenly changes his ways. Only you can make the choice to leave this relationship. Particularly if you fear for your safety or the safety of your children, seek professional help by calling a battered women's shelter, the psychiatric emergency services of your local hospital, a local suicide hotline, or other emergency hotline in your community.

• Let go of the unhealthy goal of getting the perpetrator of a past assault experience to apologize, or getting your currently abusive partner to reform and stop his abuse. Your job is to protect yourself against further abuse and to begin to rebuild your life.

• Recognize other people's voices in your overthinking and reject the unhealthy ones, particularly your perpetrator's claims that the abuse is your fault.

• Work with a therapist, friends, clergy, survivor groups, and anyone else who helps you. Eventually, you will be able to create a new image of yourself as a survivor rather than a victim.

13

Moving Our Society
to Higher Ground

The strategies I've described in this book are intended to help you overcome your personal bouts of overthinking. As a society, however, we can fight against the forces that propel many women into overthinking. We can't legislate away many of the sources of fretting, but we can make choices, as individuals and as a collective, that reduce their influence.

Change the Historical Tide

If our elders are less prone to overthink than we are, we have a lot to learn from them. They have a wisdom that comes from handling the many crises they have faced in their lives. Their wisdom can provide answers to the questions we fret about. The evidence that older people don't ruminate much suggests that they understand how to cope with adversity, overcome obstacles, build relationships, and deal with loss. Learning how they cope can give us insights on the deficits in our own coping abilities and ideas for new strategies for coping.

Our culture, however, worships youth rather than revering our older members. As a result, not only do we ignore the lessons that our elders can teach us, we create role models from people too young and immature to be wise. This may be one reason we live in a vacuum of values. If the movie and sports stars we worship have the value system of a spoiled adolescent, the messages we take from them will not help to build a solid philosophical or spiritual base for our lives.

Worshiping youth also creates standards for our physical appearance and fitness that may simply be impossible for us to attain any longer. Thus we ruminate about how old we look, how weak we are, and the inevitable health problems that come with age.

We can reverse our role models, however, with our conscious daily choices. As consumers, we can tune in to TV shows and buy books that celebrate older people as much or more than we purchase media that glorifies youth. We can seek to attain fitness levels that are appropriate for our age, and demand that the fitness industry help us do so, rather than torturing ourselves trying to become twenty again.

On the personal level, we can pay attention to our elders, and listen to what they have to teach us. Sometimes it is difficult to see and hear their wisdom. When we look to a grandparent or other elderly person, all we may see is disability and decline. We may try either to fix their problems or avert our eyes because we can't bear to look at them. This keeps us from seeing the rich, fascinating lives that many of them led, and which they would love to tell us about. But if we can just listen long enough to our elders, we will learn about courage and persistence, about living a principled life, about love and loss.

Not all elders are wise, of course. Some are ruminators and have a sour perspective on life. But we can find wise elders in our community, in biographies and personal accounts, and in historical writings. For example, Danielle, a forty-five-year-old professor of biology at a small liberal arts college, sometimes felt that she would never be a nationally recognized researcher in her field, as she had hoped when she finished graduate school. Her teaching load was heavy, so she wasn't as productive in research as she wanted to be. Her experiments never seemed to be good enough to be published in the top journals. Danielle's parents had been blue-collar workers and didn't really understand why Danielle was dissatisfied with her career—they thought it was fantastic that Danielle had an advanced degree and was a professor in a college, regardless of whether or not she was famous. Danielle's ruminations about her career were finally quashed when her husband gave her a book by Richard

Feynman, the Nobel Prize–winning scientist. During his life, Feynman focused on the "pleasure in finding things out," rather than the acclaim of others for his discoveries. Danielle was inspired by Feynman to adjust her focus to the deep joy she felt when she realized something new or made something work in her research, and to the gratification she got from teaching biology to students. So even though Danielle did not feel her own parents were much help in addressing her ruminations, she found a new perspective through the writings of another elder.

Fill the Vacuum of Values

Many of us who live with a vacuum of values frantically search for principles, ideas, how-to tips that can help us feel more whole. We allow ourselves to be constantly bombarded with information from multiple sources—the popular media, the Internet, the press, politicians, our friends, our family, our coworkers. These sources give us all kinds of subtle and not-so-subtle suggestions about how we should behave, how we should think, whom we should admire, what objectives we should strive for. It is difficult to hear that quiet, calm voice of our own deeply held beliefs amid this din. Yet if we do not begin listening to that voice we will not be able to reject the destructive messages imposed by others.

So how do we turn down the volume? We must spend more time quietly alone. But when we are working full-time, perhaps ten or twelve hours a day, managing a family and a social life, trying to keep up our education and technical skills, getting some exercise in, and on and on, there can be no room left to be quiet and alone. Our culture also rewards multitasking—reading the *Wall Street Journal* while you run on the treadmill, answering your e-mails while you're driving on the highway, helping your kids with their homework while you're also making dinner. Thus even when we try to be quiet and alone, we are tempted to fill that space with another activity as well, to make it even more productive. I once knew a pastor who said he had decided to set aside thirty minutes to meditate and pray each morning, but then thought he could get his morning jog in at the same time. After about a week, he realized he wasn't doing a good job of jogging or praying.

It takes dedication to carve out a time and protect it from all distractions so that we can listen to our voice. Many of us have lost touch with the ability to get quiet, so it can take a great deal of practice and discipline to regain that ability. Most people find they reap tremendous benefits from a regular practice of getting quiet and meditating, praying, or just listening. They feel more peaceful and calm. They feel more grounded in beliefs they are willing to uphold with their actions.

Of course, some people just find themselves overthinking when they sit down for some quiet time. The strategies described in this book for personal control of overthinking can help. For example, you may yell "Stop!" to yourself when you are sliding into overthinking. Some people find handing over their worries to prayer moves them onto higher ground. If they simply can't get hold of their negative thoughts, they may need to concede for the moment and find something active to do to break the grip of their thoughts.

We need to spend more time quiet and alone as families as well. We're constantly racing with our children from one activity to another—ball games, practices, recitals, parties. Many families seldom have dinner together at home or spend a weekend day just being together rather than in some organized activity. Yet, one of the best predictors of children's successful emotional development is spending regular quiet time with their families at evening meals and in other rituals that provide them the time and space to connect with one another for more than a moment. Parents need this time to really listen to their children and understand what is happening in their lives. And children need this time to communicate with their parents and feel a part of a cohesive family.

We cannot, as a society, choose leaders who represent our best values if we do not, as individuals, spend the necessary quiet time discovering and refining these values. Otherwise, we end up either letting other people make choices for us or going with the candidate who has the best ad campaign. We have an obligation not only to ourselves but to current and future generations to connect with our values and make choices as a citizen that reflect these values. Again, this takes time and turning down the volume.

Get Outside Yourself

Although we need to connect more with our deeply held values, our tendency to peer at our belly buttons suggests we also need to spend more time outside ourselves, appreciating other people's perspectives. Providing service to others, particularly those less fortunate than ourselves, can be especially helpful in this process. So much of what we ruminate about—our weight, our boss's grumpiness, a dumb remark we made—withers in comparison to the needs and problems of other people. Spending time coaching, counseling, and giving love and support to people in need can give us a more realistic outlook on how unimportant some of our ruminations are, helping to lift our eyes up to our vital life goals. By joining a social service association, an environmental rights organization, or a political activism group, by getting involved with a group of people who are committed to some of the same fundamental things you care about most in this world, you can give your life a focus beyond the banal events of the day and the "he said, she said, how could I have said that?" ruminations that can drag us down.

Often our navel gazing and sense of entitlement are reinforced by our friends, who are champion navel gazers themselves. You don't want friends who deny their own problems and your concerns, but you also don't need friends who pull you down into overthinking by being chronically critical, anxious, or complaining. You may need to seek out new friends who approach life as a challenge rather than a burden, and who evoke your strengths rather than drain your energy.

Where do you find such friends? You may find them in volunteer organizations that serve causes that are important to you. Sometimes just radiating your own positivity will draw positivity out of friends, and attract new people who are also looking for positive friends. For example, Rosanna casually announced at the weekly staff meeting in her law office that she had decided to replace every complaint she would normally make during the staff meeting with a constructive suggestion for improvement in the workplace. At first, her coworkers were taken aback when Rosanna responded to their complaints not with her own renditions of what was wrong but with an idea for a solution to the problem that had just been aired. Within a couple of weeks, the entire atmosphere of the staff meetings had changed from one of chronic negativity to one of positive change.

Think how powerful a change could take place across our society if each of us could, like Rosanna, shift from navel-gazing negativity to an attitude of positivity and constructiveness. Positive emotions broaden our perspective and make us more creative, so an increase in our own positive emotions will make us much more effective as individuals and as a culture.

Rise above Entitlement

The poisonous entitlement values of our society—the beliefs that we deserve whatever we want and that other people can't be allowed to get the best of us—are a major source of overthinking. Again, there are many choices we can make as consumers to reject these entitlement values. For example, turn off the TV shows that feed these values by featuring people who are fighting for them—the "people's court" and talk shows that glorify silly confrontations between people in conflict.

As individuals, we can also choose to live and proclaim attitudes that contradict entitlement values. Instead of always focusing on what we deserve in a situation, we can focus on how the situation can be resolved to everyone's benefit. This has obvious applications on the job, and many business leaders advocate taking a "win-win" approach to business negotiations and conflicts.

As parents, we often fixate on winning in arguments with our children. Entitlement values encourage us to focus on getting the respect we deserve as parents. This just leads to impasses, however, or to our children giving in but silently resenting our pigheadedness. If we can put aside our need to win the position we deserve and concentrate on helping our children understand our perspective—and listening to theirs—we can build our relationships with our children and have a mutually satisfying conclusion to the conflict. As a result, neither we nor our children will have as much to overthink and our children will learn important communication skills that help them build a less ruminative society.

If other people get more than we do, or win in a conflict with us, the entitlement values tell us to "sue the bastards!" or otherwise take retribution. Sometimes that will be the appropriate response, but often we are trying to protect our self-esteem. We can actively counteract the entitlement values by refusing to allow our social win-loss record to influence our self-worth.

Harriet, for example, was arguing in a school board meeting against the adoption of a new math curriculum at her daughter's elementary school. She felt strongly that it was a faddish program that had not been well tested, and she presented evidence to support her view. Eleanor, however, argued vehemently for the new math curriculum, describing its success in other schools. In the end, the school board voted to adopt the new curriculum. Eleanor strutted around after the meeting looking triumphant. One of the other mothers approached Harriet to express her condolences at the loss. Harriet simply sighed, and said, "I hope Eleanor is right and this new curriculum is a success. If it is, the children will benefit. If it isn't, we'll revisit this decision next year." Harriet rejected the idea that her loss to Eleanor meant anything about her worth as a person, tried to be as gracious as possible, but stood by her belief that the math program should not have been adopted. As a result, she lifted the entire situation above the morass of entitlement values and proved she was better than those values.

In addition to modeling an anti-entitlement attitude in our own lives, we can insist that our children and even our leaders rise above these negative forces. When we hear them resorting to an us-against-them attitude, claiming special privileges they do not need, blaming other people for their troubles, we can challenge them to take personal responsibility. With our children, this can require putting aside our own desires that they be "first" in everything. With our leaders, it can mean rejecting the seductive arguments that our society or group deserves more than others. Only then will our children, and our fellow citizens, put their minds to solving problems and overcoming obstacles rather than overthinking what they deserve.

Reinforce Long-Term Perspectives

To combat our penchant for quick fixes, we can focus more on a long-term perspective on our important goals. I have encouraged you to do this as an individual, to "raise your sights," as a way of overcoming personal overthinking. As a collective, we can demand that our leaders devise programs that fix community problems for the long term rather than providing a short-term fix that will only last to the next election day. As consumers, we can learn to recognize when a quick fix is being offered—a quick profit in the stock market that reinforces short-term corporate thinking, a fast-acting pill that will make us feel better for a while but will not overcome our problems—and reject these solutions in favor of ones that may take longer to implement but will endure.

With our children, we can teach the value of building skills and strengths for the long term rather than reinforcing a quick-fix approach to problems. For example, rather than giving in and providing them with the answers to their difficult homework problems just to get the paperwork done, we can insist they build their skills by doing the homework themselves, while providing them with encouragement and an appropriate level of help. Or rather than jumping in and solving a conflict between two of our children, we can help them communicate better with each other and come to their own solution.

It's easy to accept quick fixes for our children when we're too busy to help them build for the long term. If they are constantly getting messages from us, however, that shortcuts are okay, they can generalize that message in horrible ways—cheating to get good grades; popping pills to be better athletes, more alert students, or to feel better about themselves; having sex to win boyfriends or girlfriends. Taking the time to help your children build for the long term, and teaching them to reject the multitude of quick fixes they are offered to cope with growing up, is a core task of parenting. If our children can put aside quick fixes for a long-range perspective, they will make better decisions for their lives and as citizens, and will take setbacks more in stride. This will give them much less to overthink as they pass through life.

Give Women Less to Overthink

It seems pretty obvious that one way to help women overthink less is to give them less to overthink—fewer chronic strains in their daily lives, such as inadequate pay or spouses who don't respect what they do, and fewer traumatic events such as sexual assault. Of course, this is what the feminist movement has been fighting for over the last several decades. Does the fact that women are still impoverished, compared to men, are disrespected in their relationships, and are the frequent victims of assault mean that the women's movement has failed? I do not believe so. Tremendous gains have been made in women's rights to equal pay, equity in relationships, and against violence toward women. We have a long way to go, however.

As citizens, we can fight against the forces still keeping women down by choosing progressive leaders, advocating for legislation against sex discrimination, supporting domestic violence shelters, proclaiming a "zero tolerance" attitude toward violence against women, and getting behind dozens of other initiatives designed to overcome the negative social conditions women face. In their personal lives, women can refuse to accept second-class citizenship in their marriages and partnerships, in their workplace, and in other domains of life.

This means rocking the boat in our personal lives, and that can be hard. If our male partner is violent, it can be dangerous. In such cases, the only solution may be to exit the relationship, perhaps with the help of others (see chapter 12 for ideas on how to overcome overthinking a violent relationship and escape it).

Even if your male partner is not violent, he may resist changes in your pattern of relating to each other, particularly if this pattern favors him. It can be helpful to keep in mind that insisting that your relationship become more equitable—that he respect your work, your preferences, and who you are, and that he carry his load of work at home—will not only improve your quality of life but will send critical messages to your daughters and sons about how to relate to the opposite sex.

Joining forces with other women who are trying to make changes in their own lives and in our culture can also be helpful. It can provide an outlet for sharing and a source of support. It can provide resources to help effect changes in your personal life. For example, you may learn from other women how to get the job training you need to move out of a dead-end pink-collar job. Groups of women working together can be an unstoppable source of positive change in society.

Change Women's Self-Definitions

It's not just outside forces that keep women stuck in overthinking. Women's self-definition as the emotional caregivers to everyone in their lives sets them up for vigilance and worry and despair. This self-definition has to change for overthinking to be eradicated. It can be difficult for an individual woman to recognize this in herself. Women can see it in each other, though.

Carrie was one of those emotional workhorses who was always taking care of other people's problems. At work, if an extra report needed to be written, everyone turned to Carrie to do it, if she hadn't already volunteered. If a coworker needed a shoulder to cry on, Carrie's was always available. If there was a conflict between people, Carrie spent hours trying to smooth it out. Everyone loved Carrie, but she was emotionally and physically exhausted by being the supreme caregiver. One day, after Carrie agreed to give a presentation that no one in her company wanted to give, her friend Laura burst into her office and started yelling, "Will you stop it? Why did you volunteer to give that presentation? You know that's Ted's responsibility! Why did you rescue him again? You're wrecking your health doing everyone's job! And Ted turns to the other women in our group expecting we will do his work for him as well!" Carrie was stunned. She never realized how much her excessive caregiving was affecting the other women in her group as well as her own well-being.

Fostering relationships with other women—either in friendships or as part of social action groups—can give us a perspective on ourselves that helps us to realize the negative self-definitions that are feeding our overthinking. As part of a group, we can also help to educate women and girls about achieving a balance between taking care of others and taking care of ourselves.

Encourage Our Daughters
and Each Other to Cope

We are great at nurturing our daughters' emotional sides. We pay attention to their feelings and encourage their expression. We empathize
with their concerns. We are not so great at nurturing our daughters'
skills at active coping. They need to learn to move from expression of
their feelings and concerns to solving the problems that brought about
their worries. We can help them by teaching the strategies described in
this book and by living those strategies in our own lives.

We can also encourage our sisters and women friends to move from
overthinking to action. We can empathize with their concerns and give
them the emotional support they seek. We do not need to be an "uh-
huh" friend, however. Instead, we can help them pull out of overthinking by suggesting some of the strategies described here, and help them
think through possible solutions to their problems. Then they may be in
the position to do the same for us in the future!

There are many pathways into overthinking, but many pathways out
as well. We can overcome our tendency to get stuck in overthinking and
build more satisfying and successful lives. We'll be better as individuals
and as a society, if we do.

NOTES

1: *What's Wrong with Overthinking?*

1. S. Nolen-Hoeksema, "Gender Differences in Depression," in *Handbook of Depression*, ed. I. Gotlib and C. Hammen (New York: Guilford, 2002).

2. S. Nolen-Hoeksema and J. Morrow, "A Prospective Study of Depression and Post-Traumatic Stress Symptoms Following a Natural Disaster: The 1989 Loma Prieta Earthquake," *Journal of Personality and Social Psychology* 61 (1991): 115–21.

3. S. Nolen-Hoeksema and J. Larson, *Coping with Loss* (Mahwah, N.J.: Erlbaum, 1999).

4. S. Nolen Hoeksema and C. G. Davis, "Thanks for Sharing That: Ruminators and Their Social Support Networks," *Journal of Personality and Social Psychology* 77 (1999): 801–14.

5. Nolen-Hoeksema and Larson (1999), p. 87.

6. Details of this study can be found in S. Nolen Hoeksema, J. Larson, and C. Grayson, "Explaining the Gender Differences in Depressive Symptoms," *Journal of Personality and Social Psychology* 77 (1999): 1061–72.
You might conclude that women are just more willing to admit to overthinking than men, because it is less stigmatizing for women to do so. A study I conducted with Lisa Butler, who was a Stanford graduate student at the time, gave us more confidence that women were not just more willing to admit to overthinking than men. We asked a group of 54 women and men who did not suffer from depression or any other psychological malady—they were just average people who volunteered for a psychology experiment—to read an extremely sad story while sad music was playing in the background. We knew from previous work that this was an effective way of putting people into a temporarily sad mood, and indeed it worked in this study as well. The participants rated themselves as much more sad, blue, or depressed after reading the story than they had been when they walked into our laboratory.

We then gave these people the choice of doing two different tasks, explaining that we only had time left for them to do one of the tasks. Actually, we were interested in which task they would choose to do, given that they were in such a sad mood. One of the tasks was essentially an overthinking task—in it people focused on how they were feeling and how their lives were going. The other task had little to do with overthinking—it had people sort the countries of the world by geographic location. We described the two tasks to the study participants and then observed which task they chose. Ninety-two percent of the women who were in a sad mood chose to do the overthinking task, while only 8 percent chose to avoid overthinking on their sadness. In contrast, less than half of the men in a sad mood (46 percent) chose to do the overthinking task, and the majority of the sad men chose to avoid brooding by doing the other task. The results of this study gave us much more confidence that women actually do focus more on their moods and lives when they are down and depressed than do men. Details of this study can be found in L. D. Butler and S. Nolen-Hoeksema, "Gender Differences in Response to Depressed Mood in a College Sample," *Sex Roles* 30 (1994): 331–46.

7. S. Nolen-Hoeksema and J. Morrow, "Effects of Rumination and Distraction on Naturally Occurring Depressed Mood," *Cognition and Emotion* 7 (1993): 561–70.

8. S. Lyubomirsky, N. D. Caldwell, and S. Nolen-Hoeksema, "Effects of Ruminative and Distracting Responses to Depressed Mood on Retrieval of Autobiographical Memories," *Journal of Personality and Social Psychology* 75 (1998): 166–77.

9. S. Lyubomirsky and S. Nolen-Hoeksema, "Effects of Self-Focused Rumination on Negative Thinking and Interpersonal Problem Solving," *Journal of Personality and Social Psychology* 69 (1995): 176–90.

10. Ibid. See also S. Lyubomirsky, K. Tucker, N. D. Caldwell, and K. Berg, "Why Ruminators Are Poor Problem Solvers: Clues from the Phenomenology of Dysphoric Rumination," *Journal of Personality and Social Psychology* 77 (1999): 1951–60.

11. Lyubomirsky and Nolen-Hoeksema (1995).

12. Lyubomirsky et al. (1999).

13. A. Ward, S. Lyubomirsky, L. Sousa, and S. Nolen-Hoeksema, "Can't Quite Commit: Rumination and Uncertainty," *Personality and Social Psychology Bulletin*, in press.

14. S. Lyubomirsky and S. Nolen-Hoeksema, "Self-Perpetuating Properties of Dysphoric Rumination," *Journal of Personality and Social Psychology* 65 (1993): 339–49.

15. C. Rusting and S. Nolen-Hoeksema, "Regulating Responses to Anger: Effects of Rumination and Distraction on Angry Mood," *Journal of Personality and Social Psychology* 74 (1998): 790–803.

2. If It Hurts So Much, Why Do We Do It?

1. G. H. Bower, "Mood and Memory," *American Psychologist* 36 (1981): 129–48.

2. J. Miranda and J. B. Persons, "Dysfunctional Attitudes Are Mood State Dependent," *Journal of Abnormal Psychology* 97 (1988): 76–79.

3. R. J. Davidson, "Affective Style, Psychopathology, and Resilience: Brain Mechanisms and Plasticity," *American Psychologist* 55 (2000): 1196–214.

4. G. L. Klerman and M. M. Weissman, "Increasing Rates of Depression," *Journal of the American Medical Association* 261 (1989): 2229–35.

5. S. Nolen-Hoeksema, "Gender Differences in Coping with Depression Across the Life Span," *Depression* 3 (1995): 81–90.

6. S. Nolen-Hoeksema and Z. A. Harrell, "Rumination, Depression, and Alcohol Use: Tests of Gender Differences," *Journal of Cognitive Psychotherapy: An International Quarterly*, in press.

7. C. M. Steele and R. A. Josephs, "Alcohol Myopia: Its Prized and Dangerous Effects," in *Readings in Social Psychology: The Art and Science of Research*, ed. S. Fein (Boston: Houghton Mifflin, 1996), 74–89.

8. N. Schwarz, "Feelings as Information: Implications of Affective Influences on Information Processing," in *Theories of Mood and Cognition: A User's Guidebook*, ed. L. L. Martin (Mahwah, N.J.: Erlbaum, 2001), 159–76.

3. Women's Unique Vulnerabilities

1. For a detailed review of the literature on gender differences in depression and rumination, see S. Nolen-Hoeksema, "Gender Differences in Depression," in *Handbook of Depression*, ed. I. Gotlib and C. Hammen (New York: Guilford, 2002).

2. N. Barko, "The Other Gender Gap," *The American Prospect*, 19 June–3 July 2000, 61–63.

3. S. Nolen-Hoeksema, unpublished data, University of Michigan, 2002.

4. S. Nolen-Hoeksema, J. Larson, and C. Grayson, "Explaining the Gender Difference in Depressive Symptoms," *Journal of Personality and Social Psychology* 77 (1999): 1061–72.

5. F. J. Crosby, *Relative Deprivation and Working Women* (London: Oxford University Press, 1982).

6. M. P. Koss and D. G. Kilpatrick, "Rape and Sexual Assault," in *The Mental Health Consequences of Torture*, ed. E. Gerrity (New York: Kluwer Academic/Plenum Publishers, 2001), 177–93.

7. S. Nolen Hoeksema, "Contributors to the Gender Difference in Rumination," paper presented to the annual meeting of the American Psychological Association, San Francisco, August 1998.

8. D. Belle and J. Doucet, "Poverty, Inequality, and Discrimination as Sources of Depression among Women," *Psychology of Women Quarterly*, in press.

9. Nolen-Hoeksema, "Contributors to the Gender Difference in Rumination."

10. A. Feingold, "Gender Differences in Personality: A Meta-Analysis," *Psychological Bulletin* 116 (1994): 429–56.

11. R. C. Kessler and J. D. McLeod, "Sex Differences in Vulnerability to Undesirable Life Events," *American Sociological Review* (1984): 620–31.

12. V. Helgeson, "Relation of Agency and Communion to Well-Being: Evidence and Potential Explanations," *Psychological Bulletin* (1994): 412–28.

13. S. Nolen-Hoeksema and B. Jackson, "Mediators of the Gender Difference in Rumination," *Psychology of Women Quarterly* (2001): 37–47.

14. L. Feldman Barrett, R. D. Lane, L. Sechrest, and G. E. Schwartz, "Sex Differences in Emotional Awareness," *Personality and Social Psychology Bulletin* 26 (2000): 1027–35.

15. W. Pollack, *Real Boys: Rescuing Our Sons from the Myths of Boyhood* (New York: Random House, 1998).

16. J. Dunn, I. Bretherton, and P. Munn, "Conversations about Feeling States between Mothers and Their Young Children." *Developmental Psychology* (1987): 132–39; E. E. Maccoby and C. N. Jacklin, *The Psychology of Sex Differences* (Stanford, Calif.: Stanford University Press, 1974).

17. Nolen-Hoeksema and Jackson, "Mediators of the Gender Difference in Rumination."

4. Breaking Free

1. S. Lyubomirsky and S. Nolen-Hoeksema, "Self-Perpetuating Properties of Dysphoric Rumination," *Journal of Personality and Social Psychology* 65 (1993): 339–49.

2. S. Nolen-Hoeksema and J. Morrow, "Effects of Rumination and Distraction on Naturally Occurring Depressed Mood," *Cognition and Emotion* 7 (1993): 561–70.

3. J. Morrow and S. Nolen-Hoeksema, "The Effects of Response Styles for Depression on the Remediation of Depressive Affect," *Journal of Personality and Social Psychology* 58 (1990): 519–27.

4. S. Nolen-Hoeksema, unpublished data, University of Michigan, 2002.

5. G. A. Marlatt and J. Kristeller, "Mindfulness and Mediation," in *Integrating Spirituality in Treatment*, ed. W. R. Miller (Washington, D.C.: American Psychological Association Books, 1999).

6. Z. V. Segal, J. M. G. Williams, and J. Teasdale, *Mindfulness-Based Cognitive Therapy for Depression: A New Approach to Preventing Relapse* (New York: Guilford, 2002).

7. J. Kabat-Zinn, *Full Catastrophe Living: Using the Wisdom of Your Body and Mind to Face Stress, Pain, and Illness* (New York: Delacorte Press, 1990).

8. Nolen-Hoeksema, unpublished data, 2002.

9. J. W. Pennebaker, *Opening Up: The Healing Power of Confiding in Others* (New York: Morrow Books, 1990).

10. S. Folkman and J. T. Moskowitz, "Stress, Positive Emotion, and Coping," *Current Directions in Psychological Science* 9 (2000): 115–18.

11. B. L. Fredrickson, "What Good Are Positive Emotions?" *Review of General Psychology* 2 (1998): 300–19.

12. D. D. Danner, D. A. Snowdon, and W. V. Friesen, "Positive Emotions in Early Life and Longevity: Findings from the Nun Study," *Journal of Personality and Social Psychology* 80 (1998): 804–13.

5. Moving to Higher Ground

1. S. Lyubomirsky, "Why Are Some People Happier than Others?: The Role of Cognitive and Motivational Processes in Well-Being," *American Psychologist* 56 (2001): 239–49.

2. A. J. Stewart and E. A. Vandewater, "The Course of Generativity," in *Generativity and Adult Development*, ed. D. P. McAdams and E. de St. Aubin (Washington, D.C.: American Psychological Association Books, 1998); D. P. McAdams, H. M. Hart,

and S. Maruna, "The Anatomy of Generativity," in *Generativity and Adult Development*, ed. D. P. McAdams and E. de St. Aubin (Washington, D.C.: American Psychological Association Books, 1998).

3. A. Ward, S. Lyubomirsky, L. Sousa, and S. Nolen-Hoeksema, "Can't Quite Commit: Rumination and Uncertainty," *Personality and Social Psychology Bulletin*, in press.

4. M. E. McCullough, "Forgiveness as Human Strength: Theory, Measurement, and Links to Well-Being," *Journal of Social and Clinical Psychology* 19 (2000) 43–55; M. E. McCullough, "Forgiveness: Who Does It and How Do They Do It?" *Current Directions in Psychological Science* 10 (2001): 194–97.

5. C. vanOyen Witvliet, T. E. Ludwig, and K. L. Vander Laan, "Granting Forgiveness or Harboring Grudges: Implications for Emotion, Physiology, and Health," *Psychological Science* 12 (2001): 117–23.

6. C. E. Thoresen, F. Luskin, and A. H. S. Harris, "Science and Forgiveness Interventions: Reflections and Recommendations," in *Dimensions of Forgiveness*, ed. E. L. Worthington, Jr. (Philadelphia: Templeton Foundation Press, 1998).

7. D. Burns, *Feeling Good: The New Mood Therapy* (New York: Morrow, 1980).

6. Avoiding Future Traps

1. See C. S. Carver and M. F. Scheier, *Attention and Self-Regulation: A Control-Theory Approach to Human Behavior* (New York: Springer, 1981); or R. S. Wyer, Jr., ed., *Advances in Social Cognition* (Hillsdale, N.J.: Erlbaum 1981).

2. J. Crocker and C. T. Wolfe, "Contingencies of Self-Worth," *Psychological Review* 108 (2001): 593–623.

3. P. B. Baltes and M. M. Baltes, *Successful Aging: Perspectives from the Behavioral Sciences* (New York: Cambridge University Press, 1990).

4. C. S. Dweck and E. L. Leggett, "A Social-Cognitive Approach to Motivation and Personality," in *Motivational Science: Social and Personality Perspectives*, ed. E. T. Higgins (Philadelphia: Taylor & Francis, 2000).

5. C. G. Davis, S. Nolen-Hoeksema, and J. Larson, "Making Sense of Loss and Growing from the Experience: Two Construals of Meaning," *Journal of Personality and Social Psychology* 75 (1998): 561–74.

6. J. Frank, *Persuasion and Healing: A Comparative Study of Psychotherapy* (Baltimore: The Johns Hopkins University Press, 1973).

7. Married to My Worries: Overthinking Intimate Relationships

1. T. Joiner and J. C. Coyne, *The Interactional Nature of Depression: Advances in Interpersonal Approaches* (Washington, D.C.: American Psychological Association Press, 1999).

2. J. M. Gottman and R. W. Levenson, "The Social Psychophysiology of Marriage," in *Perspectives on Marital Interaction*, ed. P. Noller (Clevedon, England: Multilingual Matters, Ltd., 1988).

8. Family Matters: Overthinking Our Parents and Siblings

1. S. Nolen-Hoeksema and J. Larson, *Coping with Loss* (Mahwah, N.J.: Erlbaum, 1999).

9. The Parent Trap: Overthinking and Our Children

1. S. Nolen-Hoeksema, unpublished data, University of Michigan, 2002.

10. Always on the Job: Overthinking Work and Careers

1. T. A. Roberts and S. Nolen-Hoeksema, "Gender Differences in Responding to Others' Evaluations in Achievement Settings," *Psychology of Women Quarterly* 18 (1994): 221–40.
2. S. Nolen-Hoeksema, unpublished data, University of Michigan, 2002.

11. Toxic Thoughts: Overthinking Health Problems

1. S. Lyubomirsky, F. Kasri, and O. Chang, "Ruminative Style and Delay of Presentation of Breast Cancer Symptoms," manuscript in preparation, Department of Psychology, University of California, Riverside, 2001.
2. S. Nolen-Hoeksema and J. Larson, *Coping with Loss* (Mahwah, N.J.: Erlbaum, 1999).
3. S. E. Taylor, M. E. Kemeny, G. M. Reed, J. E. Bower, and T. L. Gruenewald, "Psychological Resources, Positive Illusions, and Health," *American Psychologist* 55 (2000): 99–109.

12. Can't Get Over It: Overthinking Loss and Trauma

1. S. E. Taylor and J. D. Brown, "Illusion and Well-Being: A Social Psychological Perspective on Mental Health," *Psychological Bulletin* 103 (1988): 193–210.
2. M. J. Lerner, *The Belief in a Just World: A Fundamental Delusion* (New York: Plenum Press, 1980).
3. S. Nolen-Hoeksema and J. Larson, *Coping with Loss* (Mahwah, N.J.: Erlbaum, 1999).
4. C. G. Davis, S. Nolen-Hoeksema, and J. Larson, "Making Sense of Loss and Growing from the Experience: Two Construals of Meaning," *Journal of Personality and Social Psychology* 75 (1998): 561–74.
5. C. G. Davis and S. Nolen-Hoeksema, "Loss and Meaning: How Do People Make Sense of Loss?" *American Behavioral Scientist* 46 (2001): 726–41.
6. A. Ward, S. Lyubomirsky, L. Sousa, and S. Nolen-Hoeksema, "Can't Quite Commit: Rumination and Uncertainty," *Personality and Social Psychology Bulletin*, in press.

RESOURCES

Many good sources of information on mental health are available in books and on the Web. Below I've listed some of my favorites.

Books

David Burns wrote the first edition of *Feeling Good: The New Mood Therapy* in 1980, but it is still one of the most respected self-help books available, particularly in its updated 1999 version. Burns describes how you can counteract negative thinking using the techniques of cognitive-behavioral therapy, which has become one of the most widely used and best-validated psychotherapies for depression and anxiety.

Another good self-help book based on cognitive-behavioral therapy is *Mind Over Mood* (1995) by Dennis Greenberger and Christine Padesky. Edward Hallowell's book *Worry: Controlling It and Using It Wisely* (1998) has many useful tips for overcoming worry.

Kay Redfield Jamison has written two wonderful books about her own battles with depression and mania: *An Unquiet Mind: A Memoir of Moods and Madness* (1995) and *Night Falls Fast: Understanding Suicide* (1999). Jamison's books are terrific not only because she is a good writer, but because she is a researcher of mood disorders and communicates this research clearly to lay audiences.

Andrew Solomon's memoir of his journey through chronic, severe depression, *The Noonday Demon: An Atlas of Depression* (2001), chronicles the medical world's various answers to his depression with an eloquence that has made this a bestseller.

World Wide Web Resources

If you feel you need to consult a psychologist or psychiatrist but don't know how to find one, there are several Web sites that will help you locate counselors. These include the Web sites for the American Psychological Association (www.apa.org), the American Psychiatric Association (www.psych.org), and the Association for the Advancement of Behavior Therapy (www.aabt.org). Each of these Web sites also has information about depression, anxiety, and other mental health issues.

The National Institute of Mental Health is the primary source of funding for research on depression, anxiety, and other mental health problems in the United States. The Web site for the NIMH, www.nimh.nih.gov, is loaded with information on mental health, including fact sheets and resources for professionals.

The National Depressive and Manic Depressive Association, at www.ndmda.org, provides basic information about depression, resources for people with mood disorders and for their families, and offers advocacy activities on behalf of people with mood disorders. Log on to find the NDMDA peer-run support group for people with mood disorders in your area.

Each year there is a nationwide National Depression Screening Day designed to call attention to depression and bipolar disorder, educate the public, and provide free screening and referrals for depression for the public. To find out more about this year's screening day, go to www.mentalhealthscreening.org/depression.htm.

The Anxiety Disorders Association of America provides a great deal of information on anxiety disorders and resources for seeking help at their Web site, www.adaa.org.

The National Center for Post-Traumatic Stress Disorder is a consortium of research institutions and clinical care facilities dedicated to research and treatment for post-traumatic stress disorder. To find information on its activities and training programs, go to www.ncptsd.org.

At www.mentalhealth.org/suicideprevention/ you can learn about the efforts of the National Strategy for Suicide Prevention, a collaboration among several branches of the U.S. government to prevent suicide. This site provides a lot of information about suicide, a hotline number for people contemplating suicide (1-800-SUICIDE), and more information for friends and family members of people who attempt suicide.

ACKNOWLEDGMENTS

This book is based on a large body of research I have conducted in collaboration with several wonderful scholars, and I want to thank them for their colleagueship: Sonja Lyubomirsky, Judith Larson, Andrew Ward, Jannay Morrow, Joan Girgus, Cheryl Rusting, Sheena Sethi, Christopher Davis, Wendy Treynor, Richard Gonzalez, Zaje Harrell, Barbara Fredrickson, and Tomi-Ann Roberts.

Todd Shuster, my literary agent, encouraged me to move my research out into the general public and was instrumental in providing me with an opportunity to do this. Deborah Brody at Holt shepherded and shaped this project to its completion. My sincere thanks to Todd and Deborah—it has been a delight working with you!

Finally, thank you to my family, who continually offer unconditional love support—Richard, Michael, Catherine, John, Marjorie, and Renze.

INDEX

activities
  benefits of physical, 65–66
  cultivating positive emotions
    through, 75–78, 115–17
  problem-solving through, 93
  sharing in intimate relationships,
    150
affective neuroscience, 37
age
  adapting goals to fit realities of, 113
  adopting elders as role models,
    243–45
  tendency to overthink based on,
    38–41
alcohol
  binge drinking as quick fix, 45–46
  negative effects of, 63–64, 193–94,
    199
  negative self-image and, 127
amygdala, brain, 37–38
anger
  accepting/moving on from, 161
  overdeveloped sense of entitlement
    and, 43–45

overthinking amplifying, 30–31
overthinking career and, 197–201
overthinking loss or traumatic
  events and, 223, 226–28, 231–33
anxiety
  dealing with, 126–27
  overview of, 8
appearance, 5

baby boomers, 40–41
Baltes, Margret, 113
Baltes, Paul, 113
Belle, Deborah, 51
belly-button culture
  intimate relationships and, 134
  overview of, 46–47
  serving others as cure for, 247–48
Benson, Herbert, 72
bereavement, see loss
Bereavement Coping Project, 22–23
binge drinking, see alcohol
binge eating
  as distraction, 63
  meditation aiding, 72

biology, 119
Bower, Gordon, 34
brain
    affective neuroscience and, 37–38
    emotions and, 34–37
brainstorming sessions, 89–91
Brown, Jonathon, 221
Burns, David, 101

cancer
    coping with, 205, 216–20
    dangers of overthinking, 207–8
    depression and, 19–23
    family support and, 213–14
    friends' support and, 214–15
    hope/optimism and, 219–20
    hospice and, 235–38
    stories, 206–16, 225–40
    see also loss
career, 184–204
    conquering overthinking, 197–204
    overthinking and, 184–88
    story, 188–97
    women's status and, 46–51
catharsis, anger and, 44–45
cognitive therapists, 118
concentrative meditation, 71
conflict
    avoiding situations and, 105–6
    avoiding within family, 164
    controlling overthinking, 7, 68–69
    intimate relationships and, 134
    over goals, 113–14
coping
    Bereavement Coping Project,
        22–23
    elders as role models for, 243–45
    forgiving one's family and, 163
    with health problems, 205
    with loss or traumatic events,
        235–37
    with problems, 253
counselors, 199

courage, developing, 81–83
Coyne, James, 135–36
Crocker, Jennifer, 111
Crosby, Faye, 49
cultural influences on overthinking,
        38–47
    belly-button neurosis, 46–47
    loss or traumatic events, 222–24
    overdeveloped sense of entitlement,
        42–45
    parenting, 165–68
    quick fixes, 45–46
    values, 41–42
    workplace instabilities, 184–85
    younger generation, 38–41
culture, higher ground, 243–54
    cooperating for positive change,
        251–52
    discovering/refining values, 245–46
    encouraging coping, 253
    entitlement issues and, 248–49
    learning from elders, 243–45
    reinforcing long-term perspectives,
        250
    serving others, 247–48
    women's self-definitions, 252

Danner, Deborah, 77
Davidson, Richard, 37
Davis, Christopher, 22–23
death
    overthinking and, 19–23
    positive emotion strategies and,
        76–77
    serious illnesses and, 210–11, 218
    see also loss
deep thinking, 14–15
dependency, 135–36, 143, 149–50
depression
    following loss, 19–23
    meditation as aid for, 72
    overthinking and, 24–28
    problem-solving and, 28–29

traumatic events and, 17–19
younger generation and, 40
discrimination, workplace, 186–87
distorted lens effect
    defining, 15
    getting healthier perspective,
        80–83
distractions
    effect on anger, 30–31
    effect on depression, 28
    effect on thinking, 7, 26–27
    positive, 61–63, 65
    unhealthy, 45–46, 63–65
drug addiction, 72
Dunn, Judith, 54
Dweck, Carol, 114–15

eating, binge
    distracting through, 63
    meditation aiding, 72
elders
    goal adaptation in, 113
    learning from, 243–45
    overthinking not affecting, 38–41
emotions
    accepting/moving on from,
        160–63
    belly-button culture and, 46–47
    brain processing of, 37–38
    distorted lens effect of negative,
        15–16
    health problems and, 217–18
    negative, 7–8, 14–15
    overthinking epidemic and, 3–4
    positive, 75–78
    reasons for negative, 203
    sexual abuse and, 241–42
    triggering networks of thoughts,
        34–37
    women's awareness of, 53–56
entitlement values
    family issues and, 152–53
    forgiveness counteracting, 98–100

overview of, 42–45
rising above, 83–85, 248–49
workplace issues, 185
exercise, 61–62
expectations, lowering
    accomplishing goals by, 114
    family matters and, 160, 163–64
    loss or traumatic events and, 233
    of other people, 96–98

faith
    answering "why" questions with,
        119
    breaking free with, 70–72
    loss or traumatic events and,
        222–24, 227–28, 239–40
    problem-solving through, 89–91
    serious illnesses and, 211, 218
family, 152–64
    accepting emotions about, 160–62
    asking for help from, 72–74, 119
    building roles outside, 181–82
    buried issues in, 156–61
    developing more complex view of,
        182–83
    discovering/refining values, 246
    entitlement obsession and, 152–53
    loss or traumatic events and,
        222–24, 232–33
    overcoming overthinking about,
        162–64
    resenting sacrifice made for,
        157–58
    self-definition coming from,
        152–53
    support during health problems,
        213–14
    see also parenting
fear, *see* death; loss; panic attacks
Feldman Barrett, Lisa, 53–54
feminist movements, 251
Feynman, Richard, 244–45
financial dependency, 135

Folkman, Susan, 76, 115
forgiveness
    family matters and, 163
    intimate relationships and, 150
    negative self-image and, 127
    problem-solving and, 98–100
Frank, Jerome, 118
Frederickson, Barbara, 76–77, 115
friends
    answering "why" questions with,
        119
    asking for help from, 72–74
    broadening base of, 124
    getting perspective with, 124–25
    loss or traumatic events and,
        222–24, 232–33
    overcoming self-defeating patterns
        with, 199
    positive and constructive, 56,
        214–15, 247–48
Friesen, Wallace, 77

Gen-Xers, 40
generation, younger, 38–47
    belly-button culture of, 46–47
    entitlement obsession in, 42–45
    need for quick fixes in, 45–46
    overthinking and depression in,
        38–41
    vacuum of values in, 41–42
genetics, 119
goals
    focusing on primary, 7
    lack of achievement of, 105
    letting go of unhealthy, 108–15,
        201, 242
    reinforcing long-term perspectives,
        250
    striving for work-related, 186
Gottman, John, 143
guilt
    family matters and, 160–62
    parenting and, 167

harrassment, workplace, 186–87
health problems, 205–20
    coping with, 205, 216–20
    dangers of overthinking, 207–8
    forgiveness improving, 100
    letting go of unhealthy goals and,
        111–12
    positive emotions beneficial to, 77,
        219–20
    potent material for overthinking,
        205
    story, 206–16
    support of family and, 213–14
    support of friends and, 214–15
Helgeson, Vicki, 52
hobbies, 62
hope, 219–20
hospice, 235–38

infidelity, 150
insight
    finding meaning/understanding in
        loss, 239–40
    meditation, 71
    overthinking not giving, 60
    understanding your personal story,
        117–20
    see also meaning
insomnia, *see* sleep
Instant Calm (Wilson), 71
Internet, 219, 235

jobs, *see* career
Joiner, Thomas, 135–36
Josephs, Robert, 45–46

Kabat-Zinn, J., 72
Kessler, Ron, 52
Klerman, Gerald, 40

Larson, Judith, 19
Lerner, Mel, 221–22
Levenson, Robert, 143

Lewinsohn, Peter, 59
longevity, positive emotions and, 77
loss, 219–20
    avoiding thoughts of, 221–22
    depression following, 19–23
    discovering strength in, 230–31
    family, friends and, 232–33
    finding meaning/understanding in,
        239–40
    gaining new perspective from, 224
    infusing with momentary positive
        emotions, 76–77, 235
    moving forward in the face of,
        236–37
    notion of unfairness in, 228–30
    questions arising from, 222–24
    steps for overcoming trauma of,
        240–42
    story, 225–40
Ludwig, Thomas, 100
Lyubomirsky, Sonja, 25, 60, 86–87, 207

Maccoby, Eleanor, 54
Marlatt, Alan, 71–72
McCullough, Michael, 99
meaning
    faith tested by possibility of death,
        211
    loss/traumatic events and, 222–23,
        227–28, 239–40
    serious illness evoking existential
        questions, 218
    see also insight
medications, 46
meditation
    breaking free with, 70–72
    discovering/refining values,
        245–46
men
    depression in, 24–25
    emotion discouraged in, 54
    reaction to others' traumatic events,
        52

    reaction to women talking about
        feelings, 143
    status of women compared to, 49–50
mindfulness meditation, 71
Miranda, Jeanne, 36–37
Morrow, Jannay, 25, 65
mothering, *see* family; parenting
multitasking, 245

neediness, 135–36
negativity
    controllability of, 55
    distorted lens effect of, 15–16
    distractions freeing you from, 62
    finding simple reasons for, 85–86,
        203
    parents reinforcing moods of, 54–55
    power of, 7–8
    suppression of, 14–15
    triggering more negative thoughts,
        34–38

obsessive-compulsive disorder (OCD)
    comparing overthinking with, 14
    meditation aiding, 72
occupation, *see* career
optimism, 219–20
overthinking
    anger and, 30–31
    brain organized for, 34–38
    death and, 19–23
    defining, 9–11
    depression and, 24–25
    distorted lens effect of, 15
    epidemic of, 3–5
    escaping from, 5–8
    generational, 38–41
    negative effects of, 25–31
    nonoverthinkers vs., 19
    powerful effects of, 16–19
    primary types of, 11–12
    testing potential for, 12–13
    what it is not, 13–16

overthinking, overcoming
    activities bringing positive emotions,
        75–78
    avoiding certain situations, 105–6
    creating positive self-image, 125–28
    developing multiple sources of self-
        esteem, 120–24
    developing positive emotions
        strategies, 115–17
    engaging physical activities, 65–66
    engaging positive distractions, 61–65
    finding new friends, 124–25
    finding your story, 117–20
    letting go of unhealthy goals, 108–15
    not letting thoughts control you,
        68–69
    overcoming depression, 27
    overcoming weaknesses, 107
    prayer or meditation, 70–72
    quick reference guide for, 78–79
    scheduling overthinking hours,
        69–70
    stopping for moment, 66–68
    talking with others, 72–74
    understanding that it hurts, 59–60
    writing down thoughts, 74–75
overthinking, triggers for
    families, *see* family
    health problems, *see* health
        problems
    intimate relationships, *see*
        relationships
    parenting, *see* parenting
    work and career, *see* career

panic attacks
    loss or traumatic events and,
        226–27, 238
    meditation aiding, 72
parenting, 165–83
    change motivated by love for
        children, 178–79
    confronting husband's behavior
        toward children, 175–80

cultural influences on, 165–67
developing roles outside family,
    181–82
examining expectations, 171–74
guilt, 172–74
long-term perspective vs. quick fix,
    170–71, 250
regular quiet time with family, 246
reinforcing negative moods in
    children, 54–55
rising above entitlement values,
    248–49
self-forgiveness and repentance,
    173–74
story, 168–69
unhealthy patterns in, 169–70
see also family
passivity, *see* overthinking, overcoming
past events
    overthinkers focus on, 14
    negative memories of, generated by
        depressed overthinkers, 26–27
Pennebaker, James, 75
performance
    anxiety, 125–28
    comparing with others, 86–87
    workplace evaluations of, 187–88
Persons, Jacquelyn, 36–37
perspective
    developing healthy, 80–83
    developing through writing,
        200–201
    finding new friends with, 124–25
    loss or traumatic events increasing,
        214, 230
    positive emotions broadening,
        76–77, 115
    reinforcing long-term, 250
PET (positron emission tomography),
    37–38
physical activity. *see* activities
positive emotions strategy
    cultivating, 115–17
    overview of, 76–77

positron emission tomography (PET), 37–38
post-traumatic stress disorder, 17–19
poverty, 51
prayer
    breaking free with, 70–72
    handing worries with, 39
prefrontal cortex, brain, 37
prescription medications, 46
problem-solving, *see also* culture, higher ground
    accepting emotions, 83–85
    banishing uncertainty, 94–95
    brainstorming, 89–91
    changing or accepting situation, 88–89
    effects of depression on, 28–29
    effects of overthinking on, 11–12
    encouraging women in, 253
    finding simple reasons for distress, 85–86, 203
    forgiveness and, 98–100
    getting healthier perspective, 80–83
    higher values and, 91–92
    listening too much to others, 100–101
    lowering expectations of others, 96–98
    not tending to support each another in, 55–56
    overthinking work and, 187–88
    positive distractions aiding in, 61
    quick reference guide, 102–4
    stop comparing ourselves and, 86–87
    taking small actions, 93
    talking with friends or family, 73
    writing down thoughts and, 75
Prozac, 46
psychodynamic therapists, 118
psychological dependency, 135–36
psychotherapy, 118–19

quick fixes
    intimate relationships and, 134
        learning to like current circumstance vs., 88–89
        long-term perspectives vs., 250
        overcoming, 107
        overview of, 45–46
        parenting and, 166, 250
        switching jobs as, 185
quiz, on overthinking potential, 12–13

rant-and-rave overthinking, 11
reference guide
    overcoming trauma, 240–42
    problem-solving, 102–4
    strategies for breaking free, 78–79
relationships
    affect of overthinking on, 16, 22–23
    broadening base of, 124
    changing or accepting situation, 88–89
    destructiveness of overthinking, 133, 137–42
    leaving abusive, 242
    letting go of unhealthy goals, 112
    liberation from, 142–51
    women's dependency on, 135–36, 143, 149–50
    women's emotional overinvolvement in, 51–53
relaxation exercises, 126–27
The Relaxation Response (Benson), 72
religious beliefs
    answering "why" questions with, 119
    breaking free with, 70–72
    loss and traumatic events and, 222–23, 227–28, 239–40
    problem-solving through higher values, 89–91
    serious illnesses and, 210–11, 218
retribution
    forgiveness vs., 99–100
    rant-and-rave overthinking leading to, 11
Roberts, Tomi-Ann, 187

role models, elders as, 38–41, 243–45
role-playing, 176–77
Rusting, Cheryl, 30

schedules, overthinking hours, 69–70,
    82
Schwarz, Norbert, 47
self-concept
    belly-button culture and, 46–47
    career or work important part of,
        184
    changing women's, 252
    creating positive, 125–28
    increasing sources of self-esteem,
        123–24
    positive emotional experiences and,
        117
    sexual abuse and, 242
    tragedies and, 221–22
self-confidence
    banishing uncertainty, 94–95
    developing, 81–83
    parenting and, 167
    positive self-imagery and, 125–28
self-worth
    broadening base of, 149–50
    developing in workplace, 202–3
    developing roles outside family,
        181–82
    evaluations in workplace and, 187–88
    increasing sources of self-esteem,
        123–24
    intimate relationship feeding
        negative, 136
    investing in children's success, 174
    letting go of unhealthy goals, 111
serotonin reuptake inhibitors, 46
service, 247–48
sexual abuse
    initiatives designed to overcome, 251
    overthinking and, 49–50
    steps for overcoming trauma of,
        240–42
    women's depression and, 24–25

sexuality, 134
"should" overthinking
    escaping, 100–101
    letting go of unhealthy goals, 113
siblings, *see* family
sleep
    engaging activity when unable to,
        65–66
    health concerns and, 209–10
    scheduling thinking hour away
        from, 70
Snowdon, David, 77
social
    comparisons, 86–87
    friction, 23
    power, 34, 46–51
society, *see* cultural influences on
        overthinking; culture, higher
        ground
sorrow, 7–8
spirituality
    answering "why" questions, 119
    breaking free with, 70–72
    loss and traumatic events and,
        222–23, 227–28, 239–40
    problem-solving through, 89–91
    serious illnesses and, 210–11, 218
status
    stop making social comparisons,
        86–87
    of women in society, 46–51
Steele, Claude, 45–46
stories, finding your own, 117–20
suppression, 14–15

talking, 72–74
Taylor, Shelley, 219, 221
Teasdale, John, 71–72
therapists
    answering "why" questions, 118–19
    overcoming self-defeating patterns,
        199
Thoreson, Carl, 100
"thought police," 66–68

thoughts, *see* brain
traumatic events, 219–40
    avoiding thoughts of, 221–22
    depression following, 19–25
    discovering strength in, 230–31
    effects of overthinking after,
        17–19
    family/friends in, 232–33
    gaining new perspective from,
        224
    infusing with momentary positive
        emotions, 76–77, 235
    moving forward in the face of,
        236–37
    notion of unfairness, 228–30
    questions arising from, 222–24,
        239–40
    reaction to other people's, 52,
        232–33
    steps for overcoming, 240–42
    story, 225–40
    see also sexual abuse

uncertainty
    banishing, 94–95
    loss or traumatic events and,
        236–37
unfairness, notion of, 228–30

values
    activities connecting to, 124
    career issues and, 185–86
    discovering/refining, 245–46
    exercising through community
        action, 62
    intimate relationships sustained
        with, 134
    parenting and, 166
    problem-solving through, 89–91
    rising above entitlement,
        248–49
    vacuum of, 41–42
Vander Laan, Kelly, 100
Vanfossen, Carol, 144–49

vanOyen Witvliet, Charlotte, 100
victimization, of women, 49

wage gap, 46–47
Ward, Andrew, 25
Weissman, Myrna, 40
White, E. B., 119
Wilson, Paul, 71
women, 46–56
    affected by overthinking, 3–5
    changing self-definitions of, 252
    current opportunities of, 3
    dependency of, 135
    depression and, 24–25
    emotional awareness of, 53–56
    emotionally overinvolved with
        others, 51–53
    escaping from overthinking, 5–8
    lack of social power, 34, 46–51
    resenting sacrifices made for others,
        157–58
    working together for positive
        change, 251–52
    workplace issues, 186–88
    see also generation, younger;
        parenting
Women and Depression study, 24–25
work, *see* career
World Series Earthquake, 1989, 16–19
worriers, 13–14
writing
    brainstorming sessions and, 89–91
    committing thoughts to paper,
        74–75
    developing new perspective with,
        200–201
    health problems and, 217–19
    overcoming sexual abuse trauma by,
        241

yeast effect
    overview of, 9
    story of, 9–11
youth, *see* generation, younger

About the Author

SUSAN NOLEN-HOEKSEMA, PH.D., is a professor of psychology at the University of Michigan. She received her B.A. from Yale University and her Ph.D. from the University of Pennsylvania. Her award-winning research has been funded by major grants from the National Institute of Mental Health, the National Science Foundation, and several private foundations. She is the author of five professional books and numerous articles, and lives in Ann Arbor, Michigan, with her husband and son.